TIMING ANALYSIS OF REAL-TIME SOFTWARE

A practical approach to the specification and design of real-time embedded software with an emphasis on timing correctness. The method uses the Q-model – A technique which adds explicit timing parameters to data flow or object-modelling diagrams, supported by a flexible time-selective, process interaction mechanism.

by

LEO MOTUS

Tallinn Technical University, Estonia

and

MICHAEL G. RODD

University of Wales, Swansea

PERGAMON

U.K. Elsevier Science Ltd, The Boulevard, Langford Lane, Kidlington, Oxford, OX5 1GB, U.K.

U.S.A. Elsevier Science Inc., 660 White Plains Road, Tarrytown, New York 10591-5153, U.S.A.

JAPAN Elsevier Science Japan, Tsunashima Building Annex, 3-20-12 Yushima, Bunkyo-ku, Tokyo 113, Japan

---

First edition 1994

Library of Congress Cataloging in Publication Data

Timing analysis of real-time software: a practical approach to the specification and design of real-time.../by Leo Motus, Michael G. Rodd – 1st ed.
p. cm.
Includes bibliographical references (p.) and index.
1. Real-time data processing. I. Rodd, M.G. II. Title.
QA76.54.M68 1994
005.2–dc20
94-28551

British Library Cataloguing in Publication Data

A catalogue record for this book is available from the British Library

ISBN 0 08 0420265 (hardcover)
ISBN 0 08 0420257 (flexicover)

Printed and bound in Great Britain by Redwood Books, Trowbridge

CONTENTS

Acknowledgements

Like most technical books, this one has evolved over some years; its roots lie in the Republic of Estonia, where, some ten years ago, Leo Motus began to wonder how time-based software could be produced in a fashion which would result in reliable, efficient and cost-effective code. He was inspired by the work of Quirk and Gilbert of Harwell in the UK, and found that their ideas offered a platform from which he could tackle the problem. He established a group around him in the Institute of Cybernetics in Tallinn, and using the Quirk ideas, developed both a deep theoretical understanding of the problems associated with time-dependent software, and a prototype computer-based tool for use in design.

At the other end of the world, Mike Rodd in his Mechatronics Research Unit in Johannesburg was attempting to introduce highly efficient automation techniques in industry there, and kept coming up against the real-time software issue. Moving to Wales in the UK, he addressed two specific aspects of automation - how to achieve acceptable, time-guaranteed performance in industrial communication systems, and how to make the emerging Artificial Intelligence tools work in real-time situations.

The two research groups came together, initially, through the International Federation of Automatic Control (IFAC) links and then, more formally, through a British Council-supported exchange programme. The Tallinn Group addressed the problems of developing the CASE tools, whilst the Swansea Group attempted to use and assess them. Their joint activity has resulted in this book.

The authors therefore owe many deep and heartfelt thanks to numerous colleagues, who have not only contributed to this text, but have provided many of the theoretical pillars on which it rests.

In Tallinn:

- A. Amenberg — developed the CONRAD database and various other aspects of the system software,
- P. Lorents — participated in the development of the language and calculus for system description (LSD and CSD),
- R. Paluoja — designed and implemented the Governor and the Editor,

- M. Pall designed and implemented the Animator,
- J. Vain designed and implemented the Evaluator,
- J. Tekko designed and implemented the range of sophisticated test algorithms and the data transformations in the Editor, Animator and Evaluator, and participated in the development of the language and calculus for system description (LSD and CSD),
- J. Kaldma and T. Tommingas are, together with the rest of the team, developing the new, advanced version of CONRAD,
- Ektaco JV A joint-venture company based in Tallinn has provided much of the computing hardware.

In Swansea, the work of Mike Rodd's AI in Real-time Research Group has the continuing expertise provided by Farzin Deravi and Gareth Digby; much of the exploration of the Q-Model and CONRAD has been undertaken by researchers Jon Holt, Allan Jones, Matthew Gibbons, Idros Abdul Hamid and Salem Al-Rowahli. Indeed much of Chapter 9 is based on Idros's and Salem's work on communication protocols, supported by colleagues in the Swansea-based company, the Institute for Industrial Information Technology Ltd., especially Ivan Izikowitz.

Much of the more recent work on the use of CONRAD has been supported by the UK's Science and Engineering Research Council (SERC) ACME Directorate, who have funded work aimed at using the design techniques in real-time industrial inspection applications.

In producing this text, the brunt of the work has fallen on the capable shoulders and technical expertise of Felicity McEwen of the School of Engineering in Swansea. She was ably supported by Joy Knight of the Institute for Industrial Information Technology Ltd. Sue Rodd translated the South African/Estonian Engineering English of the authors into Standard English.

The authors wish to thank Professor Andrew McGettrick of Strathclyde University for his invaluable assistance in improving the readability of sections of this text, and also to the many students who have test-run prototypes of the book.

Finally, the authors wish to express their sincere appreciation to their employers for the on-going support they have received, both in producing this text, but even more so, in allowing them to continue the basic research which gave rise to it.

PREFACE

Engineers are under increasing pressure to design complex computer-based control systems which are safe, reliable, predictable and able to cope with the occurrence of faults - both within the control systems and within their associated real-world, dynamic applications. So far, though, the attention of system designers has been focused on finding the correct algorithms to implement the required supervision. It is becoming increasingly evident, however, that such a single-minded isolated focus cannot ensure the correct and reliable operation of any resulting overall system. Too many plant failures are still occurring - often through subtle and seemingly inexplicable problems relating to the complex interactions which must necessarily occur between computers, between computers and plant-processes, and also within the plants themselves.

This book sets out to address this fundamental design issue - handling the extremely complex problem of system interaction. It is suggested that the answers lie buried in the so-called "abstract" world of computer science, and so the book also attempts to bridge the gap between computer theory and engineering practice. It does not pretend to be a designer's handbook; rather, it discusses the nature of the complex problems involved, especially those relating to time-based interactions. To tackle these problems, it introduces a simple, engineering-relevant (but mathematically-sound) tool for expressing and analysing interactions; this tool can indeed provide the basis for a future generation of design tools - illustrated here by the description of a prototype implementation of a CASE environment, completely based on the proposed methodology.

The approach presented is founded on the principle that it is essential, at the very first stage of any engineering design, to study not only the control algorithms, but also all possible system interactions. These occur not only within the resulting computer structures, but also within the real-world processes being supervised and (of the utmost importance) between the external processes and the complex, typically multi-computer based, control system. Handling these interactions is not a trivial problem, given that they are normally dependent upon time - and the true nature of time is now being recognised as a highly sophisticated concept. It is impossible, for example, to guarantee absolutely that the real-time clocks which form the time-references for individual real-time computers, can be synchronised if they are located in different computers. (Indeed, as Physics tells us, they <u>never</u> can be!). As a result, items of time-dependent data arising from different sources can never be directly compared. Another example of the complexity of the problems which must be appreciated, is the fact that in real application processes the time-scales involved will be different: days, minutes, milliseconds, etc. These time-scales must, of course, be related back to those of the controlling computing devices - each of which can have independent timing characteristics, often operating under the supervision of non-deterministic operating systems.

It is suggested, therefore, that before the specification and subsequent design of any control algorithms, a verifiable framework for the system must be developed. This should describe, explicitly, all the possible interactions within the final, overall system - including the target real-world application. Clearly, some of the fine detail will not be known at such an early design stage; therefore, it is essential that the framework is carried through the whole life cycle of any system design project. This on-going support is vital in ensuring that all possible interactions can continually be exposed, and their effects analysed.

To provide such a framework, however, requires an in-depth understanding of the fundamental nature of real-time systems, which, unlike traditional non-real-time computer applications (such as data processing or scientific computation), include essential characteristics of:

- genuine, forced parallelism,
- cyclic and aperiodic task execution, and
- time-selective communications.

In addition, it is essential in such systems to appreciate, and hence pay due design attention to, the nature of time - given that it will largely dictate most interactions.

Currently, most tools used in the design of real-time systems tend to ignore the problems mentioned above, and only attempt to handle them via extensions, or add-ons, to well-accepted software engineering techniques. It is shown in this book that this situation is undesirable. Design should *start* with the detailed consideration of all possible interactions; this must *not* be left until the end, as is normally done now - if, indeed, it is done at all!

The key to addressing the interaction problems must lie in the use of a mathematically-sound technique for modelling time-based interactions, within the internal computing system as well as in the associated application environment and in the interfaces between the two. Without such an approach it will be impossible to subject the system under design to any form of correctness evaluation; the infinite number of possible interactions which can occur in the final operational system implies that it will be totally impossible ever to test the system fully, either before or after installation. The only possible approach to this classic dilemma of software testing must lie in the use of mathematically-provable modelling and analytic techniques.

To this end, the use of the Quirk modelling methodology (the so-called "Q-model") for software specification, together with its accompanying formal and informal analytic techniques, is introduced here. It is shown how this approach provides a practical design platform for describing time-based interactions in complex systems. Of particular importance is that, unlike the current unsatisfactory performance of many of the other formal design methodologies, in real, practical engineering contexts, the Q-model has been found amenable to use by engineers who are not deeply skilled in abstract computer software design techniques. Although the Quirk methodology involves an extremely simple (but very versatile) mechanism for describing and analysing all possible interactions, it has a strong verifiable mathematical foundation; this is introduced in an appendix.

Fundamental to the underlying theme of the book is the need for a clear appreciation of the essential nature of real-time systems and the related concepts of time. In both cases the approach adopted here is not based on deep, abstract philosophies, but rather on pragmatic, practical engineering experience. This is where this unusual book starts - exploring the true nature of real-time systems and, specifically, the influence of time on such systems. Indeed, it is quickly discovered that many of the critical considerations have largely been ignored elsewhere in the existing literature.

To put the ideas into a contemporary context, recent developments in CASE tools are reviewed; this is necessary for providing the basis for later suggestions as to what should be included within future, consolidated software engineering environments. The review also highlights the general lack of suitable tools, and briefly mentions the shortcomings of some current offerings. It also provides a source of reference to other possible approaches.

Techniques are then introduced to support the development of the design framework mentioned previously. Herein lies the core of this book: the identification, justification and practical application of a pragmatic formalism which can be used for describing the highly complex time-based interaction of processes in real-time distributed computer-based systems in their real-world, dynamic applications. Having both informally and formally introduced the Q-model and its accompanying analytical techniques, their use is illustrated - initially by reference to two classical problems, one drawn from the engineering world and the other, deliberately a classic "reference problem" from the hallowed halls of computer science. In both cases, the point illustrated is the ability to create a framework for the subsequent development of algorithms; the examples do not set out to solve the practical problems but, rather, to specify a platform from which final solutions can be determined.

These initial simple examples are followed by an actual design exercise involving the specification and design of part of an OSI-based communications protocol stack. The stack itself is unique, not only in that it is being designed to implement the normal OSI-defined protocol logical functions, but also because, as part of a global project relating to real-time industrial communications, the stack's time-related performance is absolutely critical. This study illustrates several points: Firstly, it shows how an actual, albeit prototype, CASE tool (called CONRAD, and currently under development) is used to support the total life cycle of the design of a complex, interacting system. Also, the study illustrates how, once a time-related process-interaction model of a complex distributed system has been created, this model can be analysed and its temporal performance evaluated. As a result of this analysis, the system model can be modified by altering the characteristics of the specified processes and their various interactions, so as to achieve differing performance characteristics. Also, at each stage the model gives very important indications of possible practical implementations.

The book thus shows how the principles which are introduced can be used to form the basis of a new generation of software engineering tools; tools which not only provide a framework for subsequent algorithm and implementation design stages, but which remain as an integral aspect of the design process, available for use at all stages of that process to verify the interactions which will occur within the system as a whole.

CHAPTER 1

Characteristics of Real-Time Software

Embedded, or real-time, computing systems are increasingly being used to ensure the effective operation of a wide range of human activities, including administration, financial management, manufacturing and process control. Each of these applications is heavily dependent upon the particular user, or user-population, and necessarily reflects the particular characteristics of the application.

For economic reasons, such embedded systems are constructed, wherever possible, by the use of standard components. From the hardware point-of-view this idea is feasible - particularly over the last decade when standardised hardware has really became available "off the shelf" - in the form of either personal computers or, at least, processors based on standardised bus-structures, - such as the VME-bus components. There are, of course, serious problems which arise from attempts to interconnect products from different vendors, or to adapt standard hardware solutions to very specific needs of an application - particularly when specialised interfacing is required. Despite these difficulties, though, we are much closer to having available a collection of relatively standardised hardware components, than ever before. It does, however, still require effort to ensure total compatibility.

In the software arena there is much less standardisation - despite all that has been discussed in terms of the attraction of the "re-use" of software products. As a result, it is even more difficult to identify common software structures and components than it is in the hardware field; this is particularly evident when we move into embedded applications. We must agree that there are some common *names* for significant components of software - for example, operating systems, databases, etc. Undoubtedly, these names do indicate some degree of standardisation; however, when we actually do get down to trying to wrap our customised software around, say, a standard UNIX operating system, we end up having to add a significant number of additional components. Having said this, though, it must be added that, as with hardware, there is no doubt that we are moving towards a far more rational approach to software, and the concepts of re-usable software, as well as the use of standard software platforms (such as UNIX), will undoubtedly be realised in the decades ahead.

Despite the emergence of standard components, we must still realise that when we begin to design software, just as in the case of hardware development, actual implementation details are not particularly relevant. The specification and selection of an operating system or database belongs to the latter stage of design. Indeed, assuming that we know the solutions can be dangerous at the earliest, or specification, stage - typically because we probably have insufficient information available to proceed to such detail. At the early stages we must of necessity work with relatively abstract terms, which should be chosen so that they remain useful throughout the evolution of the software.

But we must not be too idealistic about this - it is common practice to find that it is necessary for designers, at the early stages, to have some idea of the future system, and to keep in mind some general concepts of the way in which they are going to actually implement a system. We have all gone through the phase of protesting that design should be "top-down". In practice, real designers know that they never begin any design without some idea of what the final product will look like. We suggest that this applies equally to software, as to hardware design. We believe that design takes place from both ends and is effectively a combination of top-down and bottom-up analysis. Although we would like to delay the final, fine implementation details until as late as possible, we will always have at the back of our minds, even at the earliest stages, some idea of the implementation details. Even the most experienced design engineers tend to make the hardware/software decision at a relatively early stage - despite the claims to the contrary of "academic" design experts (who, typically, have never actually done any real design).

In this chapter we will point out some of the general characteristics of embedded software, emphasising particularly those features which do not relate to any specific application and which can be discussed at the early stages in the development of a system. We start by describing factors which influence software behaviour, and we insist that in our world of real-time systems, a fundamental requirement is to ensure that our embedded systems behave correctly in the "time" domain. Of course, many methodologies have been proposed for assisting in the structuring of software. However, we suggest that many of these are derived from non-real-time application areas and, as a result, are not particularly helpful when attempting to describe embedded, deterministic systems. We believe that what is required is a simple abstract approach. In order to move towards this we conclude this chapter by listing the particular characteristics of embedded software, highlighting particularly those that are not present in the software of so-called *closed systems*.

1.1 CLASSES OF PROGRAMS

A significant number of computer programs run independently of the world that exists outside the computers on which they are executed. Once the initial data has been provided to them, execution may proceed. Provided that the underlying computer systems function correctly, the program being executed has no serious reason to interact with the surrounding world. *In principle*, all the "causal" relationships which can possibly influence the program's execution are completely determined beforehand (at the design stage) and can therefore be anticipated during execution. It is important, though, to emphasise "in principle" - most software errors, even in relatively simple applications, are caused by our inability to appreciate all possible causal relationships.

Typical examples of such programs can include: stand-alone, scientific or commercial, computational programs and dedicated artificial intelligence processing tasks, such as proving a theorem or pattern recognition. Even though such systems solve problems through dialogues with human users, we can consider the user to be a part of the computer system.

A characteristic of these programs is that their interfaces to the surrounding worlds may be easily described. Even if they permit some influence from the outside, this comes from one source - usually from a single human user. Any indeterminacy in their execution or their environment, is contained within the computational algorithms, and/or within the inherent properties of the computing system. By an analogy to thermodynamics, we choose to refer to computer systems which run programs in this fashion, as *closed systems* [See Figure 1.1].

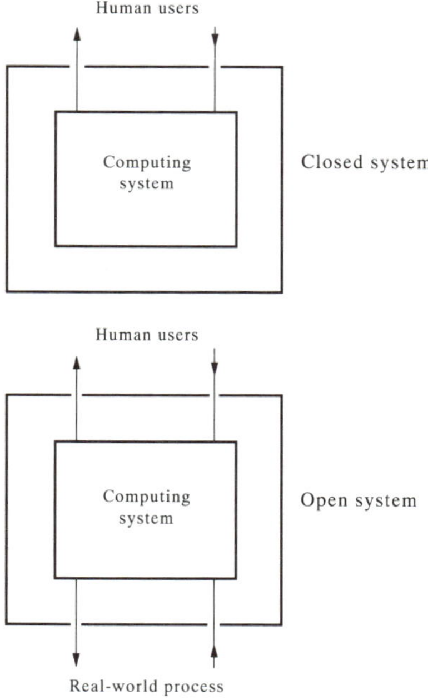

Figure **1.1** Open and Closed Computer Systems

In contrast, there exist (again using the engineering analogy) *open systems*. These are computer systems executing programs which interact with the real-world surrounding the computer system. The functioning of such systems is strongly influenced by the information provided by, and/or activities occurring in, the physical processes in their surroundings. Here, it is not usually possible to identify a single source influencing the behaviour of the program. As a result, we are not normally able to locate all the causal relations which must be catered for in any resulting program or, indeed, even in the associated computing system(s). The factors influencing the functioning of programs are often located outside the computer system, and are not controllable (and, sometimes, not even observable) by the programmer or by the user.

Strictly speaking, such an open system is formed as the result of the cooperation of programs with their underlying, supporting, computer hardware. Therefore, when developing an open system's "functional specification", we do not usually need to discuss the final implementation of its functions, as these may be implemented in either software or hardware. In practice, though, we must acknowledge that most experienced designers generally do have some implementation mechanism in mind - even at the earliest stage in design. Real design is always a mixture of top-down and bottom-up methodologies!

1.2 EMBEDDED SYSTEMS AND REAL-TIME SYSTEMS

The main concern of this book is the introduction of methods which may be used to tackle the fundamental problem in the design of open systems. This problem relates to how we can assess the behaviour of a computer system (consisting of both software and hardware) when it is cooperating with its surrounding, real-time, real-world environment. Clearly, *real-time systems* form a class of open systems. A real-time system is taken here to be a computing system that has been *embedded* in a target system, and that functions as an inseparable part of that system. As shown in Figure 1.2, the embedded system interacts both with its application and with its users, but its overall objective is to control, with the assistance (maybe) of users, the total operation in the applications working within the environment. Examples of real-time systems include control systems for aeroplane and aerospace automation, engine supervision and robotics, and process control systems.

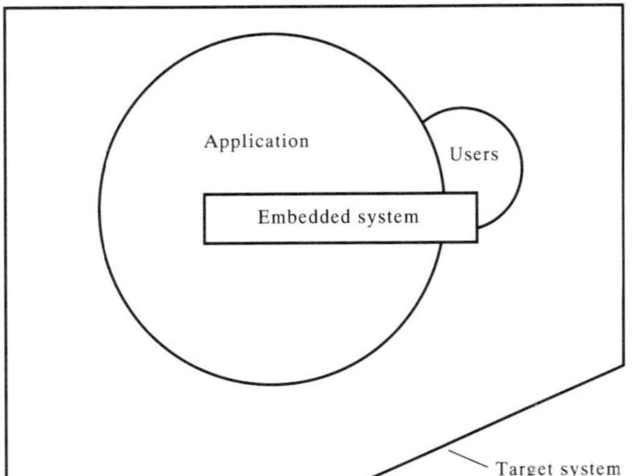

Figure **1.2** Interaction between an embedded system and its environment

This definition of a real-time system does not contradict definitions given elsewhere, where the emphasis has often been only on the sheer nature of the interaction between the computer(s) and processes supporting real-time. We prefer our approach as it indicates that the attributes of being *embedded* and of interacting *directly* with the target system are of primary importance. Ensuring the correspondence of time-measures in the cooperating systems is viewed a *consequence*, rather than as an initial assumption.

We should also note that whilst the more traditional term has been "real-time systems", the term "embedded systems" appeared during the mid-1970s, mostly be in connection with the development of the programming language, ADA. At the same time, though, many engineers who were attempting to implant microprocessors deeply into the hearts of control systems, and were already talking about "embedding" these processors. In the ADA world, of course, the developers were setting out to produce a language for so-called "embedded systems", and here they were tending to refer to military-type systems in which the computer was locked-up deep within a system which would be sent into the field. It does appear, however, that the equivalence of these terms has been almost universally accepted, but we feel it is useful at this stage to support the argument by discussing this issue further.

A common thread in the various definitions of "real-time systems" is the concept of the timeliness of the interactions which must occur between the computer system and its environment. Indeed, this is the key problem and correctly emphasises the necessity of matching the dynamic behaviour of a computer system to that of its surroundings.

However, the use of the term "time" has become very casually used, and when one reviews the literature on real-time systems, whilst a main topic of discussion is "time", definitions and interpretations differ. One finds in most texts, for example, that the properties of time, for example, its granularity, topology and global nature are presented in a variety of contexts. Undoubtedly these characteristics are extremely important, fundamental issues, but they are by no means the only ones which need to be understood.

We think that such a heavy emphasis only on time in real-time systems has generated a degree of misconception about the fundamental nature of the systems, some of which are widely propagated (see comments in the paper by Stankovic (1988)). Misconceptions relate, for example, to the apparent need for high performance and very short response times. This can, of course, be true, but only in particular sub-classes of real-time systems. Whilst certain classes do require high performance, this aspect is definitely not the only consideration. The point is that if one focuses only on a narrow aspect of the problem, attention tends to become concentrated on the underlying computer system, and not on the target system, which is formed by the computer system, the user and the applications acting together. Each of these 3 components mutually influences the others.

This is not just an academic argument! The difficulty is that computer systems are really the focus of attention of two communities. On the one hand there is the so called "data-processing community", which studies and implements programs for closed systems. On the other hand, there is the so-called "real-time" system community, which works with open systems. It is clear that the mutual understanding between these two communities (who, after all, use the same vehicles for processing their systems) would be much better if we were able to fix the areas of common problems, so that both could understand why the systems have fundamental differences. The danger has been that, too often, systems for use in the real-time field are simply taken from the data-processing field, and made to run faster - either by clever programming tricks, or simply by using faster hardware.

The term "embedded system" encourages a focus on the truly important properties of a "real-time system", and hence a shift away from defining real-time systems as being purely those which are fast enough! When we think of the problem of *embedding* a computer into a total, target system, then we must focus on guaranteeing the correspondence between the dynamic and functional behaviour of the system embedded, and that of the target environment. The point here is that we have to ensure that the embedded and target systems function as inseparable entities. The acceptance of this idea will ensure that the problem is understood by persons sitting on both sides of the great computer divide!

Once this point is clear then we have to investigate ways of ensuring the correspondence between the dynamic and functional behaviour of the two systems which are involved - i.e., the embedded system and its surroundings. From a functional point-of-view, the problems posed to programmers in any computer application are much the same - essentially, they have to write code which solves a defined series of problems. The difficulties in understanding the fundamental problem, though, arises when we begin to discuss a system's dynamic behaviour. In the case of traditional data-processing algorithms, the dynamic behaviour of the system is totally determined by the algorithms, together with their initial data and the properties of the computer system. In the case of embedded systems, however, the essential part of the stimuli which influence the dynamic behaviour of the software is generated in the target environment. The complexity of this environment is typically too high to be completely understood and controlled by the embedded system alone.

Clearly, one of the most reasonable ways of considering the influence of the application on the embedded system is to fix, for both, a common basis for measurement. Since most of the processes we wish to control are time-varying dynamic ones, it becomes evident that a sensible basis will be the temporal interaction based on, say, physical or astronomical time. We can then base the required behaviour of the embedded system on the dynamic behaviour of the application, using this common time base.

It is important, though, that in guaranteeing the correspondence of the dynamic behaviour of the embedded and application systems, it will not be sufficient just to have timely interactions between the two systems. This will be demonstrated later in the book where we will see that we also have to maintain the time selectivity of the data which is exchanged between the two systems. The point here is that in many cases the nature of the embedded system is such that the most recent data which has been produced by the application system is not necessarily that which must be used immediately. This seemingly strange concept relates to the fact that we need to have consistency in our embedded system, and in many cases this can over-ride the need for high-speed responses. Consider, for example, operators who wish to get an accurate picture of the state of the process which is under the control of their embedded system. The data which needs to be observed is not necessarily the latest data which has been acquired by the computer; what *is* required is that all data which is displayed is correct at some specific instant of time in order that the operator can make a consistent response to the observations made.

The implication is that we really need to reconsider our concept of a "correct" program. Traditionally, when we are attempting to prove that programs are functionally correct, we do not consider such time selectivity - the program is assumed to consume the most recent, available data. However, as we will see continually throughout this book, the need for correctness in the dynamic behaviour of the system requires us to look in detail at the time at which data is received. We simply cannot assume that functional correctness will ensure dynamic correctness. Our attention, must therefore be given to proving the correctness of the dynamic behaviour of the total system rather than just the functional correctness of the components. We believe there are numerous methods with satisfactory ability to handle the functional characteristics of the components, but that there is a serious lack of tools to ensure a system's correct dynamic performance.

Finally, it is interesting to note that independently of our work, and with a slightly different argument, the same conclusion, that of preferring the name "embedded" to "real-time", has been reached by a major group in Europe [Kuendig (1987)].

1.3 INFLUENCING FACTORS

In the section which follows we will discuss some of the major factors which seem to enforce certain requirements on the software engineering methods which must be applied in the development of software for embedded systems. There are clearly two aspects which influence the characteristics of our embedded software - firstly, the dynamic characteristics of the application and secondly, the algorithms which we use, and the computing configuration. It is particularly important to note that in all that we do, the first priority must be given to the requirements and constraints imposed by the application system. It is very clear that the embedded computer configuration and its algorithms must be adjusted to the needs of the application. Unlike a automatic banking teller, our chemical process will not wait for any delay in its embedded controlling computer! In the automatic teller, the customer will only get irate and deal the machine a swift kick. The chemical process, however, could well run out of control.

A somewhat less obvious aspect to consider is the total life cycle of embedded systems. An embedded computer system will function as part of an inseparable new system, and the properties of this newly created (target) system will often differ substantially from those of the original application system. A common experience is that when we begin to add some degree of intelligence to any system (for example, an aircraft computer control system), users see new possibilities and, hence make new demands upon the embedded controller. It is therefore common experience that there will be a high demand for flexibility and modifiability in embedded software. In turn, though, any small modifications can result in new functionality in the application system, which often results in even more demands on the embedded system.

1.3.1 The target system

The success, or otherwise, of a new system depends typically on the opinion of its users! Normally the users have a deep knowledge of the application (e.g., the operator of a process control system, a person accepting reservations in an airline booking system, or the laymen who manipulate such systems - a case in point being a remote bank terminal). In all these cases, however, the users are not, as a rule, specialists in computers or programming. Therefore, it is far more important to satisfy the requirements of the layman than the computer professional, in the case of an embedded system. As a result, we must always take into consideration the psychology of the user. Professional users might be satisfied, for example, by communications using complex terms to which they are accustomed, but these would not be acceptable to the user of a bank terminal. As a result, it is evident that it is important for the functionality, structure and behaviour of an embedded system to reflect the real needs of all the users.

This concept has long been used in the theory of large-scale systems [Mezarovic (1970)], and in more specific terms, in the theory of automatic control. Here, the idea is seen in the concept of an "inverse system" being the ideal controller. According to this concept, the structure and parameters of a control algorithm are uniquely determined by the structure and parameters of the system to be controlled (see, for example, [Petrov (1980)]).

The complexity of the target systems which we would consider in the context of this book, however, is greater than that of the dynamic systems which have normally been considered by the theories of automatic control. This fact hinders our immediate application of the inverse system concept in the development of embedded systems. The idea, nevertheless, is useful - especially at the specification and maintenance stages, when close co-operation with users is essential.

As one of the guidelines to our approach we use a slightly modified interpretation of the inverse system concept, which we call here the *principle of symmetry*. The idea is that an embedded system should be designed such that maximum reasonable correspondence is maintained between its structure and parameters and those of the application system.

The main problem, of course, is the sheer complexity of our applications. In the theory of large-scale dynamic systems [Mesarovic (1970)], as well as in software engineering (see, for example, [DeRemer (1976)]), a system is studied by parts, in that we first study the structure of the system, and then develop algorithms for each structural unit. The resulting structure, often hierarchical, is normally obtained by applying step-wise refinement and, in theory, by using a top-down approach [Linger (1977)]. Of course, we know that in practice step-wise refinement and a top-down approach seems to mimic the information processing in our own human minds [Miller (1955)].

In this book we shall concentrate only on studying a system's structure so as, at the later stage, to be able to select algorithms for implementing structural units. We describe the structure of a complex embedded system, and its application environment, in terms of the interaction between structural units and focus our attention on the need for careful specification and design of the structure of the embedded system.

On this basis, it is important to look at several features of the application system and see how these influence the structure of the embedded system which will be responsible for controlling it.

Firstly, the geographical distribution of the application will influence directly the associated computer configurations, but, in many cases will only indirectly affect the properties of the embedded software. However, the more distributed the software is, the more difficult it is to ensure a close correspondence between the dynamic properties of the software and those of the system which it is supporting. If, for example, our application system is scattered across a large area, we might be forced to implement the embedded system over a computer network. This network introduces additional dynamic properties - typically the indeterminacy which can occur in the time taken to transfer messages across the network. In most cases, the network performance is also highly dependent on the load characteristics of the chosen network. In many situations this load may increase by several orders of magnitude under certain circumstances - for example, under critical fault conditions. It is common knowledge that an increase in network traffic can, for example, produce exponential increases in message transfer times. Here we have a problem; therefore, although these problems belong to, and occur during, the implementation stage of a system, we have to be well-prepared to cope with them. Unless we have specified the absolute, desirable dynamic characteristics of the embedded system, we will simply not be able to deal with the contingencies which always, in practice, occur.

It is useful here to highlight the fact that most embedded systems which have been designed to be dependent upon, say, an ethernet-based communications structure, perform well under normal, average-load conditions. However, if the designers had taken the trouble to assess the possible load which could occur during catastrophic conditions, they would have seen that the system they developed would not be able to cope - specifically because ethernet performs worst under heavy load conditions! This is a particularly critical condition as it means that under the worst possible conditions, when we desparately need our control system to take over supervision, and handle a dynamically critical environment, we cannot place any reliance on the automation which we have introduced!

Turning to the question of the functionality of the system, we have already mentioned the principle of symmetry, in that the embedded system should display a structure similar to that of the application system. This is particularly true at the specification stage, but equally true at later stages where we will also have to make design decisions based upon other criteria, such as performance, economy and fault-tolerance. It is for this reason that modifications to an existing embedded system should be referred back to the first stage, right back into the specification, since at this point we have the best possible correspondence between the functional descriptions of the structures of the two systems.

One initial consequence of this is that any parts of the application system which may have to be updated, modified or changed, will need to be specified with special care. Also, the corresponding dynamic characteristics of the embedded system must leave room for such changes.

It is also important to note that a close-coupling between the functional aspects of an application (such as extensive material transfers and the up-dating of databases) will normally be reflected in the embedded system by the intensity of information exchange between its corresponding parts. Again, reflecting the principle of symmetry, such close-coupling is often accompanied by the necessity to synchronise activities corresponding to the processes which are taking place in the functionally-connected parts of the embedded system.

It is also common experience that when developing a control system for closely coupled applications, the need for global optimisation will normally appear as a prime design characteristic. This is simply a fact of industrial life, because once we begin to integrate the various components involved in a total process, it is natural to strive towards maximum throughput.

Next, we must recognise that the behaviour of an application is guided essentially by the laws of nature, (in the case of technologically based processes), or is well-regulated by the users, as in banking. It is vital that we distinguish between the inherent nature of the behaviour of our application and the image (or perception) of that behaviour that we have captured. The quality of our image, essentially our model of the application system, depends on the knowledge that we have obtained, and will often be limited by our ability to store and process existing knowledge. Such incomplete knowledge will require us to approximate complex causal relationships. This will make it even more important to check at the earliest possible moment that these relationships are reasonable. Furthermore, we will of necessity be dealing with models of the application system, and need to have confidence in these at the specification stage.

As a result, we can distinguish two basic patterns in the functional behaviour of a model of an application system. Firstly, certain functions are activated by causal relationships. For example, a chemical reaction starts as soon as the necessary concentrations of chemicals are added or a suitable temperature is reached. Likewise, in a banking operation things happen when customers enter their requirements into a terminal. On the other hand, though, some functions are often activated without any obvious reason, i.e. without any direct causality. This might be, for example, the request by an operator to display the process status or an occurrence of some abnormal alarm condition.

It is clear that the better defined the application and its functional requirements are, the simpler it is to handle causal relationships. This issue of simplicity is becoming extremely important as we begin to recognise the difficult task that we have in ensuring that all the possible causal relationships in a complex system are fully defined and catered for.

It is useful here to remember that in the case of closed computer systems, the question of causal relationships is relatively easy to handle, for example, by using classical techniques of concurrent programming (see for example, [Chandy and Misra (1988)]). The point here is that because the environment is well-understood and does not interfere with the execution of the programs, we can handle any form of parallelism which might occur, in a straightforward, well-defined manner. However, in the case of open computer systems such as those which we are dealing with here, we have to cope with situations in which both causal and non-causal events can occur!

It is worthwhile here to discuss why such non-causal activation is necessary in most embedded systems, especially as we feel that in future we need to move towards a reduction of such effects.

A useful starting point is the recognition that we often have to provide hourly or daily status reports. The event that triggers such reports could be a time-instant (i.e., at a specific time of the day it is necessary to print out a report). Alternatively, it could be a request coming from outside the computer system - say, from an operator. Due to the complexity of the application and the problems of formal description of the behaviour of that system, the embedded software clearly has to operate on the basis of a relatively simplified description. The most obvious simplification is to replace an imprecise or complex causal relationship by a timing constraint. This timing constraint can fix an activation instant with respect to another event, which is, in turn, activated by a causal relationship. We might then be faced with a request to activate an embedded system function at seemingly random time instants!

However, in many cases, the key processes in an application are continuous (or batch-continuous) in time. Examples here include chemical reactions or the flight of a missile. In order to monitor and control a continuous process, the computer system must cyclically measure the process's state. The same is also true for the control outputs from the computer. It is obvious that all tasks must be ordered in time.

It is for these, and other similar reasons, that time, and timing constraints, are non-trivial in the case of embedded software. As a result of the need to approximate causal relations in the application, a *time axis* must be introduced to determine activation instants, and to impose constraints on successive activations, of different software processes. Such time usage is well known to programmers of real-time systems and is inherently applied in many operating systems through the use of watch-dog timers and related exception-handling functions. However, much less has been discussed about the implication of introducing other aspects of time into programs. For example, the cyclic repetition of tasks in an embedded system often leads to specific problems in intertask communication. Usually when tasks are activated according to defined causal relationships, there is no problem - each task consumes the available data. However, in the case of embedded systems there are two complications. Firstly, we may have to represent causal relationships by timing constraints; secondly, the application can impose its own constraints on the data that is available (or appropriate) for consumption. This takes us back to the problem of the time-selectivity of data.

Both these points imply that we have to be time-selective in the communication of data between tasks in an embedded system. This is a particularly important point, as the time-selectivity of intertask communication is not normally required in other classes of software, and so intertask communication, based on temporal considerations, has not been well-developed.

In summary, we believe that we need to get a sound, comprehensive understanding of time in software and be able always to guarantee that embedded software matches the true requirements of an application - not only functionally, but also in terms of the complex timing relationships. We would go further and state that the reliability and safety requirements of the total target system are highly dependent on these timing relationships. As a result, the specifications of the software must reflect these requirements of the application as early as possible in the design cycle.

1.3.2 The embedded system

An embedded computer system normally consists of hardware - including possibly, processors, memory units, interfaces to the application, data communication devices - and of software, which controls the functioning of the hardware. In an ideal situation we should be able to start by defining what the embedded system has to do without paying any attention to how it is to be done. Provided that there are no technical or economic limitations, this approach will clearly give the best results from an application point-of-view. There are, however, at least two prime reasons why we cannot puritanically stick to the ideal! Firstly, we have to accept that we are faced with certain technological and economical limitations in building, buying and using computers. In the practical world of engineering design, we simply cannot afford the long iterations which would occur if we were to examine all possible solutions to a particular specified problem. Secondly, certain aspects in our description of "what is to be done" can become important to consider carefully purely because of the sheer technical limitations of the computers which are available to implement solutions. Thus, for example, our specifications might call for certain processing times which are simply non-realisable with the hardware currently available.

In view of these points (amongst others) we suggest that a combined approach is necessary in specification. Essentially, we should not only specify "what", but should describe the specifications in a framework which keeps in mind the "how" aspects of the problem. In this latter aspect of "how", it is necessary for us to bear in mind the various classes of computer systems which can (currently) be found. This is important as it will give us some idea as to the approach we should take in terms of the framework to be adopted.

In essence, we can identify the following basic computing structures:

- single-processor computers,
- multiprocessors with use of common memory,
- multiprocessors without the use of common memory, and,
- computer networks.

Clearly, there are many other possible computer structures, some of which are mixtures of these, but this simple classification does provide a useful starting point.

Let us begin with the single-processor computer. Here, the first programs that were developed were sequential and used the processor in a monopolistic way. The next step was to multiprogram, followed by the introduction of the so-called multitasking-mode. In this mode of operation, several communicating programs were executed in "pseudo-parallel". Pseudo-parallel is used here to denote the fact that programs only "seem" to be executed in parallel; essentially each of the "simultaneously" executed programs is actually using the processor monopolistically - each getting a turn at using the resources. Clearly, multitasking is the absolute minimum facility needed in successful embedded software, as it does allow a single processor to be used for a multiplicity of jobs. One of the first process-control applications (Texaco in 1959, as discussed by Bennet (1988)) was based on multitasking.

From the programmer's point-of-view, multitasking on a single processor and the parallel execution of programs on a multiprocessor with common memory differ only in the necessary run-time support. In a multitasking processor, the switching between tasks (normally controlled by a program status word) is the key to the operation, whereas in the multiprocessor solution (with common memory) the synchronisation of access to common memory fields is of top priority. In the latter case, various techniques, such as semaphores, critical intervals, and Hoare's monitors have been introduced (see, for example, [Andrews (1983)]).

The introduction of synchronisation tools, such as semaphores, was, however, not sufficient to guarantee successful functioning of parallel programs. It became interesting to forecast the effects of replacing the strict ordering of executing sequential program operators by a partial ordering. Also, in connection with such parallel operations, new problems became important, such as the avoidance of deadlocks. As a result, formal methods of describing and analysing parallel programs were created to handle these new problems. A common drawback, however, to many of these early techniques was that they closely followed the code of a program.

Historically, the next move was to the use of (seemingly, high-bandwidth) local area networks for communication and the adoption of multicomputers which did not share common memory. As a result, programmers faced many new problems, including the synchronisation of, and communication between, communicating programs, without using shared variables. New communication methods emerged, based, amongst others, on the exchange of messages [DeNicola (1981)]. Communication protocols also became important, especially when dealing with networks. However, whilst all these tools were being developed for use in closed computer systems (since most of the theoretical work was going on in the computer science environments), the industrial application of these techniques was largely neglected. Embedded, or real-time, software was, for a long period left to non-professional programmers, such as control and mechanical engineers.

Things began to change in the 1980s, and have moved to the current point where much theoretical and practical research is being carried out in order to satisfy the specific needs of embedded-software users (for example, see [Izikowitz (1989)]). It is important to note, however, that from the point-of-view of embedded software specification, it does appear that the basic implementation-related problems, relating primarily to hardware configurations, have been investigated and are well-understood.

In terms of specification it is useful, therefore, as a starting point, to concentrate on what can be referred to as the second generation of formal methods for parallel programming, as these are slightly closer to the problem statements and, less burdened by operational or implementational aspects [Hoare (1978)], [Milner (1983)].

1.3.3 The software life cycle

The concept of a software "life cycle" was originally suggested by researchers involved in the administrative support of software development and maintenance. The idea, well-accepted in other aspects of engineering, turned out to be useful and has become one of the cornerstones of software engineering.

In a classical design life-cycle, one can distinguish three phases: problem statement, solution implementation and maintenance [Lehman (1980)]. The problem statement phase for embedded systems includes an analysis of the application system in its environment, the specification of the requirements of the (future) embedded system and a statement of the goals of the total target system.

A "requirements specification" is one of the documents which will initiate the software development process. This will list the underlying goals of the embedded system, the major problems to be solved and any general constraints (often economic) that have to be satisfied. In the process of developing the requirements the designers will distinguish functional as well as non-functional requirements - the latter including aspects of safety, fault-tolerance, and information throughput. Further extensions of the requirements specification, caused by defining behavioural requirements characterizing the dynamic properties of the future system, lead to detailed behavioural specifications. The analysis of the behavioural specification is a major concern of this book.

Historically, though, the specification of *algorithms* has been the starting point for software specification. The approach has been to describe algorithms in a way which is simple, avoids ambiguity, and facilitates the verification of the necessary properties of algorithms and their resulting implementation. If we merge the behavioural specifications with the specification of algorithms, we get the "logical design" of an embedded system. Logical design is, inherently, an important pre-implementation step in developing distributed systems - for at this stage we have a full description of the future system, typically (and preferably) without any physical implementation details. At the logical design stage it is possible (and appropriate) to prove that the system described (so far) is consistent, contains all the necessary information and is not in contradiction with any of the constraints imposed on it. We can do this without reference to any particular computer architecture.

The implementation phase consists of traditional programming activities such as the physical design of software for the specific computer configuration, the choice of implementation language(s), coding, module and system debugging and testing, and documentation development. This phase has been thoroughly studied and is supported by good tools. The problem statement and implementation phases in particular, may, in practice be allowed to overlap in time. This means that we often start on implementation before the logical design has been completed - with the result that solutions often do not fully meet their goals, since these might not be completely defined.

We are, increasingly, realising that the maintenance phase covers the largest part of the software life cycle, both time-wise and money-wise! In this phase, remaining errors are corrected, but it will also include the many modifications to the software, caused of necessity by changes in requirements. This is normally a result of users not being able to define their requirements fully before the system is installed and its potential is realised. In many cases, completely new software has to be introduced, mainly because of the high cost of modifications - see, for example, [Belady (1982)]. A noteworthy, if not major, component of the software maintenance cost also comes from the necessity to study the structure of the software when it needs to be modified - necessary in order to find the appropriate place(s) for modification and to avoid side-effects.

As a result of practical experience, especially by large users of computer systems, it is generally accepted by the software engineering community that the initial phase of software development needs more attention. It is evident that this phase is an important source of errors and discrepancies; most errors are introduced through insufficiently checked functional and non-functional requirements, and are only discovered during later phases in the life cycle. It is  intuitively obvious that errors discovered during the problem statement phase are not as expensive to correct as errors discovered during, or after, the implementation phase. Consequently, requirements and resulting specifications need thorough checking and verification. This is possible, provided we can introduce more rigour into the earlier phases of software development. The resulting effect will be that the problem statement phase becomes more costly, but there will be a substantial reduction in the cost of implementation and maintenance. This, is the practical justification for adopting the methods presented in this book!

1.3.4 The software life cycle for embedded systems

Embedded systems are characterised by their reactive nature - they interact directly with their surrounding application. In such systems the computer is built into a technical or natural system, and becomes an inseparable part of it. The resulting "target" system - which consists of the embedded computing system and the technical/natural application system - has new properties. These new properties may not necessarily have been either present, or important enough to be noticed, when the requirements for building the system were formulated. This is why it is so often necessary to modify embedded software soon after its introduction!

It is useful, from a control engineer's viewpoint, to realise that something similar happens when we close a control loop in an automation system. Typically, this is because the dynamic properties of the object being controlled change under the influence of the controller - the total, new system has characteristics which are not necessarily the sum of the characteristics of the two, previously separate, systems.

Giddings (1984) has described coping with this phenomenon as the "accommodation of uncertainty" into software design. In a classical "waterfall" model of the life cycle (see, for example, [Lehman (1980)]) this necessity to modify software which, in theory corresponds exactly to its specification, leads to iterations throughout the whole "waterfall" life-cycle model.

Boehm (1986) has suggested a "spiral" model of the software life cycle, and this can be considered as a general philosophical model of evolution. At each new "winding" of the spiral, we can, on the basis of newly available information, enhance or change decisions made earlier. A central place in Boehm's spiral model of the software life cycle is given to the notion of "prototypes". These ideas are strongly recommended in this present text.

An effective use of such a spiral model will imply that we have good tools for the elicitation, storing and extensions of knowledge about a software project and its environment. Based on [Boehm (1986)] and [Greenspan (1986)], the prime aspects of software engineering, as applied to embedded software, may be summarised as:

- ways of achieving a rapid convergence of "specification-to-prototype" pairs which occur in the spiral model,

- methods to elicit, store and use knowledge of the embedded system, the application system, and reusable software and hardware products, and

- the development of tools to support the automatic handling of the above problems.

1.4 HIERARCHY OF VIRTUAL MACHINES

Up to now we have visualised a computing system, including both hardware and software, as a "black box", and we have not assumed any inner structure. It is intuitively clear that the factors discussed in the previous sections apply, in different degrees, to different parts of the software and hardware. Therefore, it is important to fix the parts of the system which we are going to specify and study.

The range of target systems which we must deal with when designing embedded systems is highly non-homogenous in respect of their physical and dynamic features. Just think of the following possible applications - land-based and flying vehicles, power distribution systems, assembly conveyers, chemical processes, and engine controllers!

The computer hardware used for implementing and executing the software will also differ substantially from application to application - it could involve a single processor, multiprocessors, or networks of distributed processors. This just picks out one system aspect, and would be difficult to find even two identical hardware configurations at two locations of the same technological process!

In order to be able to analyze formally a particular stage in the software development process, we will have to extract some common properties and identify some recurring problems in a seemingly chaotic and disparate collection of possible applications. A reasonable way of introducing order into this diversity seems to be to use the concept of "virtual machines". This concept has historically been used to describe and analyse system software. An orthodox interpretation of this concept was given by Goldberg (1974), who applied it to describing computers with special architectures which facilitated the execution of several abstract machines on the same hardware.

A looser interpretation of the concept, though, given in Lawson (1981), suits our needs better. Here, a virtual machine is seen as a collection of computing and communication hardware, equipped with the necessary software, having an exactly defined interface to its surroundings. Making use of this definition, we can decompose any computer system into a hierarchy of virtual machines. An example of such a decomposition is given in Figure 1.3.

Application oriented user interface
Application programs
Compilers, interpreters, etc.
Application oriented systems software (e.g. drivers, schedulers, DBMS, communication protocols)
Operating System's kernel
Computing and communication hardware, microprograms, etc.

Figure **1.3** Decomposition of a computer system into a hierarchy of virtual machines.

The lowest layer in Figure 1.3 is considered to be the virtual machine used by the developers of the operating system kernel. This machine's communications hardware includes, besides the usual intercomputer communication devices, interfaces to application-oriented I/O devices (sensors, actuators, switches, etc.) The machine's computing hardware can be any computer configuration, including, local area networks. The problem for operating system designers and implementers relates to how much of the underlying hardware to "hide". For example, should the local area network be totally transparent to an upper-level user, or is it reasonable to find a compromise?

The second-lowest layer in the suggested hierarchy is the machine used for designing and implementing the application-oriented components of the system software. In an embedded system, we often use dedicated schedulers and specially-designed drivers for non-standard peripheral devices. We might also require different data base management systems (DBMS) for different applications.

The third-lowest level supports software implementation tools. Since compilers, interpreters, etc., are usually standard, the upper interface of the three lower virtual machines must also have standard sections supporting the execution of compilers, interpreters, etc.

In a closed computer system, these three or four lower layers are normally "packaged" by the manufacturer, and are rarely handled separately. In an open computer system (for embedded software), however, this will not necessarily be the case.

In this hierarchy the application programs do not require additional comment, but we should point out that all known types of processing will be used in embedded systems - sequential, pseudoparallel, parallel, and distributed.

Above the level of the application programs is built an interface for the non-professional programmer, who uses the services of many of the underlying levels. Examples of such application-oriented user interfaces are functional keyboards, active mnemonics, mimic diagrams, and, of more recent interest, the various windowing techniques.

The hierarchy depicted in Figure 1.3 appears as one virtual machine to the end user - such as to the pilot in an aeroplane or the operator of a chemical process. These users, interact with the embedded system in their conventional (pre-computer) way. Quite often operators will not know anything about the computer system they are manipulating. (Are **you** aware how the processor in your video recorder or washing machine operates? In fact, are you even aware if one exists?)

It is interesting to note that the hierarchy of virtual machines discussed here is similar to the ISO/OSI model used for describing computer network protocols. The fact is that they have both grown out of the same need for describing complex processes, and this has led to the adoption of the concept of a virtual machine (or an abstract machine, the term used in a more formal context).

Now that we have a way of describing details of the inner structure of embedded system software, we can also expand on the differences between closed computer systems (sometimes also called "transformational" systems) and open computer systems (sometimes known as "reactive" systems).

In essence, closed computer systems interact with their surroundings (the user) through the highest-level machine shown in Figure 1.3.

However, in an open computer system, the essential flow of information exchange with the environment is controlled, as a rule, through the lowest virtual machine (via sensors and actuators). The users of the highest virtual machine in Figure 1.3 may be looked upon as "advisors", who may change, or adjust, the functions or goals of the embedded system. They may also possibly modify important parameters, such as the set-point values of controllers. In other words, the advisor is  engaged in strategic decisions, whereas most of the tactical decision-making algorithms are built into the system, and their functioning is largely determined by desired target system.

Considering these ideas in the context of software development, we see that the problem statement phase usually merges the two upper levels in the hierarchy (Figure 1.3), and ignores all the detail of the lower levels. This is certainly an appropriate thing to do, and it will work well in the case of closed computer systems. In the case of embedded systems, however, many additional constraints are imposed by the dynamic properties of the application systems. Unlike a closed computer system, an embedded system functions in a closed loop fashion. (Always remember that the Input/Output to and from the application system is via the lowest layer of the virtual machine.)

It is imperative that the lower layers of the hierarchy must satisfy all the constraints imposed on them by the target system. In order to guarantee this we must define the parameters which determine the time behaviour of the lower layers of hierarchy, as these will affect any operating system's scheduler. This can be done by a bottom-up analysis of the software, and so in the problem statement phase, we have to determine the required values of these parameters. All the subsequent top-down development of software (i.e. specification, refinement, design and implementation) should be based on the time-related values required.

1.5 CHARACTERISTICS OF SOFTWARE FOR EMBEDDED SYSTEMS

From the very first examples of embedded systems, such as the computer control systems introduced at the end of 1950s, the supporting software has had to exhibit the following characteristic features:

- *existence of parallel activities*: In the first applications, tasks were executed in "pseudoparallel". Later on, real parallel activity was achieved, thanks to multiprocessors and computer networks.

- *on-going execution of activities*: The majority of activities in embedded software are repeated, with appropriate time constraints, in endless loops.

- *existence of time constraints*: These are real deadlines imposed on execution time of activities, and also on their communication with other activities and with the application system.

A substantial number of these features are imposed by the application environment system itself. In most technical and/or natural systems many processes take place simultaneously; therefore, in order to influence their outcome, we must handle them in parallel. The on-going execution of some parts of a system's software will also be caused by the corresponding, repetitive, nature of the application. Finally, time constraints are essential in matching the behaviour of an embedded system to that of the application: the application is in control and not the embedded system. We can use the computer to start some chemical process, but we can rarely alter its inherent reaction times.

In the following subsections we will elaborate slightly on the above features in order to gain a better insight into the functioning of embedded software.

1.5.1 Parallelism

Parallel processing of programs can be dated back to the end of 1950s. Since then, computer scientists have been involved in studying the nature, effective design, and implementation problems of parallel programs. Strictly speaking, one should distinguish between parallelism and concurrency. In the case of parallelism, we are referring to the simultaneous execution of programs (or parts thereof) which do not communicate during their execution. Concurrency, however, implies the simultaneous execution of programs (or part thereof) which communicate (and/or synchronise their activities) during execution. However, in the following we shall use the term "parallelism" to cover both cases.

The bulk of the effort towards implementing parallelism has been oriented towards increasing the throughput of multiprocessor systems, and in solving sophisticated mathematical problems in the shortest time.

These types of parallel programs are not, typically, influenced by events occurring outside the computer system during its operation. Consider, for example, a program for solving a system of partial differential equations; once started and given the initial data, the program will proceed until completion or user-termination. In this book we have used the term "closed" computer systems to characterise such programs. Parallelism, in a closed computer system, may be characterised by the following features. (Note that in the discussion which follows, "process" is not a strict term; it should be accepted intuitively as an activity with a well-defined purpose. Sometimes, "process" and "task" are used in the same sense.)

P1. The program is an implementation of an algorithm in a form of a set of parallel processes; the separate execution of a single process of a set does not usually provide results which may be used independently of the results created by the other processes.

P2. The possible number of parallel processes and their synchronisation conditions, are determined only by the given algorithm and the computer system on which the program is being executed. The actual number of parallel processes may be manipulated by the human designer.

P3. The timing constraints on the execution of the parallel processes may only become evident if the overall permitted time for executing the given algorithm is limited - typically by the user.

P4. The activation of the parallel processes is determined by causal relations (stated in the algorithm) and the processes are explicitly co-ordinated to each other.

Computer controlled systems date back to the late 1950s. However, the software for such computer controlled systems (which provide examples of embedded software) was for a long time developed by control engineers and other non-professional programmers. Only recently has embedded software (real-time software) attracted the attention of computer scientists. In the following, we suggest features of such embedded software which resemble, to some extent, the features (P1 - P4) described above.

EP1. A program is the implementation of a collection of algorithms which often exchange information, sometimes in a very sophisticated fashion. However, although the program may often be considered as a set of parallel processes, separate execution of a single process of the set might provide separately usable results.

EP2. During the problem statement phase the number of algorithms which must function in parallel, together with their synchronisation conditions, are determined by the application. These constraints cannot normally be changed by the designer, as they relate to the physical process involved. At the implementation phase, the constraints on the parallel execution of algorithms must be satisfied, and it might be necessary to introduce parallelism, just as in P2 above.

EP3. The application imposes constraints on the start times of the various parallel processes, and also on the times and contents of information exchanges. In addition, each process might have an allowable execution time, as in P3 above.

EP4. The majority of start times of parallel processes are determined, not by corresponding algorithms, but by events occurring in the application environment. Because of our incomplete understanding of the application, these events are not always causally related to each other. As a consequence, some parallel processes may, of necessity, be started independently of each other.

It is evident that properties P1-P4 and EP1-EP4 both characterise systems of parallel processes. The prime difference between the two classes, however, lies in the degree of freedom left to the system designer. In other words, the difference lies in the number and nature of the constraints imposed by the environment surrounding the computing system in which the execution of the programs occurs.

In practice, the two classes of parallel programs differ substantially; these differences turn out to be fundamental when we start developing theories for analysing, and subsequently proving, the properties of the programs (or their specifications). Therefore, we suggest that a clear distinction must be made between the two forms of parallelism.

> *Definition 1.1*: A system of parallel processes satisfying properties P1-P4 is said to be *non-forced parallel*.

Examples of such systems are programs for solving number-crunching problems. Designers may change, at will, the number of parallel processes - this may be done by merging processes or splitting others into parallel parts - depending upon what the hardware configuration will allow. Most current research in parallel programming deals with non-forced parallel systems.

> *Definition 1.2*: A system of parallel processes satisfying properties EP1-EP2 is said to be *forced parallel*

Forced parallel systems, as a rule, interact directly with their surroundings, and this normally occurs without human interference. The outside world determines, right from the specification level, the processes which must be executed in parallel. The system designer is not able to change the number and synchronisation conditions of these processes. It is possible, though, that the system designer may add some non-forced parallelism at a later stage.

Note 1: In theory, and especially at the specification stage, it is normally possible to make a clear distinction between the two forms of parallelism. However, when we move closer to implementation and compare the timing requirements of an application to the performance capabilities of the associated embedded system, the situation often becomes blurred. It may turn out that some of the processes, specified as forced parallel, could actually be implemented in pseudoparallel. It may also turn out that some processes, specified as sequential, must in practice, be implemented on several processors, possibly as a set of non-forced parallel processes.

Note 2: Forced parallelism is similar, in an engineering sense, to the forced parallelism which is used in electrical circuit theory.

Having appreciated the importance of the inherent nature of embedded systems, it is evident that the problems to be solved during the specification of software should be handled in the following order.

The first and most general problem, and at the same time the problem closest to the target system, is that of describing and analysing forced parallel processes. Moving closer to the logical design, but still in the specification stage, there is the necessity to decompose one (or several) forced parallel processes into smaller units. The need for decomposition is not caused by the application, but by software engineering considerations or by having insufficient computing power. Such decompositions may lead to non-forced parallel processes.

Finally, the software of the embedded system will be presented in the form of communicating sequential processes which can be executed in parallel. Thus, the last step in the problem statement phase is to specify algorithms for implementing communicating sequential processes. Again, it must be pointed out that the application of innovative, or special purpose computer architectures, is considered to be an implementation problem, and is therefore not considered in this book.

1.5.2 Synchronous, asynchronous and truly asynchronous processes

Currently, the theory and practice of parallel programming lends to the adoption of two principles for co-ordinating the concurrent execution of processes - depending on whether the processes may be executed synchronously or asynchronously.

Conventionally, two processes are called synchronous when they are activated by the same event (e.g. a clock tick), according to a strict schedule. In the case of asynchronous processes there is no strict schedule. Instead, each process has a number of triggering conditions which are usually manipulated by other processes, or events, in the system.

Asynchronous execution is usually interpreted as demonstrating true causality, together with the possibility of a degree of time uncertainty. A process is activated after its triggering conditions have become true, but not necessarily at the triggering instant. The handling of both synchronous and asynchronous modes of process execution are supported by well-known formalisms (see, for example, Petri-nets in [Peterson (1981)]). Synchronous and asynchronous modes are not disparate. Milner (1983) claimed that a synchronous mode can be described as a special case of an asynchronous mode; Awerbuch (1985) claimed that an asynchronous network can be used to model the functioning of a synchronous network. Varshavskii (1986) suggested that the basic difference between synchronous and asynchronous modes can be seen when analysing the performance, reliability and technical complexity of the devices involved - and claimed that the asynchronous mode gives better results.

Synchronous and asynchronous modes of execution are both necessary in embedded software. However, an additional mode for the execution of communicating processes is required. In accordance with the properties (EP1-EP4) of forced parallel processes, one must often activate a process, even if not all of its triggering conditions are present. To be more precise, the application can activate a process without caring whether or not its triggering conditions are true. For example, it could happen that the computation of a control signal must go ahead to satisfy the requirements of the application - even if new data from a sensor has not been received. The quality of the controller's output will certainly decrease, but an accident can be avoided. Remember that the application, and not the embedded software, will always "drive" the total system.

We use here the term "truly asynchronous" to denote the execution mode of two communicating processes in which the processes are repeatedly activated at independently chosen time instants.

> *Definition 1.3*: Repeatedly executed communicating processes are executed in a truly asynchronous mode if their activation instants are mutually independent.

If we knew the causal relationships which bind together the activation instants of truly asynchronous processes, there might be no need for a truly asynchronous mode. This is usually the case in closed computer systems. In embedded systems, however, truly-asynchronous modes have been used in many cases; however, it appears that nobody has ever explicitly pointed this out. We cannot avoid using the term, since as will be seen later, the truly-asynchronous mode is handled separately by our suggested formal model (the Q-model). Also, this mode of operation provides a good explanation for the seemingly random appearance of some of the timing errors (see Chapter 7 of this book).

Examples of truly asynchronous modes are the activities necessary in loading a chemical reactor (see a software specification, in [Motus (1984)]), and primitives in operating systems for robots, as described in [Schwan (1985)]. (Schwan refers to the truly-asynchronous mode as the "asynchronous execution of processes with the possibility of unused data").

Clearly the situation relating to the term asynchronous is still very confusing. To resolve this critical issue, we chose here to refer to the truly asynchronous mode as *"ASYNCHRONOUS"*, and relegate the more traditional term asynchronous to the word *"SEMI-SYNCHRONOUS"*

1.5.3 Time parameters determining software behaviour

So far in this chapter we have considered the analysis of the qualitative properties of embedded software. In this section, we will try to fix the quantitative time parameters which are necessary to determine the behaviour of implemented software. We will also point out some of the ways of determining the possible values of these parameters.

As has been said before, the guaranteed behaviour of embedded software is necessary to ensure its correct influence on the application. The time-related behaviour of software is usually obtained by constructing a schedule for co-ordinating the execution of processes. However, such a schedule may contain a remarkable degree of indeterminacy; many processes may be activated by events taking place in the application environment, and the computer system may not be aware of them before they actually occur.

In the problem statement phase of the software life cycle, particularly when we are working on the requirements or functional specifications, it is easy to include additional characteristics into the description of the problem - provided we know what to include! Our fundamental approach adopted here is that characteristic parameters, limiting the possible behaviour of the resulting embedded software, must be found by a bottom-up analysis of the proposed software - and in particular, from any scheduler responsible for co-ordinating its execution.

We are interested here only in schedulers for hard real-time applications, since most embedded systems work in a time-critical environment. There seems to be consensus on what parameters are necessary here - see, for example, [Reghbati (1980)], [Stankovic (1985)], [Ma (1984)]. The following parameters are normally required for scheduling. We should note, however, that when undertaking the development of specifications we will need to adopt definitions which are applicable both to software as well as physical processes. (This will be discussed in detail in Chapter 4.)

- *start time*: the time instant when a task is activated.
- *computation (or execution) time*:- the time interval between the start time and the termination time of a task. (We will, from here onwards, use "execution" time in order that the term is seen to be applicable to both physical and software processes.)
- *deadline*: the upper limit for the termination of a task.
- *activation period*: the interval between two successive start times for a task.

When scheduling non-periodic tasks, start time and activation period are not normally necessary, and such tasks are scheduled dynamically as the need arises. This is normally based on their execution times and deadlines.

In more sophisticated scheduling algorithms, particularly those supporting distributed systems, two additional parameters may be required - any communication delays incurred per message transferred, and average times spent by tasks in queues.

Scheduling algorithms, based on the above listed parameters, have been developed for both single- and multi-processor computers, and for networked systems. At the specification stage, however, we must address two questions - how to obtain estimates of these parameters, and whether the given set of parameters is sufficient to analyse the interaction between the behaviour of embedded system and the application. The simplest answer to the first point would be obtained from an analysis of the dynamic properties of the application system! In real-life, however, we can get figures only for key processes interacting directly with the environment, and can only estimate start times, deadlines, etc., by analysing the required dynamic behaviour of the target system. For the rest, we need to either to find causal relationships binding them to the key tasks, or to determine their time parameters by using other heuristic considerations. An additional difficulty, from the scheduling point-of-view, is that estimates of time instants are often available only as time intervals.

Knowledge of the nature of the application often enables us to determine estimates for the frequency of execution of non-periodic processes. In fact, at the specification level, it might be reasonable to consider these as periodic processes, with random execution intervals. This assists greatly in the performance analysis of various possible hardware configurations, and will be important when proving the consistency of timing constraints.

The parameter "execution time" is special and deserves additional attention. This parameter is essentially determined by the co-operation of an algorithm and a computing system. At the specification stage we are only able to make an estimate of the allowable execution time, and this estimate may be used later on when selecting suitable algorithms and/or processors. Clearly, communication delays and average times spent in queues will depend heavily upon the specific hardware configuration selected and upon system software utilised (such as, the communication protocols adopted and the operating systems selected). At the specification stage, these parameters will usually be hidden in the allowable execution-time estimates.

It should also be noted that when specifying a system, a task could, in reality, be a physical process, say existing in the embedded systems environment. In this case "execution time" could well be a physical time, not related to any software process.

The question that must still be faced is whether the set of parameters is sufficient to match the required behaviour of the embedded system to its environment. Clearly, the set of parameters adopted is necessary for scheduling the tasks in the computer system, and this set will have been formed with certain background assumptions. We will try, in subsequent chapters, to emphasise the more usual assumptions, and use these to point out some of the potential difficulties which arise in specifying embedded systems.

It is also natural that, in addition to the above-mentioned time parameters, qualitative constraints on the *order* of task executions must exist - most likely specified at the start of the tasks. When developing a schedule, we will probably have to assume that the given time parameters are not in contradiction with the qualitative constraints on execution order. However, at the specification stage, such an assumption is too strong. Practice has shown that the potential inconsistency of time and ordering constraints becomes especially acute when dealing with repeatedly executed (periodic and aperiodic) tasks. This is a problem of specification and/or program verification. A more serious problem, closely connected with timing parameters, is the time-selective nature of process (task) interactions. In practice, much of the data produced by the application system is never consumed. At the same time, the usefulness of the data produced often depends upon the interval between the actual time of data production and the instant when the data is required to be consumed. Consequently, a time-critical data item must have an associated *validity-time interval.* The difficulty is that for some data items, the validity-time interval is determined by the environment, and for others, by the embedded system! Data validity-time intervals may also implicitly influence the scheduling algorithms, and their values must therefore be estimated carefully.

Another fundamental problem is connected with the somewhat abstract notion of "simultaneity". Any precise time instant is nothing more than a comfortable abstraction - just try to imagine an instantaneous event in Nature! Even more difficult, and far more practical, is the problem of guaranteeing that two events will ever take place simultaneously.

Usually, when we speak of the simultaneity of two or more events, we actually mean that the events take place within a given time interval. Consequently, it is necessary to obtain a correspondence between the notions of simultaneity in the application and in the final target system. This has a special importance in a distributed system; for example, in the required precision of clock synchronisation in different processors. In Chapter 2 of this book, three intervals - tolerance, equivalence and simultaneity - are introduced, to provide a better understanding of this problem.

CHAPTER 2

Time Concepts in Embedded Software

The previous chapter ended with a brief introduction to the time parameters which might impact the behaviour of software in embedded systems. This behaviour is manageable, as long as the factors which influence the execution remain *within* the computing system. It means that whilst we are dealing with software which is only guided by internal-computer events, we are implicitly making two profound assumptions:

- that we know all the values of the time parameters necessary for constructing scheduling algorithms for hard real-time application software, and

- that the given parameter values and any other constraints imposed upon the behaviour of the software system are not contradictory.

The first of these assumptions is certainly true when we deal with the scheduling of existing tasks - since here, at least, we can measure all the necessary parameter values. At the implementation phase, however, the second assumption is usually totally forgotten in practice - meaning that it is always assumed to be true! Now, when dealing with the specification of embedded software, the truth is that on the basis of experience we normally have to fix certain time constraints which are acceptable to the application. We must be aware, however, that estimates of any restricting conditions, usually (obtained from different application experts) need not be consistent. We have, though, to deal with the problem of proceeding from a specification, through design and on to an implementation, in a way in which the specified time constraints *will* be satisfied by the end product.

In order to guarantee this, we first need to have a good understanding of the nature of time in embedded systems. This is where we immediately encounter defined terms which are not strictly defined, such as "real-time" and "real-time system". The notion of "real-time" is obviously fundamental to embedded software. Unfortunately, the interpretations of the term "real-time" still lack consistency and depend heavily on subjective points-of-view.

Stankovic (1988), amongst others, started the process of demystification the term and, together with a series of papers by Kopetz and his colleagues, has largely cleaned-up the role of time (and real-time) in the implementation stage of software, as well as in the context of computer hardware (see for example, [Kopetz (1990)]).

We will take another step along the same road and discuss time-usage in programming, taken here from the point-of-view of embedded software specification, by establishing a general framework for time-bounded terms in programming. As a by-product, another view of the difference between closed and open computer systems will result.

2.1 UNDERSTANDING REAL-TIME

General agreement has been reached on defining the *functioning* of a real-time system - DIN Standard 44300 proposes, for example, that real-time functioning is "an operation of a computer system in which the programs for processing of incoming data are constantly operational so that the processing results are available within a given time interval; depending on the application, the data may appear at random or at predetermined times" (DIN 44300).

Arguments about the essence of "real-time" itself, however, still do not show any clear move towards an agreed and unambiguous definition. One of the goals of this chapter, therefore, is an attempt to clarify the situation, and we begin by suggesting that the attribute "real-time" does not denote time as such! Rather, it characterises a computer system's ability to establish correspondences between different time-measuring and/or counting systems.

This understanding is in accordance with the picture of a real-time system as being a computer system that functions in direct and immediate interaction with one or more technical and/or natural systems (the latter systems normally form the environment that embraces the computer system, also called the surroundings of a computer system). Usually, within each system, there exists distinct time-measuring/counting method(s). For successful co-operation it is essential that the computer system (which is supposed to influence the behaviour of the other systems in a clearly-defined direction) is able to understand, analyse and forecast the functioning of its partners.

Inherent Difficulties. One can distinguish two areas of difficulties which hinder understanding and agreeing upon the basics of real-time systems. The first follows from the fact that a real-time system must be considered as part and parcel of its environment - consequently, different specialists with different understandings and priorities will be involved in various aspects of system analysis, design and operation.

A second source of difficulties, pointed out by Kurki-Suonio (1991), is that in the design process resulting finally in a real-time system, it is often needed to consider real, existing systems, as well as their models. Often designers mix up which is which, and one has to be aware of what belongs to the models of reality and what are properties of a real systems.

Traditional approaches. Computer scientists have for many years studied so-called "reactive systems" - computer systems with on-going interactions with their environments, (see, for example, [Henziger, Manna and Pnueli (1992)]). These classes of reactive systems are usually in contrast to those referred to as conventional, transformational systems - computation-oriented systems which have strictly limited and well-guarded interaction with their human users. From an engineering point-of-view, reactive systems can be considered to embrace both soft and hard real-time systems - a good definition of these is given by Hoogeboom and Halang (1991).

Reactive and transformational systems resemble thermodynamically open and closed systems, as was mentioned in the previous chapter. Reactive systems are information-wise open, whereas transformational systems may be considered as information-wise closed systems. This analogy adds to the importance of studying real-time computer systems and their environments together, and to the importance of establishing clear correspondence between time-counting methods in the interacting partners. The analogy also helps to understand the essential differences between reactive and transformational systems, and to emphasise the peculiarities of hard real-time systems as a sub-class of reactive systems.

Two important aspects of reactive systems are of special interest:

- In addition to the well-known synchronous and asynchronous modes, the possibility of truly asynchronous interaction between processes, i.e. the start times of interacting processes can be truly independent of each other. This mode often results from incomplete knowledge of possible causal relationships and/or their substitution by timing constraints.

- Time-selective interprocess/intercycle communication. This is closely related to the wide-spread (mis)understanding that real-time systems consist of non-terminating programs. In many cases it is sensible and, even more, correct to consider a non-terminating program as the repeated activation (maybe for an infinite number of times) of a terminating program - this results in the concept of the cyclic execution of terminating programs, which, in turn, introduces explicitly the problem of time-selective interprocess/intercycle communication.

In this chapter, then, an attempt will be made to highlight the basic properties which ensure the timing correctness of software. These are given in three classes - performance-bound properties, timewise correctness of events and data, and time correctness of interprocess communication.

2.2 SOME PRAGMATIC TERMS USED IN SOFTWARE PRACTICE

We have previously suggested that the most important problem to be faced in the design of real-time systems is in matching the behaviour of co-operating dynamic systems - one of which is the computer system. In our opinion, time seems to be the most suitable tool for expressing and, subsequently, proving this match.

Hermann Kopetz (1990) stated that in real-time systems time and data form an *atomic unit of information*. This does not mean, however, that time can be considered as just another variable. The computing science community has learned over the past decades that time handling, its modelling and its presentation in computers is difficult and needs special care. We suggest here that the necessary paradigms are already present, and that the majority of the required theory is available. The problem to be solved seems to be the selection of a well-founded minimal and sufficient set of paradigms, theories and notions.

This selection problem can be illustrated by looking at a typical list of questions which can be asked, in any given practical situation, about the characteristics of time Shoham, (1988):

- Is time discrete or continuous?
- Is time unbounded?
- If time is continuous, is it dense, and if so, is it complete - in other words, can continuous time be modelled by rational or real numbers?
- Is time branching or linear; cyclic or acyclic?
- If time branches, should past and future be handled differently?

(We should note here that philosophers often show confusion by using the term "real time" to denote the fact that time has been modelled by real numbers [Benthem (1991)].)

The previous list of questions can be extended by adding problems relating to the manipulating of different time scales (see, for example, [Corsetti et. al. (1991)], and by considering the wide variety of possible ways that may be used to define time when specifying a system's requirements (see, for example, [Halbwachs (1992)]).

In the following section, some of the time-bound terms used in practice are surveyed. The terms are classified according to three different standpoints of the observer - time as seen by an "implementor", time as seen by a "verifier" and time as seen by a "specifier". Terms are grouped according to their most frequent use in a system's life-cycle.

2.2.1 Time as seen by an "IMPLEMENTOR"

These are terms that usually take their origin from the implementation stage in the software life-cycle. For the "implementor" the only aspect of the final systems which really matters is the computer system; the rest of the world is a model. The model is rather detailed in the case of a real-time system (a reactive, open computer system), and may be very schematic in the case of a transformational (closed) computer system.

The "implementor" is interested in time to provide a basis for organising the execution of programs, or to be used in handling implementation-bound problems, such as scheduling.

The following four definitions are taken from Kopetz (1984).

Physical time - a reference is established by counting cycles of a physical, strictly periodic process (ticks of a physical clock). Usually there is a measure to express the distance of one tick from another, i.e. physical time is usually a metric time.

Logical time - a reference is established by counting specified significant events during the execution of a program (logical ticks). The time, i.e. the distance between two adjacent logical ticks, is not measurable. Most often the "implementor" is interested only in the order of logical ticks (events).

Absolute time - a reference is established in relation to a global event for a given system (e.g. the origin of absolute time may be the instant of switching the system on).

Relative time - a reference is established in relation to a local event in the given system. Usually we may have more than one relative time simultaneously in a system. In the case of distributed programs (i.e. those executed on multiprocessors or across a computer network), one has to distinguish between **global time** and **local time**, depending on whether the reference is valid for the whole system or only for a part of it. Global and local attributes may be used for both logical and physical time. As a rule, absolute time is global and relative time is normally considered to be local.

Only one absolute time may be defined in a system; however, within one and the same system several relative times are usually in use. Whenever necessary, a correspondence between physical and logical time may be established. Then, since the other types of time - absolute, relative, global, and local - are derivative terms, one will have a set of comparable times. The metric properties of the physical time are used as the basis for comparison.

A common feature of the above-defined terms is that they are intrinsic to a program (or to a system consisting of a program and a computer). The same terms may be used in a real system (in an implemented program) and in its formal models. The set of terms enables the introduction of total ordering (natural for sequential programs and for the interleaving models of concurrency), as well as the partial ordering of events (e.g. for a maximal parallelism model of concurrency).

2.2.2 Time as seen by a "VERIFIER"

This viewpoint is typical during the design and testing stages of the life cycle. The "verifier" is interested in all the possible executions of a program, and usually concentrates on certain properties of a program - e.g. "safety", "liveness" and "fairness". Time is often reduced to the ordering of events (i.e. logical time), without really using the metric properties of time. This approach is valid and works well - even for many reactive systems (see, for example, [Kurki-Suonio, Systä and Vain (1991)]).

"Verifiers" work, as a rule, with computational models of programs. Consequently, the time they use need not (but may) be related to a time used by the "implementor".

The temporal logic community, for example, is using linear time and branching time. **Linear time** allows a "verifier" to concentrate on the universal properties of a program, i.e. on the properties that hold for all execution sequences of that program.

Branching time considers the collection of all execution trees generated by a program, and usually helps to concentrate on its existential properties - i.e. there exists at least one execution sequence with that particular property. Emerson and Halpern (1986) compare branching versus linear-time temporal logics, point out the advantages of both, and give a slight preference to the branching-time temporal logic.

Explicit metric properties have been recently introduced into temporal logic. Two basic approaches can be distinguished [Henzinger, Manna and Pnueli (1992)].

(i) The **bounded-operator** approach introduces for each temporal operator one or more time-bound versions (usually upper-bound and lower-bound temporal operators). This leads to two separate proof principles: upper-bound properties are close to liveness properties, whereas lower-bound properties closely resemble safety properties. Correspondingly, methods usable for proof of safety and liveness properties are used.

(ii) The **explicit-clock** approach uses the traditional temporal logic proof system, where time is introduced as a separate variable and must usually have metric properties (see, for example, [Ostroff (1989)]).

Some researchers argue that continuous time is needed (see, for example, [Caspi and Halbwachs (1986)]); whilst others claim that they manage with discrete time [Henzinger, Manna and Pnueli (1992)]. The arguments for and against continuous time are often linked with the computational model used ("maximal parallelism" or "interleaving" model).

Note that the "implementors" use discrete time, whereas "verifiers" use discrete as well as continuous time, and "specifiers" have many specific problems of their own. However, from pragmatic considerations, the "specifiers" tend to use discrete time.

2.2.3 Time as seen by a "SPECIFIER"

Specification is the most complex stage in the life-cycle and has the major impact on the quality of the future system. Experience has shown that up to 60% of errors discovered during implementation, testing and maintenance have their origin in the specification. The complexity of specification arises from two basic points:

- A "specifier" has, intellectually, to move from existing objects and phenomena (to be influenced by the computer system) to their formal models since during the design, verification and implementation of the system only computational models of the real world will be used. This transition, from real objects to their models, is complicated because of the infamous "semantic gap" between informal and formal descriptions

- A "specifier" has to fix time constraints on the behaviour of the computer system so as to guarantee the necessary match between the computer system and those processes in the real world that are to be influenced by the computer; a minor inconsistency here may cause a major error in an implemented system.

Representation of time constraints and requirements. Two basic problems must be faced when stating time constraints and requirements for any future system.

(i) The necessity to handle different time scales. In order to characterise activities in a particular control system, one needs to handle timing in, say, milliseconds: in others, minutes, hours or even days might be needed. When moving gradually to implementation, the different time scales are to be presented in the units of system time (usually defined by a timer in the computer system). As demonstrated by Corsetti et. al. (1991), this is not a straightforward task.

(ii) The necessity to handle time constraints and requirements given in various different ways. For example, to maintain control of a car when braking on a slippery road, the rotation of wheels must be well synchronised. One can state that the brakes on different wheels must start to work simultaneously and that the wheels are to be stopped simultaneously. This statement sounds theoretically tidy but is of no use in practice. Simultaneity here can only mean that one fixes a tolerated (admissible) difference in the wheels' angular speed. In a computer system which controls brakes, this must be translated into the actual time constraint (e.g. milliseconds) required to synchronise the angular speed of wheels.

Matching different time-counting systems. Time is obviously a widely used tool for controlling the matching of behaviour and dynamic properties of co-operating systems - especially when some of the systems are physical, real-world processes. Time provides a common measure against which one can compare the behaviour and dynamics of co-operating systems.

In terms of the above computer system, the common measure is, of course, global physical time. In practice, however, a computer system can co-operate with many technical systems which form the computer's surroundings. Some of these systems may function in continuous time; whilst others are characterised by a sequence of ordered events, for example. The notions and terms used for comparing a variety of times with the global physical time in a computer system, or with any globally accessible metric time, can be grouped into two .

(i) SYNCHRONISATION TERMS

(i.1) Tolerance interval (for (part of) a computer system's surroundings) - if two or more events characterising, or influencing, the surroundings occur within this interval, they are considered to occur simultaneously from the point-of-view of (part of) the surroundings. The tolerance interval will determine the necessary granularity of time required for describing (this part of) the surroundings.

(i.2) Equivalence interval (for the embedded (into the surroundings) computer system) - if two or more events occur inside a computing system within this interval, then they are considered to have occurred simultaneously (from the point-of-view of the embedded computer system). A trivial consequence is that the equivalence interval may not be larger than the tolerance interval for the corresponding events.

(i.3) Simultaneity interval (for the embedded computer system) is the time that elapses from the occurrence of the first of a generated group of events until the occurrence of the last event of the same group. The generating event and the group of events generated by it should be in the same equivalence interval.

(ii) ACCEPTABILITY TERMS

This group of time notions is concerned with the timeliness of events and the resulting data.

(ii.1) Validity time is a time interval during which an event in the system can be considered legal or the data resulting from this event can legally be used.

The validity time notion is essentially based on the ideology of time-stamping of data (see, for example, [Kopetz (1990)]). The validity time is usually determined by the producer of the data, who also time-stamps it.

(ii.2) Response time is a time interval during which specific input values must be accepted and corresponding output values must be generated (it could also be interpreted as a specific form of validity time). Over stressing the importance of response time in connection with real-time systems has caused a number of misinterpretations, as discussed by Stankovic (1988).

(ii.3) Time-out is used to denote a deadline for response/validity time.

2.3 WHAT ARE "TIMING PROPERTIES"?

Some of the software properties usually termed as "timing properties", or "real-time properties", or "time correctness" are discussed in this subsection. It is suggested that the timing properties be classified into three groups.

(i) Performance-bound properties comprise integral time characteristics for the system as a whole, or for a part of it. Examples of this group are **response time, time-out, and execution time** for a sequence or loop of programs. This is the most thoroughly studied group of timing properties.

The presence or absence of certain performance characteristics can be proved/evaluated by using:

- a temporal logic: more specifically either a bounded-operator or an explicit-clock approach (see, for example, [Henzinger, Manna and Pnueli (1992)], and [Ostroff (1989)]). In both cases upper and lower bounds of the properties can be verified; while the explicit-clock approach always reduces performance to safety properties, the bounded-operator approach results in liveness properties (the upper-bound case) or safety properties (the lower-bound case)

- algebraic methods [Caspi and Halbwachs (1982) and (1986)] and timed Petri-nets (see, for example, [Sifakis (1979)]) provide formulae for evaluating response time for a collection of programs whose co-operation is guided by causality (or before/after) relationship

- the Q-model formalism, to be introduced in this book, and which considers the sophisticated case of a loosely co-ordinated group of cyclically executed programs where some of the unknown (or incompletely known) causality relations may have been substituted by timing constraints; formulae are provided for evaluating upper and lower bounds for the message passing through the given collection of programs

- a simulation approach, which is probably the first, and the most widely used, method for performance studies.

(ii) The timewise correctness of events and data is concerned with execution time of programs and delays between events. The latter covers a wide variety of questions relating to:

- measuring/stating the validity time of data,
- checking whether (requiring that) data is consumed within its validity time,
- checking (requiring) the length of the specified simultaneity (or equivalence) interval,
- requiring (scheduling) repeated activation of programs (periodic or quasi-periodic execution),
- etc.

These questions have been somewhat less thoroughly studied than the performance-bound properties but are still well covered. Corresponding examples can be found in temporal logic (e.g. [Henzinger, Manna and Pnueli (1992)], in compositional verification [Hooman (1992)], in algebraic methods [Caspi and Halbwachs (1986)]), and in the Q-model.

(iii) Time correctness of interprocess communication is a typical problem of hard real-time systems, although it can also be met in other reactive systems.

Intuitively, it is clear that the time correctness of interactions is a good indication of whether or not time parameters and constraints imposed upon the interacting parties (usually independently of each other) are consistent and non- contradicting. Strangely though, little attention has been paid to the time correctness of interprocess interactions (even for the case of a non-cyclical execution of processes). Most researchers have concentrated on the transport delays which occur in the physical communication media: whilst this is certainly a very important feature, it can be applicable only at the implementation stage.

A very few researchers have investigated interaction timing in the pre-implementation stages, for example, Hooman (1992) whose assertion language enables the specification of the time instant when the interactions should start.

The case of repeatedly executed processes, where the time-selectivity of the transmitted data really becomes important, has drawn even less attention. Time-selective interactions were first introduced by Quirk and Gilbert (1977), and the ideas were further developed by Motus (1983). As will be shown later in this book, the concept of time-selective interaction, if properly handled, forms an excellent tool for checking the consistency and non-contradiction of time parameters and constraints imposed upon the interacting parties.

Time-selective interaction means, in a nutshell, that the data required by the consumer (addressee) must be of a certain, predetermined, age - i.e. not too old and not too new. This age requirement remains unchanged throughout all the execution cycles of the interacting parties, even if they are activated with different periods. The idea is based on the understanding that in real-time systems the most recent data are not necessarily the most suitable for consumption - for example, the requirements of the data integrity, in many cases, override the traditional desire for the most recent information.

From a traditional point-of-view, the consequences of adopting time-selective interaction can seem heretical - it becomes possible that the consumer process may never consume some of the messages sent to it, whereas some other messages may be consumed several times. As a by-product, this concept explains, and enables the forecasting of timing errors that occur at seemingly random instants, caused by a saw-tooth graph of a non-transport delay occurring inevitably during the interaction of truly asynchronously executed processes (see Chapter 7).

It seems probable that the lack of attention which has been devoted to interprocess communication, and time-selective interaction in particular, is caused by an incomplete understanding of the essence of time in real-time systems. The interaction is complex and different time parameters, constraints, requirements, and possibly different philosophical concepts of time, are involved.

2.4 THE PHILOSOPHY OF TIME

The time-bound terms mentioned in the previous sections reflect the pragmatic attitude of programmers - notions of time being introduced only when they were inevitable! Little attention has been paid to fully understanding and appreciating the role of time in the software process, and this has largely hindered the development of theoretically well-founded software engineering environments for real-time systems. The rest of this chapter introduces a possible interpretation of time in software as a combination of several well-understood philosophical concepts of time: it is suggested that this approach might help to clarify the situation.

The philosophical essence of time is still an object of active research. An extensive survey of contemporary time research can be found in [Benthem (1991)], [Denbigh (1981) and [Shoham (1988)]. It is useful to note that, as a rule, only one basic concept of time is used in each major research area. However, as we have found, in the computing arena, it seems necessary to utilise 3 concepts of times, and these will be introduced in the following sections. It is important to note that what follows is not merely a theoretical exercise but, in our opinion, essential to understanding the complexity of timing relationships in real-time computing systems.

Time in theoretical physics is just like any other space co-ordinate; it has no intrinsic direction, and is fully reversible.

Time in thermodynamics, and in other evolutionary sciences (e.g. biology), has a fixed intrinsic direction and is, in general, not reversible. Under strict assumptions (e.g. complete control of the causality) it is sometimes possible to reverse time for a brief period.

Time in our conscious awareness (e.g. psychology) has a fixed direction, its origin is always at the present moment; therefore strict distinction is made between Past, Present and Future. ("Time started for me the instant I met him/her!")

In theoretical physics and thermodynamics, the observers of time stay outside of processes under study; this is why all events happening in time are equally real to them. In our conscious awareness the only real events take place in the Present; events that have taken place in the Past and events that will take place in the Future differ substantially from the present ones and from each other.

The computing world can be characterised, with a slight exaggeration, by two opposing schools of thought. One school advocates the use of logical time - if no events occur in the system, time does not proceed. The other school advocates the use of physical time - metric properties of time are essential and time forms a basis for measuring system properties. Obviously the school of thought that uses only logical time is well-suited to transformational computer systems, where the only real processes exist within the computer. The case of reactive systems (real-time systems) cannot, in general, be covered using only logical time - which will cover only exceptional cases of real-time systems.

2.5 EXAMPLES OF USING DIFFERENT TIME CONCEPTS IN SOFTWARE

The following examples demonstrate how and why the time concepts traditionally used in different research areas have come to be used in programming.

2.5.1 Time concept of theoretical physics

Programs in informational closed computer systems (i.e. transformational computer systems) operate very much like models of Nature in theoretical physics - in both cases it is assumed that all the causal relationships are known and can be controlled by the programmer/experimenter. This assumption is true, provided that the structure of programs and the properties of the computing system do not change during the execution of the program. Since we know and control all the causal relations in transformational programs, the time can be reversed almost at will - exactly as we do in theoretical physics. As an example, just think of the possibility to "undo" some already completed action and "redo" it later (in some CAD system, or in a word processor).

The most sophisticated and complete usage of this time concept as described in [Jefferson (1983)], where the "virtual time" notion, which is equivalent to the above-described global time, is introduced. For reversing the direction of time, Jefferson uses a "time-warp" mechanism. In fact, virtual time is an additional co-ordinate of the program's state space. In this approach each process of the program executes in its own (local) time, which has a correspondence with the (global) virtual time, and sends messages to other processes whenever necessary. Each message is time stamped with its virtual sending time (a local time mapped into the virtual time). A process accepts messages in the order of their arrival and checks that their virtual sending times are increasing. Whenever a message is received that is preceding in its sending time the already processed messages, the time-warp mechanism is applied and the process's local time is set back. All the more recent messages are annihilated by returning corresponding "anti messages" to their senders. In this way the time-warp mechanism guarantees time integrity of the concurrently executed processes.

2.5.2 Time concept of thermodynamics

In an informationally open computer system (a reactive system) the assumption that all the causal relationships are known is not justified. The surroundings, into which the computer system is embedded, are, as a rule, too complicated to be completely formalised. Even if a complete and formal model of the surroundings exists, the computing power of the embedded system is not sufficient to consider all the required details. The other assumption - that we can control all the causal relationships - is even less well-founded. Imagine, for example, a computer controlling the loading of a chemical reactor. It is impossible in practice to "undo" the loading of a component after it has been loaded and the resulting reaction has started.

Consequently, time in open computer systems is normally not reversible and has a definite intrinsic direction. This means that time in real-time systems is, as a rule, employed exactly as it is in thermodynamics or biology.

Another application of the thermodynamical time concept can be found in temporal logic (see, for example, [Emerson and Halpern (1986)], [Henzinger, Manna and Pnueli (1992)] and [Ostroff (1989)]). Here, temporal logic assertions are based on infinite sequences of events - ordered according to increasing time. It is not possible to "redo" the history according to the verifier's will. In order to change the history, one has to go several steps backwards and modify the transition system (i.e. a complex comprised of a computer system and its surroundings, or the corresponding computational models) that generates the history. Similar problems can be met by using algebraic methods [Caspi and Halbwachs (1986)].

2.5.3 Time concept used by our conscious awareness

Processes in real-time applications are typically executed repeatedly - periodically, quasi periodically, or aperiodically - and are terminating. This paradigm is preferable to the competing paradigm which claims that processes in real-time systems are non-terminating. The cyclically executed terminating process' paradigm saves us from the necessity to work with non-terminating processes; it also explicitly emphasises the necessity to reason about repeatedly activated, interacting processes - the number of activations of which may be theoretically infinite.

Temporal logic, in spite of all its virtues, is rather cumbersome in handling time problems for repeatedly activated processes (see, for example, [Allen (1984)]). This is a direct consequence of the use of thermodynamical time which implicitly forms the time basis of temporal logic. Repeatedly activated terminating processes also necessitate the introduction of time-selective interprocess communication [Quirk and Gilbert (1977)], [Motus (1983)], which is not easily analysable in temporal logic or Petri-nets.

For describing the timing properties of interprocess communication, especially in the case of repeatedly activated processes, it seems natural to use time in the same way as it is used in our conscious awareness. This means that time is relative, and the time instant of requesting data is taken to be the origin of the relative time. When the process requesting data is activated at another time, the origin of the relative time is defined anew. The required age of the data is described with respect to the origin of the relative time used in connection with this particular interaction.

Such an interpretation of relative time is close to the time concept as used in our conscious awareness. By applying this concept of time for each pair of interacting processes, a set of internal relative times is formed. This time concept has been used by Quirk and Gilbert (1977), Motus (1983), and Caspi and Halbwachs (1986).

2.6 MIXED USE OF MULTIPLE TIME CONCEPTS

In the previous section examples were given emphasising the usage of one or other, but always a single, philosophical concept of time in programming. We suggest, however, that in order to enable the full analysis of timing properties - i.e. performance-bound properties, timewise correctness of events and data, and time correctness of interprocess communication - it is necessary to use several time concepts simultaneously.

The analysis of timing properties is possible only with a suitable mathematical model of computations; simulation cannot give the required level of confidence. It is essential that the model captures the necessary multitude of time notions - otherwise the analysis will cover only part of the timing properties.

For example, a timed Petri-net is based on causality relationships and locally defined delays for forwarding the causing factors. Since causality is usually non-reversible, one can deduce that only the thermodynamically time concept is used in timed Petri-nets. As a consequence, performance analysis is perfect, timewise correctness of events and data is analysable to a certain extent, but time-selective interprocess communication can not be handled. Since temporal logic is implicitly also based on the thermodynamical concept of time, the same arguments can be applied for characterising its ability to analyse time properties.

We will in later chapters, introduce the Quirk- or Q-model. [Quirk and Gilbert (1977], [Motus (1983)]. It will be seen that this is based on the thermodynamical time concept, but it also relies substantially on the use of several relative times (similar to time as used in our conscious awareness) - one for each process and one for each pair of interacting processes. For each process the thermodynamical time advances in grains defined by the execution time interval and/or by the repeated activation interval. Thermodynamical time is reversible inside one grain, if necessary. This multitude of times forms a solid basis for analysing all the previously-listed timing properties of a system.

2.7 SUMMARY

This chapter has taken a pragmatic look at the question of time and how it becomes an essential aspect of programming in situations in which programs have to interact with real-world, physical processes, which obey the laws of Nature, rather than the laws of computer science. It is suggested that such timing considerations are fundamental, and are far from trivial - especially when we attempt to bring together complex embedded systems with even more complex applications. In all that follows in this book, the question of time will remain ever present, and will be seen to be a key-parameter in the consideration of all software development methods.

CHAPTER 3

A Review of Embedded Software Description Methods

In this chapter we will introduce some software description methods and their associated tools, which are, or are claimed to be, applicable in the development of embedded systems. Our goal is to look at these against the background of the requirements discussed in the previous two chapters. The basis provided here will serve to indicate trends and help to put techniques introduced later in this book into context. The review will also provide a basis for seeking alternative strategies.

Historically, serious difficulties in meeting deadlines and budgets in software projects, and in matching user expectations to delivered capabilities, and problems with software quality, reliability and maintainability, gave rise in the 1970s to a discipline (or activity?) called *software engineering*. Like so many other new terms, *software engineering* suffered from serious mis-interpretation, and was, and often still is, confused with programming: the so-called "humble programmers" soon started to call themselves "Software Engineers".

One of the underlying ideas of software engineering is that creating a program should be approached exactly like the creation of any other engineering object. Some of the typical software difficulties, connected with the inherent "fuzziness" of information processing, were discussed in the introduction to this book. Suppose that we have fixed, well-defined data structures and a complete set of processing rules: in this case, we have an ideal problem statement for a programmer. From this point onward, we have, in principle, formal methods for developing a program. Programming is basically an evolutionary process: however, it starts and ends with a jump!

These are jumps across the so called "*semantic gap*" which inherently exists between an application and the program that sets out to solve a problem arising from that application. The term "Semantic-gap" means that a totally different terminology is used to describe a problem in its application domain from that employed in a computer science dialect. It is usually hard, if not impossible, to prove that different words mean the same thing! The problem of the semantic gap may be reformulated as two questions: " Is the program solving the right problem?" and "Are the results obtained the solution to the problem we wanted to solve?"

Taking a closer look, we can distinguish two different semantic gaps. The first, which we are dealing with in this book, is connected with the statement of the application problem for the program designer. The other is connected with program implementation - one and the same logical program may be implemented physically on a variety of different computing configurations. The questions to be asked at this stage are connected, for example, with the cost, reliability, and fault-tolerance, of the implementation.

As in all aspects of traditional engineering, the specification should aim to overcome the semantic gap. Before we plunge into the various, almost abstract, concepts involved in specification creation and analysis, it is useful to recall the previous statement about software engineering - that software engineering sets out merely to regard the development of programs like the creation of any other engineering objects. Software engineers are doing nothing different from their engineering colleagues down the ages - simply developing an article to meet the requirements of a customer. The customer does not want to know how many coats-of-paint or wheel-nuts his desired automobile must have. Rather, he wants to say what speed it must be able to travel at, how comfortable it should be, what colour and size it should be, what its cost will be and what the length of useful service will be. Few customers will have any idea of how an internal combustion engines work, or what type of milling machine will be used to produce the cylinder head!

In software, the same applies. The challenge of software specification is to get an agreement with the customers as to exactly what they want - but in such a way that at a later stage the software engineer can produce the desired, agreed article, in as quick and as accurate a fashion as possible.

The noble aim of specification is thus to reduce the semantic-gap! There seems, however, to be little hope of totally getting rid of the gap, since it is largely caused by the philosophical problem of obtaining a formal description from a non-formal one. As a result, the first attempts at software specification were based on totally non-operational problem statements given to programmers. Increasingly, though, attention is being given to attempting to develop operational specifications, with the objective being that a program (possibly a prototype) can be automatically derived from these specifications (see, for example [Zave (1982)]). It seems that specifications will tend to become very high-level programs - even if they do become largely unreadable by non-experts!

In 1982, Duffie (1982) listed the basic steps which he considered necessary in developing distributed control systems, and these provide us with a useful starting point for our survey, since he was, in essence, addressing the embedded system problem. Duffie suggests the following steps:

- specification of requirements,
- partitioning of tasks into processes,
- an assessment of communication requirements,
- selecting of processors,
- allocating processes to processors,
- design of the communication network (if necessary),
- design of the computing hardware (if necessary),
- application and system software design, and finally,
- implementation.

From the above list it is clear that in the most cases, especially when the system includes specially designed hardware (e.g. I/O, communication systems and dedicated processors) the process of obtaining an operational specification will not be straightforward for open systems. From the viewpoint of traditional programming, however, to get an operational specification in a well-defined closed computing environment, it will be sufficient to provide an interpreter (or a compiler or program generator).

Considering the list provided by Duffie, and supported by our own experience in producing embedded systems, we tend to think that instead of a single operational specification, for embedded systems we will have to deal with a sequence of operational specifications (covering the various aspects of distributed embedded systems) which can be transformed into a converging sequence of system prototypes.

This conclusion matches well the ideas of a hierarchy of specifications as suggested by LeLann (1983), with the idea of a hierarchy of virtual machines (Chapter 1 of this book) and with the spiral software life-cycle model of Boehm (1986). Thus we feel that our suggestion has value and so it will therefore form the platform for the following survey.

Our main interest lies in the initial phases of software development, and it is remarkable how many different, and yet non-contradicting, specification methods have been suggested in the literature.

Roman (1985) distinguishes two prime aspects of specification: requirement specification and design specification. Both of these aspects have more detailed inner structures, for example, functional and non-functional requirements. (The latter we take to mean requirements relating to reliability, fault-tolerance, performance, etc.). Design specification deals separately with logical and physical design problems, but it is worthwhile to note that Roman does not mention the necessity for considering timing requirements, with the possible resulting restrictions on design specifications.

Another example of different specification aspects is given by Winograd (1979). He points out three basic aspects:

- program specification (meaning the description of corresponding algorithms),
- result specification (meaning input/output descriptions), and
- behavioural specification (describing time-related activities).

It is possible to give many more examples but this will hardly add anything new. Being pragmatic, we will take the classification given by Winograd (1979) as the basis for our review. Winograd's classification supports our earlier points (Chapter 1) about separately studying the structure and algorithms of the structural units, so as to reduce the complexity of the problem-at-hand. Later in this book we will deal with specifications which combine the "result specifications" and "behavioural specifications" suggested by Winograd; it will be seen then that these are wider than the "requirement specifications" of Roman (1985).

In the following review we will concentrate on methods and tools which have a direct impact on behavioural and result specification. For pragmatic reasons, we have ignored work which is mainly oriented to use in program (algorithm) specification.

3.1 REVIEW STRATEGY

Over the past decade the terms "Software Engineering Environment" (SEE) and "Computer Aided Software Engineering" (CASE) have gained popularity. Quite often, CASE is taken to mean a particular tool, or a set of tools, which provides some degree of automatized support for certain stage(s) in software development. SEE, in many cases, denotes a wider coverage of software development - essentially, providing an environment which usually covering several stages of software development. In this review, for simplicity, we will not distinguish between CASE and SEE - the borderline between them is vague anyway, and we will use CASE to denote both.

In the 1980s, the majority of publications in the CASE arena were aimed at non-real-time applications - see, for example, a survey by Hausen and Mullerburg (1982). In this they studied 28 different CASE systems, of which only five were intended for embedded (real-time) applications. As we go deeper and consider the ability to estimate and/or analyse time-bound properties, only two out of the five systems remain. So, only 7% of the CASE systems surveyed by Hausen and Mullerburg were applicable to the handling of timing problems.

A more recent survey by Calvez (1990) does not indicate any radical changes in interest in CASE tools for the real-time domain. As one would expect, the majority of the available tools are obtained from non-real-time CASE systems by adding components which facilitate their use in the real-time/embedded systems domain. The only exceptions, perhaps, are the ADA-bound tools. The user expectations of CASE tools for embedded systems are emphasized by Boebert (1980). Implicitly, also, the STARS (1983) strategy (Software Technology for Adaptable, Reliable Systems) is also oriented towards embedded applications.

Many research communities, however, have expressed a need for specific, dedicated, embedded/real-time CASE systems. At the present time, though, the results have not been encouraging. We can suggest three possible reasons to explain the small number of CASE tools dedicated to embedded applications:

- the market share for embedded systems, as compared to the total number of conventional computer applications, is too small to justify the necessary research,
- software engineering and computer science are not mature enough to tackle theoretically "inconvenient" real-time problems, and
- most embedded systems still tend to be programmed by control/applications engineers who have little computer science background.

In reality, these reasons probably act in combination. Moving on to the review, we need, for convenience, to adopt some classification procedures. Roman (1985), in his taxonomy, suggests the following criteria:

- formal foundations of a tool,
- scope of applicability,
- level of formality,
- universality/degree of specialization, and
- specialization area.

This five dimensional approach appears useful for developing a taxonomy of existing CASE systems. For evaluating perspective development trends, however, it might be too sophisticated.

As an alternative approach, Blackledge (1983) suggested a classification based on the building blocks used in specification. He distinguished between static and dynamic specifications. The former is based on the functional or invariant descriptions, and the dynamic specification, in his interpretation, is based on state/event or condition/event descriptions.

The use of the word "dynamic" in the above context indicates an historically interesting approach. The functioning of a system, in time, is usually studied separately from its structural and functional properties. For the simultaneous study of functional and timing properties, one needs sophisticated manipulations (see for example, [Schiel (1985)]). Such an approach, however, is not effective in studying embedded systems, since, in many cases, we will not be able to distinguish static and dynamic behaviour. According to Blackledge (1983), for example, a functional description is called "static" even if the interaction of functional parts is time selective - in other words, if it depends upon the dynamic behaviour of the system!

In the light of their suggestions, in the following review we will adopt an even simpler classification, based merely on distinguishing top-down from bottom-up approaches. This criterion is not necessarily better than any other, neither does it lead us to less-fuzzy classes. Its advantage is merely that it helps us to concentrate on the nature of the semantic gap that we want to close!

We will also pay special attention to the use of formal methods. For this reason, we point out a third group, overlapping with the above two groups: this is of tools and methods which essentially rely on some strict formalism. This has been done very deliberately because we believe that timing properties cannot be analysed without well-founded formal methods.

3.2 SPECIFICATION METHODS AND TOOLS BASED ON A BOTTOM-UP APPROACH

This group of specification methods is based, essentially, on partitioning programming activities into two levels. The first, and lower, level is comprised of modules (subroutines) written in a traditional programming language. The second, the higher level deals with building a system out of ready-made, debugged and tested modules (subroutines). This approach decomposes the verification and testing of large programs into two, comparatively-simple, tasks - thus increasing the efficiency of programming. The idea was presented by DeRemer (1976), who proposed the introduction of a new language, MIL75. According to Ludewig (1978), though, this language was never implemented. Nevertheless, it initiated a new class of programming languages - the so-called module-interconnection-languages (see, for example, [Prieto-Diaz (1986)]).

The same idea, building and verifying a program out of already-verified, -implemented and -tested modules, was published in connection with automatic program synthesis by Tyugu (1970). Probably, because of contextual differences and also language problems, (it was written in Russian), this paper was not then noticed by the emerging software engineering community.

Thus, one of the origins of a formal approach to bottom-up based CASE systems can be seen to be DeRemer (1976). Another source is probably the Wirth (1977) paper, relating to "discipline" in real-time programming. To be fair, though, it must be stated that many, if not most, real-time programmers accepted a bottom-up strategy anyway!

The following are references to some representatives of this approach. Thorelli (1983) calls his MIL-type language a "linker", and an interesting feature of his system is that it uses Milner's Calculus for Communicating Systems (CCS) [Milner (1980)] for proving the correctness of a program. A number of systems belonging to this group also have been developed in the United Kingdom:

- MASCOT (Modular Approach to Software Construction, Operation and Test), is oriented towards the development of modular asynchronous systems, in which tasks communicate via shared memory (see, for example, [Ludewig (1978)], [Dowling (1983)]). A producer-consumer scheme is used in MASCOT for communication.

- The approach adopted in the DARTS (Design Approach for Real Time Systems) and its extension for covering network implementation problems, DARTS/DA. The DARTS approach exploits ideas that are not too far from those of MASCOT, (see [Gomaa (1984), (1989)]).

- The CONIC system [Kramer (1983), (1984)], [Sloman (1986)] has been developed for distributed computer systems. In this system special care has been taken to ensure support for the possibility of introducing dynamic reconfiguration and modification. This is one of the few examples which describes methods for verifying the correctness of a system's functioning and the consistency of modifications that are to be made.

- Project PEACOCK is based on a different approach. It uses abstract data types for systematically describing and analysing software systems [Bull (1986)]. Each module is described as an abstract data type, and all modules may be executed in parallel with each other. Special languages have been developed for describing module interaction. The intention of this project was to apply one formalism throughout the whole software life-cycle.

The majority of CASE systems developed in the former Soviet Union may be classified into this bottom-up group. Some examples of the systems are given in [Pogrebnyi (1981)], [Kazmin (1984)], [Schtrik (1984)] and [Kaganov (1984)]. The EF-technology, described in [Pogrebnyi(1981)], allows module execution time to be taken into account. The system proposed by Kazmin (1984) relies heavily on the properties of a dedicated distributed operating system, PARUS, and uses first-order predicate calculus for verifying some of the program features.

Instead of attempting to distill the essence from each of the above systems, we will try to extract aspects which indicate their overall integrating influence on the progress of software engineering.

1. The common ideology underlying the approaches adopted in this group has been to introduce a specific discipline of thinking - essentially that a software system is a modular structure. Quite naturally, the resulting efforts have taken two well-defined directions:

- research into tools and methods for developing good, effective and correct modules as standard building-blocks for large software systems, and

- research into tools and methods for building well-structured, modifiable and verifiable large software systems, by the use of correctly-functioning modules, whose behaviour is usually well known.

2. The emergence of well-structured systems gave a new emphasis to the use of formal methods for verification. As a result, new methods were developed for verifying both the modules and the resulting sophisticated structures built-up from correct modules.

3. As the consequence of the previous point, new emphasis was placed on reliability and fault-tolerance studies of software systems. The ability to modify large software systems improved, and new hope appeared for the re-use of software modules.

4. Progress within this group of CASE tools gave rise to new research activities in the area of process interaction and synchronization. Many interesting results have emerged, for example the formal comparisons of process interaction using shared memory and by message exchanges [Lynch (1981)], [DeNicola (1981)], [Lamport (1985)].

Against the undoubtedly positive influence of methods from this group, one should be aware of the principal limitations of the bottom-up approach.

1. The area of application interest of the bottom-up approach remains inside the computing system (and, essentially, inside the program). The approach may result in a significant increase in the efficiency of programming, but it cannot decrease the semantic gap between the application and the program. This is the first and perhaps the most important philosophical limitation of the bottom-up approach.

2. Although many of the above-mentioned CASE systems are proposed for real-time applications, they are, as a rule, not able to analyse the timing properties of the resulting software systems. This

drawback can, at least in principle, be eliminated by extending the parameters of the system description, and by adding corresponding analysis methods. This leads us to the second philosophical limitation of the bottom-up approach. We cannot, even in theory, prove that the dynamic requirements of an application are satisfied by the dynamic properties of the computer systems, by using only a bottom-up approach. As will be recalled from the first two chapters of this book, this is one of the fundamental problems involved in developing embedded systems, and one which cannot be solved via a bottom-up approach.

3.3 SPECIFICATION METHODS AND TOOLS BASED ON A TOP-DOWN APPROACH

This group of tools arises from the serious concern about capturing the requirements of the environment, users and customers. As a rule, software development starts by fixing the environmental requirements, and then proceeds, via step-wise refinement, to the design and implementation phases. Into this group we thus have also included tools which further on in the design process, consider requirements derived from the bottom-up approach.

Any real system will consist of a non-homogeneous collection of functions which will have to be executed. According to the top-down approach, when we move away from the requirements of the application, it will be natural that a set of operators available in the specification language, will be selected heuristically. As a result a wide set of operators will be necessary to meet the wide range of possible applications. The same will be true in connection with the parameters of, and allowable relationships between, these operators. Top-down methods start from a point which is hard to describe formally, anyway, - the application domain. The heuristic nature of the necessary description tools will hinder the use of formal verification and analysis methods. Nevertheless, many CASE systems in this group do use formal methods: in the most cases, the formalisms have been added after the fundamental tools have been developed.

The first system for the requirements analysis of non-real-time data-processing applications that had real success in practice seems to be PSL/PSA [Teichroew (1977)]. This system works extremely well in its application area, although there is room for improvement. Researchers have pointed out some drawbacks of PSL/PSA; for example, it does not support parallel processing [Ludewig, (1983)], and the attribute analysis of its structural elements is not well supported [Furia (1979)]. In the later versions of PSL/PSA, the possibility of introducing accompanying simulation studies has been added. Also, users may now tailor relationships between structural elements of the description. The widely used SADT tools have adopted many of the PSL/PSA concepts [Ross (1985)].

One of the first CASE systems built especially for developing real-time applications was RSL/REVS [Alford (1977)]. In its first version performance and timing properties were analysed by simulation. In more recent versions, a limited capability for timing requirement analysis, together with the ability to support the development of distributed applications, was added [Alford (1985)], [Scheffe (1985)].

A remarkable feature of RSL/REVS is that it automatically generates a graphical representation of the specification in terms of R-nets (Requirement Networks). Five years after developing the R-net ideology, the concept was related back to the principles of finite automata [Alford (1985)]. A serious limitation of RSL/REVS, however, is that timing requirements are able to be analysed only within a single R-net [Scheffe (1985)].

The majority of the following tools and methods have been influenced by the ideas and concepts of PSL/PSA and RSL/REVS:

Ludewig (1980) suggested a tool, PCSL, for the specification of software for process-control systems. He used simplified data structures, (as compared to PSL/PSA), and paid direct attention to synchronization problems. He allowed parallel processing, and the approach is able to consider some of the important timing parameters.

The same author [Ludewig (1981)], [Ludewig (1983)] developed ESPRESO, which essentially extended PCLS. A new feature was the use of abstract data types. Unfortunately, ESPRESO pays less attention to analysing the specification than PCSL does - instead, specification implementation problems have been addressed in detail.

One of the most complete systems is EPOS [Biewald (1980)], [Lauber (1983)]. It is intended for developing process control software, and supports the whole software life-cycle. The formalism used in EPOS is the Petri-net. Based on experience and requirements in the practical use of EPOS, a subsystem for studying timing problems was added [Joho (1982)]. In this sub-system, the time-bound properties of the software under development are studied by simulation.

A novel approach to operational specification has been taken in STATEMATE (see, for example [Harel (1990)]). Here, the concentration has been on developing and using visual formalism. A substantial part of STATEMATE is a simulation-based study of the dynamic properties of the system being developed. The study is based on the use of STATECHARTS - which are extensions of finite state machines. Special care is taken to deal with state decomposition problems.

The well-known Jackson System Design Methodology, has been extended to cover real-time applications [Cameron (1986)]. It is now possible to impose time constraints on data validity, processing, etc. Data communication between processes is based on a first-in first-out (FIFO) discipline. Currently, though, little has been published about the methods used for analysing the timing properties.

Clearly, new CASE tools are emerging with increased speed, and we will therefore not try to name and describe them all. Instead, as in the previous group, we will try to find characteristics common to this group of top-down approach-based systems.

1. Special attention has been paid to studying the initial phase of software development. In earlier approaches, this phase was largely neglected by professional programmers, whereas the top-down approach has led to an awareness of the problems of knowledge elicitation and presentation.

2. Direct contacts between the actual requirements and the problems of proving the consistency of those requirements has definitely improved, through mutual understanding between programmers and their customers. Thus it has, to a certain extent, improved the quality of the resulting software - since the problem statement is more detailed and contains fewer inconsistencies. Consequently, a top-down approach is useful in reducing the semantic gap.

3. The top-down approach has served as an additional reason for developing good user interfaces for computer non-professionals.

The top-down approach starts at the application end, which, as we know, consists of a collection of non-homogeneous, physical, chemical, biological, economic, etc. processes and systems. Knowledge about these is extremely difficult to present formally, especially when trying to use the same approach and tools for all applications, and yet attempting to maintain efficient processing capability.

The drawbacks to the top-down approach can be derived from this last observation.

1. The operators and elements used in the specifications (via the specification languages) are selected heuristically, based mainly on the experience and "inner feelings" of their users. Research into the actual needs for describing various applications has not yet provided a solid foundation for a non-heuristic selection of building blocks. We therefore have to live with an array of agents, entities, stimulus-responses, processes, alphas and objects, without really knowing what the actual differences between them are! Also, for the application-oriented engineer, these terms are abstract and often meaningless.

2. As a consequence of the heuristic approach, formal methods for specification analysis are not always readily applicable. Therefore, in many cases the application of formal methods seems rather unnatural; also, the effects of their application are not always as expected.

3. Another consequence of the heuristic approach is the lack of strong timing analysis methods. The majority of systems which do provide timing analysis, apply it only to performance estimation. Typically the analysis is implemented by simulation.

4. Distributed computing problems stand, essentially, right on the borderline between the top-down and bottom-up approaches! This explains, to some extent, the difficulties with handling distributed systems, and the fact that most of the proposed methods are still not finding acceptance in real applications.

3.4 FORMALISMS IN CASE SYSTEMS

The wide range of possible formalisms currently suggested for, or actually incorporated into, software development tools, will not be dealt with here, but only briefly mentioned. The two most popular formal methods are finite automata and Petri-nets. Other formalisms can be grouped into classes of algebraic methods and classes of mathematical logic-based methods. The characteristics of the majority of methods, though, are such that they are not useful in proving complex timing correctness. As an exception, the algebras suggested by Caspi and Halbwachs (1982, 1986) and the various forms of temporal logic should be highlighted.

We have chosen here to stress only two well-defined approaches which seem to be particularly important in enabling the use of different formalisms - namely communicating abstract processes and the object-oriented techniques.

3.4.1 Communicating abstract processes

The communicating abstract processes approach is not, strictly speaking, a formalism. It is more of a concept which supports the use of various other formalisms. The value of the concept lies in its ability to separating the study of the algorithms which implement the structural elements of a system, from the study of the system's structure.

The concept of communicating abstract processes, which was in fact intuitively used for many years, was formulated and published by Hoare (1978).

The approach, based on the concept of communicating processes, combines elements of both bottom-up and top-down approaches in the specification and design of systems. According to this approach, processes in the environment and in the computing system are described as mappings from their definition domains into their value ranges. The occurrence of events is caused by the corresponding mappings.

The systematic application of communicating abstract processes offers the following possibilities:

- the description and study of data flow or control flow, as required,
- the consideration of either qualitative, or quantitative, timing restrictions imposed on the execution of mappings, and of interactions between mappings,
- a procession by the stepwise refinement of the mappings, from the requirement specification through to design and implementation, and
- the control of the complexity of each particular process, and that of the overall system, by the selection of algorithms which implement the mappings.

Some application examples of the concept are given by Reghbati (1980), Pizzarello (1982) and Roman (1983).

The first formal method for analysing the correctness of the joint functioning of communicating processes was published by Hoare (1981). This formalism is based on Hoare-Floyd's axiomatic approach, also known as Hoare's type logic, (see, for example [Apt (1984)]). This is, in fact, an application of his program verification methods, taken at a higher level of abstraction. Hoare,

(1981) assumes that all the causal relationships are known and that the message exchange between processes is based on a first-in first-out (FIFO) discipline.

A less theoretical approach has been taken in PAISLey (see, for example [Zave (1984),(1984a)]). This CASE system represents the operational specification approach, and takes care of cyclically-executed processes as well as some timing restrictions.

In the context of describing and analysing timing restrictions, possibly the best and most practical of the available formalisms is presented in [Quirk and Gilbert (1977), (1978)]. A large part of this book is devoted to an extension of the formalism suggested by them, and this will be discussed in depth in future chapters.

In summary, CASE systems based on the concepts of abstract communicating processes have several outstanding properties when compared to other approaches:

- bottom-up and top-down approaches, are combined, giving a high freedom of choice in the detailed description level,
- parallel, distributed and cyclic execution of processes are described naturally,
- no difficulties have been observed when introducing and analysing time parameters and timing restrictions, and
- many different formal methods may be used for describing separate structural elements (processes).

3.4.2 Object-oriented techniques

Another interesting concept, which can include many different formalisms and can also combine the top-down and bottom-up approaches, is the, now popular, object-oriented approach.

The key idea behind this approach is that a specification is described in terms of abstract objects, whose possible interactions are determined by explicitly stated interfaces. An object is usually an active component of the system to be described.

According to Berzins (1988), an object oriented system description should consist of all the aspects of the environment which impose restrictions and requirements on the computing system, as well as all the functions implemented by the computing system itself. There are slight distinctions made in interpreting objects given by different authors, but all recognize the basic features of objects, as stated in Goldberg (1983):

- An object is a protected data structure, with methods (procedures) for describing its processing.

- An object may have a hierarchical structure, so a "class" is an object describing data and methods which can be common to several other objects.

- A message is a request to an object for the execution of an action - often accompanied by the initial data necessary to execute that action.

Experiments undertaken by Boehm-Davis (1985) point out that an object-oriented design methodology tends to be more suitable for real-time applications than other methods i.e. those based on structure and functional decomposition methodologies. Unfortunately, no similar experimental data is available relating to comparing specification methodologies.

Another useful comparison of four different design methods for real-time systems is given in [Kelly (1987)]. Here, two of the four methods (Object-Oriented Design and Software Cost Reduction) are object-oriented, and one (PAMELA) is based on abstract communicating processes.

Somewhat surprisingly, Kelly (1987) and Calvez (1990), agree that an object-oriented approach is typically bottom-up, in other words it starts with knowledge representation in the computer. This may be true when we look at the existing CASE tools based on an object-oriented approach, but it does not hold true when we evaluate the general approach. We suggest that the present situation is caused by the pragmatic attitude of tool developers, and not by the limitations of the object-oriented approach.

In addition to our own experience, our belief is based on the comments of the authors of Smalltalk - a programming environment which must be considered as one of the major initiators of the object-oriented approach. According to Goldberg (1983), the approach was developed to obtain a better correspondence between human and computer knowledge presentation and processing. Consequently, from the point-of-view of computing system development, an object-oriented approach is natural in that we combine the top-down and bottom-up approaches!

In summary, from the details of specific tools one can discern several similarities between abstract communicating processes and object oriented methods:

- both combine (at least, in principle) the top-down and bottom-up approaches,

- both leave open (at the preliminary phases) the inner details of processes and objects,

- both allow the application of many different methods (including formal ones) of specifying, designing and implementing processes and objects, and finally

- both effectively separate the overall structure of the system to be developed from details of each structural element.

3.5 EVOLUTIONARY TRENDS IN CASE TOOLS FOR REAL-TIME APPLICATIONS

The methods and tools reviewed in this chapter have necessarily been disparate. Some tools have already been in use for a decade whilst others have only recently been suggested, and little of their practical engineering value is known.

Such a mixture was selected on purpose, since our goal was to gather together ideas and experience from a range of existing tools and methods. Hopefully, these ideas can serve as cornerstones for the development of new methods dedicated specifically to embedded software specification, design and maintenance.

From a historical perspective, one can distinguish two phases in the evolution of CASE systems and methods. The first phase lasted probably until the end of the 1970s. Experience gathered during this phase was analysed and generalized in many papers [Lehman (1980)], [Ohno (1982)], [Zave (1982)], [Winograd (1979)], [Hausen (1982)], [Abbot (1981)]. A particularly useful assessment of the major results of this first phase was presented by Balzer (1979). The eight principles, initially formulated by Balzer, are still the basis for the research in this area:

- Separate functionality from implementation.
- An application-oriented system specification language is required (presenting a model of system behaviour).
- A specification must encompass the system of which the software is a component.
- A specification must encompass the environment in which the system operates.
- A system specification must be a cognitive model rather than a design - implementation model.
- A specification must be operational (sufficiently complete and formal).
- The system specification must be tolerant of incompleteness and augmentable.
- The specification must be localised and loosely coupled.

The second phase now seems also to be complete. Its termination was marked by a wave of survey and analysis papers. [Boehm (1986)], [Greenspan (1986)], [Roman (1985)], [Prieto-Diaz (1986)], [Ross (1985)], [Alford (1985)], [Hesse (1984)], [Zave (1984)].

This second phase was characterized by the fact that the idea of operational specifications had gained popularity. This was partly due to the increased interest in operational specifications, and partly due to the increased number of embedded applications. As a result, research into, and the actual use of, formal methods, increased remarkably. Formal methods were also added to systems developed during the first phase, such as finite automata being added to RSL/REVS, and Petri-nets to EPOS. Additionally, because of practical necessity, the building of tools for timing analysis was also started. The majority of well-documented applications, however, still used simulations for studying the timing properties of specified and/or designed systems.

Based on this review, and on our own experience, we suggest the following trends which we consider will characterize the development of CASE tools for embedded real-time software in the coming years.

1. Software engineering first emerged as a discipline following the realisation that we were plunging into a so-called "software crisis", increasingly producing software with little idea of how to control its development. Early ideas on software engineering were based on studies into the static structure of programs, with the hope of facilitating the debugging, testing and maintenance of programs. Now, however, software engineering has taken two distinct directions:

    - algorithm (program) specification, design, implementation and maintenance, and
    - specification, design, implementation and maintenance of systems of interacting algorithms in which the inner structure of each particular algorithm is ignored.

2. The general problems of software engineering will be related to:

    - the introduction of knowledge bases into CASE systems,
    - the application of knowledge elicitation and processing methods for facilitating the re-use of existing specifications, designs and software products, and
    - the collection, systematization and automatic re-use of human expertise, as applied in the non-formal decision making required during the evolution of projects in a software engineering environment.

3. The demand for embedded systems is increasing rapidly. As a result, from the software engineering point-of-view there is a demand for CASE tools appropriate to developing such specialised software. New formal methods are required for timing analysis and checking the correspondence of the dynamic properties of an embedded system, the dynamic requirements of an application. Whenever possible, preference should be given to analytical methods as opposed to simulation studies. Simulation studies are analogous to software testing - one can demonstrate the presence of errors, but not their absence!

4. With the increasing role of formal methods, single-formalism-based systems are preferable to those based on multiple formalisms. Using only one formalism across several stages of the software life-cycle gives an inherent economy in a CASE system implementation, and also in terms of user education. An additional advantage is that automatic knowledge presentation and processing becomes easier. This, approach, however, should not totally exclude the use of other appropriate formalisms for particular purposes, but the required transformation from one formalism to another must be done automatically, thus ensuring that no errors are introduced.

5. Any CASE tool should accept all information as soon as it becomes available, and use it whenever necessary. This avoids the need for additional information gathering. As an example, we suggest that techniques, such as those used by Matsumoto (1981,1982) in which he investigated timing restrictions only after synthesizing the finite automaton, are inappropriate. The knowledge presentation methods, likewise, should be able to capture all the information which will be needed in the process of software development.

6. For embedded software development, two conceptually close classes of methods and tools - abstract communicating processes and an object-oriented approach are important. There are at least two reasons for this:

- both top-down and bottom-up approaches can be arbitrarily combined. This helps to decrease the semantic gap between programmers and customers, and facilitates a smooth transformation from specification through design, and on to implementation, and,

- the necessary timing parameters and cyclic execution of processes/objects fit naturally into these concepts. This enables the development of suitable formalisms for correctness analysis.

As has been mentioned in this chapter, potential candidates for the timing analysis methods have been suggested by Caspi and Halbwachs (1986) and Quirk (1977).

3.6 SUMMARY

This chapter has attempted a broad-based review of the current situation relating to CASE tools for use in the development of embedded software. Important trends have been extracted, and potential candidate approaches suggested. This book now uses these as pointers in moving ahead to propose an environment which goes a long way towards satisfying a significant section of the requirements for a specification tool for embedded software.

CHAPTER 4

The Q-Model

In Chapter 1 we analysed the aspects of embedded software which make it inherently different from traditional data processing software. These differences are fundamentally due to various timing restrictions on the parallel execution of processes, compounded by having, in practice, incomplete information relating to the causal relationships. In addition, there is the necessity for the cyclic execution of individual processes, and the need for time-selective interprocess communication. We listed in that chapter, the time parameters of processes that are considered necessary for creating an execution schedule, which will guarantee the fulfilment of the time constraints imposed by the environment of the embedded system.

In Chapter 3 we discussed some of the existing CASE tools, primarily with a view to determining to what extent the requirements for the specification of embedded software are currently being met. It appears that, with a few exceptions, the majority of existing CASE tools proposed for use in real-time applications have been developed by extending the methods used earlier for non-time-critical data-processing applications. The basic ideas behind the tools remain unchanged, and only additional subsystems have been added to cater for the handling of *some* real-time properties. It is suggested that such an approach cannot provide a tool which systematically and comprehensively covers all the requirements for the specification and design of embedded systems (see Chapter 1).

In Chapter 3 we suggested two promising approaches which can be adopted in developing a computational model for embedded software. These are based on an object-oriented approach, together with the use of techniques based on communicating abstract processes. Whilst the two approaches are conceptually close, the object-oriented approach is more general since it allows, in practice, an unlimited choice of methods for describing objects.

We have decided, though, to restrict this freedom in order to increase the efficiency and analytic power of the resulting computational model. We have therefore applied the concepts of abstract communicating processes to the description of objects and their interactions. In view of the deterministic structure of embedded systems, we also need to restrict the dynamic creation and deletion of objects.

Our goal in this chapter is to formulate a computational model which:

- meets the requirements stated in Chapter 1, necessary for modelling software for embedded systems,
- is applicable to all the software life-cycle stages involved in describing a system's behaviour, and in analysing the correspondence between the dynamic requirements of the environment and the dynamic capabilities of the computing system,

and

- is based on a general object-oriented framework and, for detailed description uses the concept of abstract communicating processes.

Since we try to avoid algorithmic details of the embedded software, at least during the initial phase of development, and concentrate rather on describing and analysing the software structure, we will describe a system as a collection of objects created from two super classes - processing objects and communicating objects.

Before proceeding with a detailed description of these objects, we will explain our initial premises in more detail.

4.1 BASICS FOR DEVELOPING A COMPUTATIONAL MODEL

Summarising much of our previous discussion, it is evident that any embedded system is a computing system which executes operations on a collection of interacting objects. From the implementation point-of-view, an embedded system may thus be described as a hierarchy of virtual machines (see Chapter 1). The end-user normally sees only the uppermost machine in this hierarchy; the instrumentation engineer usually works at the lowest level of virtual machines - this is where the data measured in the environment enters the computer system, and where decisions are delivered back to the environment for execution.

Software engineers tackling the specification, design and programming tasks all develop these virtual machines in order that the requirements of the end-user and the environment are satisfied. One of the major problems to be faced is to overcome the semantic gaps which exist between the different levels of virtual machines. This problem was discussed in detail in Chapter 1. In this current chapter we base our work on a primitive, invariant notion: the notion that there exists an element in a computer system which may be used on different levels of abstraction without a change in its semantics. We suggest that this primitive invariant element is a "computational process".

4.1.1 Informal definition of a computational process

In the 1960s processes were already being recognised as the fundamental, dynamic units of computation. Intuitively, processes were understood to be programs in execution. A number of different definitions of the concept of a process exist, but most of them can be reduced to a simple formulation:

"a process is a sequence of actions performed by a program" (see [Coffman and Denning (1973)]).

In view of the variety of definitions of a process, Coffman and Denning actually avoided the notion of "process" when they want to be more formal - they use "task" instead. Therefore, a more detailed definition of a process can be obtained by using that given by Coffman and Denning (1973), by simply replacing "task" with "process"

"A process (task) is an atomic unit of computation, whose terminal behaviour is specified but whose internal operation is unspecified and of no interest to a discussion. Depending on the application, a process can be a computer instruction, a procedure or even an entire (unitary or distributed) system."

This definition is ideal for use at different stages in the software life cycle; all we have to do is to change the abstraction level. As a result, we can describe a software system as a single process, or as a set of communicating processes, depending on how much detail we would like to see.

Further, we choose to interpret the term "internal operations" of a process rather loosely; the term may denote the execution of computer instructions, actions performed by humans, or actions performed (or caused) by the physical processes in the environment of the computing system. Such a loose interpretation is necessary at the specification stage - for we will then be able to describe processes in a computer, just as well as we can describe actions performed by humans or physical processes in the environment. The latter are important in capturing the characteristics of the interface between the embedded computing system and its environment.

Although the terminal behaviour is specified the precise internal operations of a process are not known (and are, at this stage, declared to be of no interest), for future formalisation we will require to make *some* assumptions about the inner structure of a process. In principle, we suggest that the internal operations of a process may be executed either sequentially (in a prefixed order) or in parallel (where the execution sequence of internal operations is determined dynamically).

When analysing a specification assuming a sequential nature of processes (i.e. the assumption that the internal operations are executed in a prefixed order) is useful, however, since it results in a simpler structure for a process. This, in turn, facilitates the analysis of its properties; the better these are defined, the easier will be the implementation algorithm selection. It is important, though, to appreciate that the above preference does not restrict the freedom of implementation in any way.

4.1.2 An informal introduction to process interaction within a system

Having accepted the idea of a process being a fundamental unit of computation, a software system can conveniently be described as consisting of interacting processes. An essential requirement is that the processes of the system may have to be executed in parallel. This immediately implies that time instants could exist where several processes have been started and not yet completed.

Processes may interact either:

- indirectly, when competing for resources, or
- directly, when communicating, that is, exchanging data.

Whilst analysing specifications, we can neglect any indirect interaction within processes by assuming that each process executes on a separate processor and has all the necessary physical resources. This enables us to avoid dealing with implementation problems during the initial phases of a project. When necessary, we can describe the competition for resources by introducing special processes, such as Hoare's monitors, (see [Hoare (1978)]).

Direct interaction, (in other words, communication between processes), in the majority of models has been described by the use of shared memory. The communicating processes are synchronised by the use of devices such as semaphores and critical sections. A problem, though, is that many embedded systems will not be able to support shared memory, since they tend, by nature, to be distributed. In view of this, process communication in the computation model has to be based on message exchange. In addition, we apply a "producer-consumer" scheme since we are interested in bounded time for message transfer (see [Lamport (1985)]). Formal comparison of the two classes of process communication methods is given by Zave (1976) and DeNicola (1981).

All processes in an embedded system will be started often - either periodically or aperiodically. This causes additional complications in process communication. It will often be necessary, to distinguish, for example, between different *generations of data*. These different *data generations* result from different executions of the same process. The handling of different data generations can be considered only if the message exchange mechanism has some intelligence. This concept as we shall see later in Section 4.3 will form a fundamental aspect of our approach to an intelligent message exchange mechanism.

For the sake of ease in modifying a system and in order to suppress the side-effects of changing a process, we have selected an asymmetric communication scheme. In this, the consumer of data will always know the names of its data producers - but the producer does not know anything about its consumers. Thus, independent of whether previous output data has been consumed or not, results from subsequent executions of a process will overwrite previous results, unless the message exchange mechanism has held them (say, in a buffer).

4.2 FORMAL DEFINITION OF A PROCESS

At different levels in the hierarchy of virtual machines, users will adopt different semantics to describe what a process is. A programmer, for example, will be satisfied with the explanation that a process is a "program in execution". A control engineer, though, may say that a process is the action of changing a valve position, or re-adjusting the set-point of a controller.

In order to reach a common interpretation of the word "process", the mathematical notion of a mapping has been adopted.

A process (p) *is considered to be a mapping* (i.e. a transformation) *from its domain of definition* (dom p) (i.e. set of all possible input values) *onto its value range* (val p) (i.e. set of all possible output values).

$$p\colon \text{dom } p \rightarrow \text{val } p\,.$$

Although at first sight this is a vague and abstract concept, the definition covers all the data transformations commonly used in programs. Many authors have supported this definition (e.g. Davis (1979)), and its application in traditional data processing software modelling has been successful. It should also be noted that unlike in the standard object-oriented approach, we do not want to have 2 or more copies of a process activated at exactly the same time instant: because we wish to ensure full observable behaviour. Of course, 2 or more copies of a process could simultaneously be executed but they will not have had the same start time. One actually may have simultaneous instantations of a process but under different names - just to make sure which instantation does what!

However, if we consider the fundamental requirements of embedded software, we find a number of drawbacks in the above definition which will hinder its use in models of embedded software. These drawbacks stem from difficulties in characterising the nature of a process's execution. In essence, we cannot fix when, and how often, a process is started. In systems whose functioning is guided by completely known causal relations, this knowledge is not required - a process is activated soon after all the necessary conditions for its activation have been satisfied. In such systems the most recent data is always the best!

However, when we do not know the instants of process activation, we cannot time-stamp the process's output data. It is not possible, therefore, to check the "age" of input data; consequently, we are not able to guarantee the time-selectivity of process communication. One could argue that at the system's actual runtime, we could measure time, and time-stamp all the data moving in the system. This is certainly true, but two problems remain unsolved.

Firstly, this can only be done after the system has been implemented. If we discover, at that stage, that we cannot meet some of the timing constraints, a large part of the system will have to be modified - defeating the whole objective of having specification tools.

Secondly, whilst we can measure time, and hence time-stamp all the events occurring inside a computing system, it is not always possible to time-stamp events that have occurred in the environment. This immediately restricts our ability to prove the correspondence of the dynamic requirements of the environment and the dynamic capabilities of the computing system.

To overcome these difficulties, Quirk and Gilbert (1977) had an inspiration: *process start times should be described explicitly*. The resulting process definition is as follows:

$$p: T(p) \times \text{dom } p \rightarrow \text{val } p,$$

where T(p) *is the* ***process timeset*** *which contains all the process start times.*

This new definition of a process thus provides the possibility of comparing the "age" of data to a particular starting instant. It also automatically time-stamps all process output data with the process's start times.

4.2.1 Properties of the process timeset

A process timeset is primarily determined on the basis of the dynamic requirements of the environment, although in some cases the intrinsic requirements of the computing system could also influence the value of the elements in the process timeset. Each process may, in theory, have its own independent timeset.

Since an embedded system typically functions in infinite loops, most of its processes will be activated a large number of times. Thus, there are several possible ways of defining a timeset:

- Explicitly listing all elements of the timeset, for example, fixing the first element and determining a regular interval between two successive elements

- Selecting a triggering event in the environment whose occurrence activates the process. In this case, however, it will also be necessary to estimate the interval between two successive elements of the set, otherwise it will be impossible to analyse the behavioural properties of the system.

- Selecting a triggering event in the embedded system. This case is equivalent to the traditional software system which has completely known causal relationships, in that we assume that we are in control of all the events occurring inside the computing system.

- Referring to a timeset that is already defined for another process, and fixing some additional restrictions. For example, the process could be activated simultaneously with a referred process, or the process could be activated immediately after the process referred to has completed its execution.

Pragmatic considerations will also force several restrictions upon the elements and overall properties of a timeset.

1. Elements of a timeset must be well-ordered. As soon as a partial ordering is permitted, indeterminacy cannot be avoided in respect of data consumption. Indeterminacy is not desirable in embedded systems - comments on this issue are given by Kerridge and Simpson (1986), as well as in earlier sections of this book.

2. Each timeset must have a minimal element, since all timesets must be well-ordered. We require that all timesets of a system have a common minimal element, min (T(p)) = 0. As a result of this, each system (and, in fact, each process in a system) may have its own unique time referencing system. This timing system may, or may not, be related to the time referencing systems in other processes interacting with the process we are modelling. The question of whether or not these unique time referencing systems are synchronised to astronomical time is not important from the computational model's point-of-view.

3. We can assume a finite computing power in the underlying processing system. This implies that in any finite time interval, a process may be activated only a finite number of times:

$$/ [0,t] \cap T(p) / < \infty ,$$

where / . / denotes the "power" or "cardinality" (i.e. number of elements) of a set and

[.,.] denotes a closed interval.

The same statement may be reformulated and presented as follows:

Let t, $t' \in T(p)$ where t, t' are two consecutive elements of T(p). Then, based on empirical application knowledge, it is always possible to find functions, $t_{min}(p) \neq 0$, $t_{max}(p) \neq 0$ and $t_{min}(p) < t_{max}(p)$, such that $t_{min}(p) \leq t' - t \leq t_{max}(p)$.

In summary, there are several possible ways of defining the timeset for a process:

(i) Explicitly listing all elements of the timeset, or fixing the first element and determining a regular interval between two successive elements - for example,

$T(p_i) = \{t_0, t_1, t_2, \ldots, t\}$

or

$T(p_i) = \{t: t_n = t_0 + nt_a\}$, where t_a is the regular interval between two successive elements

(ii) Selecting a triggering event in the environment whose occurrence activates the process

$T(p_i) = \{t: t_n = t(ne)\}$, where t(ne) is the instant of the *n*-th occurrence of the triggering event *e*.

In order to enable further analysis of the behavioural properties, it will be necessary to estimate the interval between two successive occurrences of the event, *e*. It should be noted that this additional information effectively reduces this case to the previous one, (i): the only difference is that the triggering event is selected from the environment.

(iii) Referring to a timeset that has been defined for another process and possibly allowing some additional restrictions caused by attributes of that process. For example, the process could be activated simultaneously to the referred process; or the process could be activated immediately after the process referred to has completed its execution; or an attempt to activate the process within its equivalence interval will be neglected.

4.2.2 Cyclic execution of a process

In practice, computer resources are always limited, with each processor having a finite power. Consequently, unless we are careful, cyclic activation of processes cannot be guaranteed, and an implemented system will not always be able to execute processes cyclically for any fixed period of time. If, say, the execution time for each process is not bounded, available resources can soon become overloaded by started, but not yet completed, processes. Any further increase in the number of activated processes, or in the processing of re-entrant copies of processes, will require multiprogramming, and hence additional time must be spent on context switching. (Context switching is the processing undertaken by the operating system, or its executive, which is necessary to undertake process swapping).

If we continue in this fashion, i.e. initiating new processes whilst others are incomplete, sooner or later the system will not be able to perform any useful (i.e. application-oriented) work, and will use its processing power solely for context switching, i.e. "thrashing" occurs.

This situation can, in principle, be avoided if we introduce a restriction on process execution time. Let us denote the execution time of process p, started at time instant $t \in T(p)$, by $\zeta\ (p,t)$. In general, $\zeta\ (p,t)$ will be random. Without discussing other possibilities here, we suggest that an estimate of the execution time be used, such that,

$$\zeta\ (p,t) \in [\alpha\ (p), \beta\ (p)]\ .$$

Here, $\alpha\ (p)$ and $\beta\ (p)$, where $\alpha\ (p) < \beta\ (p)$, are functions determined by using empirical, or theoretical, knowledge of the nature of process p. It is assumed that the execution time may have values uniformly distributed in the given interval.

By using the suggested interval estimate we are actually highlighting our ignorance of the execution time of a process. In theory, a statistical estimation based on the probability distribution of $\zeta\ (p,t)$, is possible. However, considering the difficulties associated with this, as well as the need for a robust specification and design analysis, and the necessity of obtaining the worst and the best case estimates only, we have eliminated (for the time being) the idea of correct, mathematical handling of such random variables.

It is appropriate here to make another comment on the philosophical nature of time. The time mechanism adopted for describing process timesets and process execution times has all the properties of thermodynamical time. It is irreversible, except under strictly fixed conditions. For example, we cannot usually re-execute completed process execution cycles; the results of these might have already been used to influence the environment, and we cannot undo physical processes in that environment. If necessary, we may introduce a separate system of time for describing events occurring during process execution. The only condition here is that we have to synchronise the beginning- and end-points of this time to the internal time of the system which has been used in defining the timesets. This additional system of time may, in some cases, be that of theoretical physics, in that time during the process execution could be reversible, as long as deadlines (for completion of execution) are met. In other cases, the additional time may also be thermodynamical.

It is important to note here that all process times must be bounded - without this assumption, a full analysis of temporal behaviour is impossible. The boundedness of process times is not a serious restriction from the practical point-of-view. If we expect our system to give positive results in finite time, we must also expect that all the activities taken by our system terminate in finite time. The upper bound to process execution time may, in theory, be any finite number. However, for increasing the actual benefit obtained from the timing analysis, it is recommended that the upper bounds are realistic. In many cases one has to modify one's pattern of thinking slightly to get the maximum benefit out of the timing analysis. Consider, for example, a process monitoring a telephone call in a digital exchange. The problem here is that we seem in this case, not to want to restrict ourselves to a fixed time limit for all calls. The monitoring process, however, in our thinking need not be considered to be executing exactly as long as the monitored call. If we want to measure the duration of the call, we can take a "minimum time unit" (possibly based on financial considerations!) and check periodically if the call is continuing. In this case the monitoring process is actuated periodically - each execution takes a short time.

The other purpose for monitoring a call is either for listening to it or recording it. Here the monitoring process is activated only twice - firstly when the monitored call starts (to switch on the listening/recording device) and, secondly, when the call terminates (to switch off the device).

4.2.3 State of a process

Traditionally in programming a computational process is partitioned into a set of internal states. A process is then described as a series of transitions from one internal state to another - until a terminating state is reached. A similar approach (state transitions) is used for describing the functioning of dynamic systems in theoretical automatic control.

Program verification is also normally based on proving correctness in moving from one state to the next, where certain pre- and post-conditions are related to each state. The popular finite state machine concept is also often used for formal representation of program functioning, and this is, based on having knowledge of the internal states of a process.

In our case, unfortunately, the traditional interpretation of a process state is not applicable. There are two main reasons for this:

- Firstly, the overall complexity (i.e., the total number of states) of a typical, practical system will exceed our processing and analytic capabilities, if each process in a system is represented by a set of internal states. An average embedded system will consist of several hundreds, if not thousands, of processes so if we assume that each process has ten internal states, we end up with tens of thousands of states in the system. (Maybe this is why Petri-nets are not often used in handling *real* systems?). Thus to decrease the complexity of a system description we reduce the overall number of considered states. This can be done by abstracting away the inner states of processes. Traditionally, a process is considered as a sequence of transfers from one inner state to another. When analysing timing properties we do not need (or, rather, can cope without) such detailed knowledge of each process.

- Secondly, at the specification stage, we have not, as a rule, fixed the algorithms to implement the processes. Thus, defining the internal states will be impossible! The methodology advocated in this book says that we do not need to know the detailed algorithms in order to analyse the time correctness of the proposed system. We can thus reduce the complexity of the description and return to consider the internal states at a later stage, when selecting/specifying/developing the required algorithms.

Our aim, though, is to analyse many of the properties of the specification as early as possible, so it seems to be necessary to devise a compromise solution to the question of processes and their states.

We propose that in order to describe the structure of a future system, and to analyse its dynamic properties, it is possible to neglect the internal states of processes, and let each process have only one state - a termination state. In other words, at the completion of a process's execution, its output variables will form the *new state value* of that process. The state value is thus an element in the process's value range. At the end of the next execution cycle, the process state is given a new value. As a result, a process state will have piecewise-constant graph.

The state of process p, activated at $t \in T(p)$, is an element of the process value range, val p, denoted by s(p,t), which has resulted from the particular execution at time t. The state value, s(p,t), remains unchanged until the completion of the next execution of the process.

A process state is time-stamped with the time instant of processes start - this is because this instant has the minimum indeterminacy of all the time parameters characterising a process. Random factors, typically caused by implementation details (as a result of, say, multiprogramming, or through the transport delay of messages), will have minimum influence on the process start time.

4.2.4 Common and selector processes

Processes can interact in a system if:

(i) The producer process output variables (i.e. the *value* range) and the consumer process input variable (i.e. the *domain* of definition) have a common part. i.e. when the value range and domain of definition have common elements.

(ii) The corresponding values resulting from a particular execution, are transmitted from the producer process to the consumer process.

Let us consider an example of three interacting processes (Figure 4.1), neglecting at this stage any formal graphical symbols:

We assume here that the domain of process p_1 is completely determined by value ranges of p_2 and p_3. Without pondering at this stage on the various possible ways and methods of arranging the interactions (this will come later), this situation can be described mathematically as:

$$\text{dom } p_1 = \text{val } p_2 \times \text{val } p_3.$$

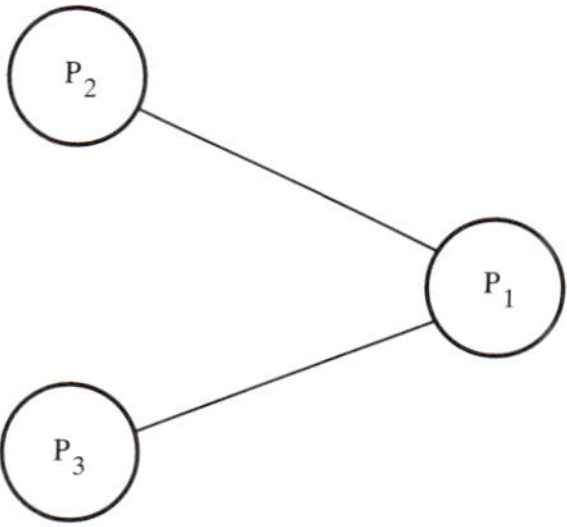

Figure **4.1** 3 Interactive Processes.

Depending on the algorithm which implements process p_1, the variable values which form an element of dom p_1 may be consumed each time it is executed. Alternatively, the selective consumption of the variable values (forming the element of dom p_1) may be performed in a fashion in which the selection depends on conditions posed by the algorithm of process p_1.

Exactly in the same way, the value range of p_1 may always consist of the same variables, or it might consist of several value ranges which are selected on the basis of the input data of the process and/or the interim results of computation. Note, that we must emphasise that actual data values are not exchanged; the approach considers only the *time* at which the data would be exchanged.

In the traditional programmer's interpretation, these situations are known as the *conditional transfer of control*, depending on input data or interim results.

In order to decrease possible indeterminacy in the behaviour of the system, it is advisable, whenever possible, to fix explicitly such conditions of control transfer. To facilitate this, we divide processes into two classes.

1. *A Common process* is an unconditionally defined mapping on the Cartesian product of all input variables, which always maps the elements in its domain into one and the same value range.

A typical example of a common process will be one which implements a simple elementary action which will not be further decomposed.

2. *A Selector process* is a mapping whose execution is influenced by explicitly defined conditions:

- it can select only some of the variables in an element of its domain,

or

- it may have more than one value range. Selection between the value ranges during a particular execution can depend upon input data and/or interim results.

A typical example of a selector process will be a process which is aggregating (combining) two or more common processes. On the input side of the selector process, an input selector will decide which of the input variables to accept. On the output side, an output selector will decide which set of output variables to assign new values to.

In terms of the process state, therefore, it can be seen that a selector process has more than one state, whereas a common process has exactly one state.

Formal methods for fixing such input selectors have been proposed by Pattison (1987). Pattison suggests the use of restriction, group and preference constraints (in the form of predicates) in reducing the size of each operand (e.g. the value range of a producer process) of the Cartesian product which defines the domain of a consumer process. The output selector is seen as a mechanism for selecting one of many different paths (possibly with different output variables) according to an algorithm implementing the selector process.

4.3 FORMAL DEFINITION OF PROCESS INTERACTION

In an embedded system, just as in any large software system, there are two seemingly contradictory requirements:

- processes must interact, and exchange data and control signals,

but

- processes should be as loosely-coupled as possible.

The latter demand becomes important at the maintenance stage, especially when the system needs to be modified. Loose-coupling obviously decreases possible side-effects caused by modifications.

In the light of these contradictory requirements, the question of process interaction is a key issue in our proposed modelling methodology. Whilst many techniques have been suggested, we start our discussion here by looking at ADA. In this language, the well-known "rendezvous" technique has been adopted: this requires symmetrical knowledge between the communication partners - "I can accept a message from you, only if I know that you were supposed to send it to me" (see, for example, [Rationale (1979)]).

We suggest, however, that the need for such symmetrical knowledge is too strong and too restrictive an assumption, especially for implementing time-selective, intercycle communication between processes. We also find that in practical situations a producer process supplies data to several consumers, and that each of these can have different requirements in terms of the "age" of the data required (see section 4.1.2. relating to the concept of age). In this case, either the producer process, or each consumer, must take responsibility for storing the required amount of data, essentially the required number of the producer's states. The resulting effect is that we have to extend the capability of each process by adding data-storage and data-handling components. A significant number of these additional facilities will be common to most processes, and the question is, whether they should be duplicated throughout the system, or whether some other mechanism should be devised.

We suggest separating such data-handling facilities from the application-oriented components in the same way as operating systems are separated from application software. This immediately enables us to adopt an asymmetric approach to knowledge between communication partners.

This approach to data exchange has the following rather pragmatic advantages:

(i) Data is transferred only when absolutely necessary; the producer has to send/store its recently produced values to be able to carry on with its computations. The consumer, however, does not need the data before it really CAN use it - at that time, only, it asks for data from the "store". The "depth" of this "store" depends on the producer's and consumer's requirements.

(ii) From the software maintenance point-of-view, it is important when changing/modifying processes that the side-effects are minimal. This is greatly simplified by the suggested approach.

When implementing this approach we naturally orientate ourselves to message passing in any of its forms, e.g. polling or remote procedure calls, etc.

We thus require that consumers know their producer partners, whereas producers do not know anything about their consumers. The producer-processes simply produces their states, and a special, logical device accepts these states, and forms the messages required by the consumers. Such a logical device is termed here a ***channel***. A channel implements point-to-point, one-way communication between two processes. Formally, a channel is a mapping of the producer process (p_i) value range (i.e. its output) onto the consumer process (p_j) domain of definition, (i.e. its input).

Thus:

$$\sigma_{ij}: \text{val } p_i \times T(p_i) \times T(p_j) \rightarrow \text{proj}_{\text{val } p_i} \text{dom } p_j$$

- where $\text{proj}_{\text{val } p_i} \text{dom } p_j$ denotes a projection of the domain of p_j onto the value range of p_i.

The idea of the projection is to emphasise that one producer does not necessarily define the whole domain of the consumer process - it is more likely that it will define only part of it. Timesets are included in the definition of a channel in order to describe, if required, the time-selectivity of the channel. It is evident that the above definition gives the consumer access to the complete history of the producer process. The time selectivity of a channel is described by means of the channel function, $K(\sigma_{ij},t)$.

Formally:

a channel function $K(\sigma_{ij},t)$ defines for each $t \in T(p_j)$, a subset of $T(p_i)$

$$K(\sigma_{ij},t) \subset T(p_i), \quad t \in T(p_j).$$

Thus consumer process p_j, activated at $t \in T(p_j)$, only has access to the states of producer process p_i, whose computations were activated at $t \in K(\sigma_{ij},t)$.

We wish to point out that the concepts of channels and channel functions were originally suggested by Quirk and Gilbert (1977).

In practice, time-sets and time-subsets are difficult to manipulate. Therefore, we find it useful to use relative "backward time", in which channel functions are given as intervals in this time. Relative backward time belongs, in the philosophical sense, to so-called "psychological" time, and is found to be extremely useful in describing process communication. Here, each pair of communicating processes has its own relative time. The origin of this time is defined by the instant of the consumer process start time which has resulted in the request for data from the channel. The basic difficulty in applying this approach to timing lies in transferring the origin of time to the producer-process's timeset. This problem is discussed in detail in the next chapter.

The channel function is thus expressed as an interval in the relative time for the associated pair of processes. We introduce a numbering scheme for the start times of the producer process p_i, and an example of this is given in Table 4.1. for the case when p_i is activated at $t_i \in T(p_i)$.

$T(p_i) =$	t_0, t_1, t_2, ..., t_i, ..., t_n, ...
numbering of elements	i, i-1, i-2, ..., 0

Table **4.1** An example of a number scheme for the producer timeset elements in relative time.

The channel function may thus be expressed as $K(\sigma_{ij},t) = [\mu, \nu]$ where μ and ν are integers. For example, $\nu = 0$ and $\mu = 1$ denotes that the consumer can get the latest state (available at the moment of the request) and the immediately preceding state, of the producer (see Table 4.1).
If $\nu = 1$ and $\mu = 1$, then only the latter is accessible through this channel.

It should be noted that the origin of relative time $(\nu = 0)$, in which the interaction between processes p_i and p_j is described, is determined by the request for data from the consumer-process, transferred then to the appropriate start time of that process, fixing thus an element of the consumer-process timeset $T(p_j)$. As the next step (described in detail in Chapter 5), one has to find a corresponding element from the producer-process timeset which is the actual origin of relative time for this particular act of interaction. Intuitively, the transfer of an element of a timeset onto another timeset depends on the relationship between the two timesets involved. As explained in the next section, different relationships between the producer and consumer processes timesets define different channel types.

4.3.1 Types of channels

Each and every process in a system may, in theory, have its own timeset. Now, since the communication between processes can require specific conditions for the synchronisation of the communicating processes, we need to provide various channel types which will take care of all possible situations. Of course, the most simple case will be that of the traditional Petri-net interaction - i.e. the completion of one process causes a partner process to start:

The major reason for requiring different types of channels is to be able to describe the relationships which can exist between the timesets of the various communicating processes. In practice, we have found four types of channels useful describing synchronisation and data communication between producer (p_i) and the consumer (p_j) processes. These types are as follows:

- *A synchronous channel*, in which $T(p_i) = T(p_j)$, in other words, one in which the two timesets coincide exactly.

- *A semisynchronous channel*, in which the timeset of the producer is given and this determines (in fact, generates) the consumer process's timeset, i.e. $T(p_i) \rightarrow T(p_j)$. This, indeed, is analogous to a Petri-type relationship, and describes an asynchronous interaction in the normal computer science interpretation.

- *An asynchronous channel*, in which the producer and consumer timesets are independent (or, possibly, we cannot prove their dependence on each other). Thus this channel performs in a truly asynchronous mode. This is usually accompanied by the fact that the timesets have different powers, i.e.

$$/ [0,t] \cap T(p_i) / \neq / [0,t] \cap T(p_j) /.$$

Now, since channels are the only mechanism for the synchronisation of different processes, we also need a channel which does not transfer data, but only synchronises process activation. This channel is called *a null channel* and it guarantees that the timesets of the processes associated with it, will coincide.

The four types of channels described above seem to cover a wide application area and the formal analytic methods developed further in this book, will consider only these forms of channels.

There are no formal hindrances, though, to extending this set of channel types, and the only additional difficulty will be that each new channel type will need to be accompanied by methods for checking correct usage.

Finally, it is important to note that as the semisynchronous channel actually implements communication between asynchronous processes in the traditional meaning of the word, the functioning resembles a transition in a Petri-net - therefore this channel can also be called a *Petri-channel.*

4.4 DESCRIPTION OF A SYSTEM IN THE Q-MODEL

In summary, the Quirk (or Q-)model has only two types of elements - processes and channels - and a system description may use only these elements.

Formally, a system described in terms of the Q-model is considered to be a pair

$$(P, \Sigma),$$

where P is the set of processes included into the system description, $P = \{p_1, p_2, p_3, \dots, p_n\}$ and Σ is the set of channels representing all described interactions which occur between the processes, $\Sigma \subset P \times P$. We note here that there is no distinction made at this point between any possible channel types: this decision will be made later in the decision process.

Each of the processes $p_i \in P$ may be considered as a system (P', Σ'). The opposite is also true: a system, (P, Σ) may be represented as a process $p''_j \in P''$, of a higher level system (P'', Σ'').

The state-of-a-system, (P, Σ), at each time instant is determined by the states of all the processes of that system.

With these formal ideas in mind, we progress in the next Chapter towards applying them in practice, and start by looking at graphical mechanisms to represent processes. We will also have to look more closely at the internal operations of the processes.

CHAPTER 5

Representation of the Q-Model

In the previous chapter we introduced the formal description of a system in terms of the Q-Model. In this approach a system is described as a pair (P, Σ), where P is a set of processes, and Σ is a set of channels responsible for implementing the necessary process interaction. This formal, mathematically-sound description can also be represented graphically, where processes are the nodes of a graph and channels are the arcs.

As a simple example, the three interacting processes introduced in Section 4.2.4, are shown in such a graphical form (Figure 5.1)

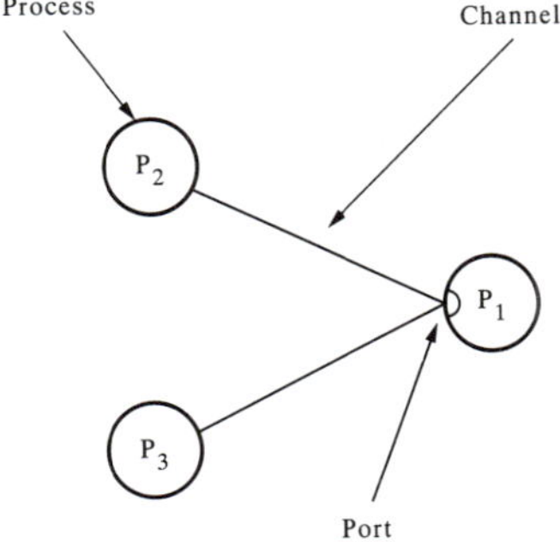

Figure **5.1**. Graphical representation of three interacting processes

For convenience, we use circles to denote common processes, and rectangles to denote selector processes. Each arc of the graph has a set of attributes, which describe channel type and function. Figure 5.2 shows these representations and also inputs via ports.

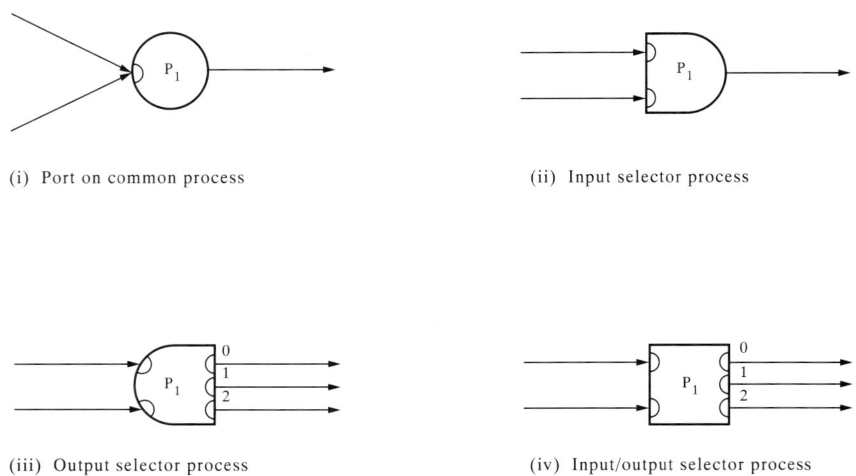

Figure **5.2** Representation of Ports and Process Type.

In this chapter we will introduce this graphical representation and also present ideas relating to the inner structure of a process. Various possible channel implementation mechanisms will also be discussed. The practical problems which result will raise important questions about precision in terms of time synchronisation. In addition, the problems of defining the origins of relative time for specifying channel functions will be analysed in respect of the different channel types.

5.1 THE INNER STRUCTURE OF A PROCESS

At the early stages of design, it is useful to assume that each process will be executed on a *separate processor* and that the *only data available* in the system is *produced by the processes* of the system. This is an important and fundamental assumption which must be borne in mind in understanding our approach. As a result, when we describe a proposed system, the description must include all (including human) of its interfaces to and from the environment. The dynamic requirements of the environment must also be represented by the properties of these interfaces, which are described as processes which:

- either *produce data from the environment* with specific, predetermined periodicity, (this reflects the required measurement, and/or monitoring, sampling frequencies), or

- *consume data* (to be sent to the environment) with specific, pre-determined age, at a specified frequency, (this reflects the actions necessary to influence, or control, the functioning of the application system.)

We should note that in a specification we will often describe the functioning of many component parts of the environment as if they belonged to the future embedded system itself. This is done because the final partitioning of functions between the computing system, conventional stand-alone controlling devices (e.g. PID controllers), and operators/users is often only done at the design stage, after the specification has been completed.

A consumer process, of course, may consume data from more than one producer-process. Usually, also, different producers will **provide different states** (in other words, different sets of output variables). In such cases, consumer processes will have separate input "ports" for each input channel. However, it is also possible that several data producers might provide exactly the same data (for example, using redundant sensors), whilst the consumer might be interested in only one set of such data. If a comparison of multiple input data being sent by the different producers is *not* required, all the channels providing that same data can be connected to the same input port.

The previous paragraph highlights a particular important aspect in the handling of input ports. Two cases are evident:

(i) **Two or more channels connected to a single port** (see Figure 5.3(i))

Here, the two channels can be considered as being "OR"ed in the sense that they are regarded as a single source of incoming messages. Thus, the triggering effects from each channel are aggregated: as a result if these triggers fall within the specified equivalence interval (defined for p_1) then only the first will be **reacted** to.

(ii) **Two, or more, channels connect to separate ports**. (see Figure 5.3(ii))

In this case, all the defined ports are always read during any resulting execution cycle. As a result it is evident that only a few combinations of channel types are meaningful: typically these would be a single semisynchronous or synchronous channel on one port, and asynchronous channels on the others.

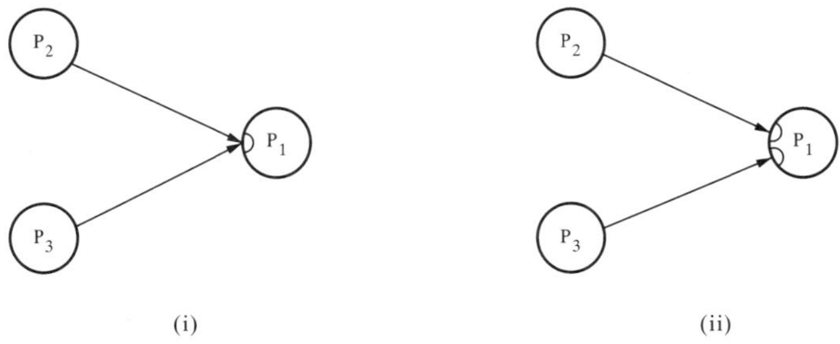

Figure **5.3** Connections to Input Ports

The structural analysis of the system description can often reveal some prohibited or dangerous combinations of input channels (see chapter 7). Such restrictions tend to be application-dependent, and therefore will not be discussed in too much detail here. The problem, though, must be fully appreciated, although, in truth, it has not yet been fully investigated (see for guidance Chapter 7). In understanding a system's operation, it is useful to assume that these different input ports are scanned sequentially in time by the process. This assumption, although not absolutely necessary, gives us a good understanding of how the process functions. The actual order of scanning the different ports is determined by the designer by fixing an allowable delay, $\eta\ (\sigma_{ij}\ , t)$, between the activation of a process and the request for data from the associated channel.

Strictly speaking, $\eta\ (\sigma_{ij}, t)$ is a random variable. By using the same argument as in the case of the process execution time, we can reach an assumption that the interval estimate should be given by:

$$\eta\ (\sigma_{ij}, t) \in [\gamma\ (\sigma_{ij}\ ),\ \delta(\sigma_{ij}\ )],\ \text{ and }\ \gamma\ (\sigma_{ij}\ ) \leq \delta\ (\sigma_{ij}\ ).$$

In Figure 5.4 a time-diagram illustrating the functioning of process p_1 (see also Figure 5.1) is presented. After short preparatory work, the process first requests data from channel σ_{21}, and then from channel σ_{31}. Computations follow, and a new state value is assigned just before the completion of the process. As soon as process p_1 has completed its execution, this new state value is sent to all output channels associated with that process. In this example, the new state value is time-stamped with t_k - the activation time-instant of this particular execution cycle.

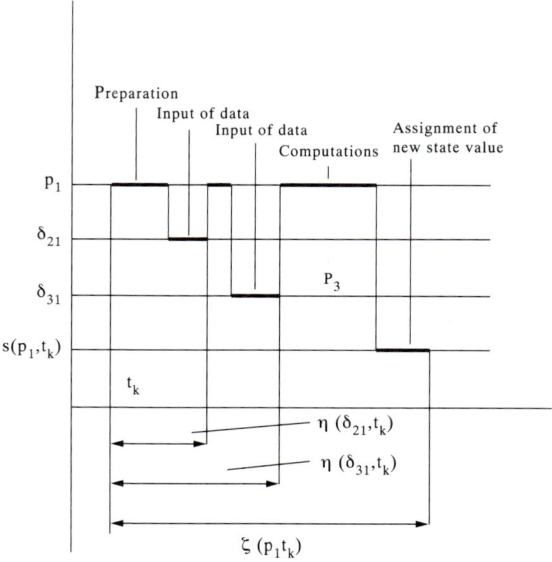

Figure **5.4** An example of a common process behaviour (see process p_1 in Figure 5.1).

In order to implement the *conditional transfer* of data and control signals, a *selector process* has been introduced. When specifying a selector process, we fix the number of possible alternative states (output ports). (Note here that a common process has only one output port and, therefore, only one state.)

For convenience, the alternative states of a selector process are numbered with positive integers. The state number "0" is assigned a new value after each and every execution of the process, and any type of channel may be connected to its associated port. The states with non-zero numbers are assigned new values which depend upon the conditions of the "output selector". The corresponding ports associated with these states can only have semisynchronous channels connected to them.

A fragment of a system, including two common and one selector processes, is shown in Figure 5.5 to explain the concepts involved.

The operation to be effected here could be one in which process p_5 has to compare two input values (from p_1 and p_4) in which its new state value should appear (in addition to that on output "0") under the following conditions:

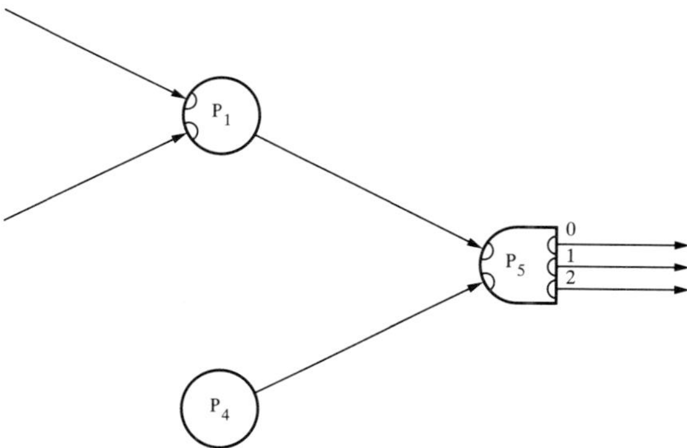

Figure **5.5.** A fragment of a system with a selector process.

- on the first output (1), if, say, $s(p_1, t_k) > s(p_4, t_i)$ (i.e. some specific condition), or
- on the second output (2), if this previous condition does not apply, i.e. if $s(p_1, t_k) \leq s(p_4, t_i)$.

It should be noted that when one of the alternative outputs is assigned a new value, the state of the other conditional outputs remains unchanged.

5.2 PRACTICAL PROBLEMS OF SYNCHRONISATION AND COMMUNICATION

The concept of channels is based on message exchange without waiting for completion or an acknowledgement. A channel receives a message from the producer process (the state of the process), and transforms it into a message as required by the consumer process (this message is thus a "time-sequence" of the producer's process states). The channel also checks the age of the data, and imposes predetermined message exchange disciplines upon the producer- and the consumer-processes, depending on the channel type and function. (Recall that a channel is an intelligent logical entity.)

The practical implementation of a channel will largely depend on the particular computing system involved. However, implemented channels will show standard structures which may easily be replicated in any application. We consider that channels will naturally form components of the system software, as they can, for example, be considered as extensions to the message-exchange primitives of operating systems.

There has always been a reluctance to accept the idea of a message exchange without waiting for an acknowledgement - mainly since it seems to reduce communication reliability. Research into interprocess communication primitives, [MacLeod and Rodd (1982), MacLeod (1983)], however indicates that high-reliability communication may still be achieved, provided that publicly-accessible global time is maintained throughout the system, and all messages are equipped with their validity time (see also [Kopetz (1985)] and [Motus (1986)]).

A further issue which must be addressed when specifying an embedded system is the actual precision required for event synchronisation. Closely connected with this question is that of the precision required (i.e. the granularity) of the system time. Typically, the first question is handled implicitly - it is either assumed perfect or often totally neglected! The granularity of the system time is similarly determined by a mystical "inner-feeling" or empirical experience, and is normally independent of the answer to the first question!

A specification however, according to our interpretation, should be a formal presentation of some rather vague ideas about the functioning of a proposed future system. To this extent, specification always tends to describe an ideal situation - examples of this include assumptions such as: each process has a personal processor; each processor has access to precise global time; many events occur strictly simultaneously; or, message exchange takes zero-time.

After implementation, however, most of the physical processors used will be shared by several processes, and message transfer time is far from negligible. In fact, message transfer time will typically be non-deterministic, and will depend heavily on the communication network's loading. Since embedded systems are often implemented via a network of processors, we face an additional problem of having many, not-quite-ideally-synchronised system clocks!

From the application's point-of-view, the specification of synchronous events (meaning events occurring simultaneously) is, also, normally just a comfortable assumption! In practice we assume that simultaneous events actually occur within certain intervals of time, which depend upon the application, and could be measured in seconds, minutes, or even hours.

Therefore, one of the tasks that must be handled during specification, is obtaining the real, practical requirements for abstract notions such as the simultaneous occurrence of events, the time actually allowed for the transfer of messages, and the minimal, acceptable granularity of time. A correct understanding and accurate definition of such aspects can result in a reduction in the project cost, largely through system simplification.

Once we have fully understood the timing restrictions imposed by our application, we can proceed to specify the structures of all the processes which will be involved in the final system. This takes us right back to handling the individual parameter applicable in process and channel specifications. In Chapter 2 of this book, a group of terms, tolerance interval, equivalence interval, simultaneity interval and validity time, was introduced. These terms must be fully appreciated within the context of a practical design.

The tolerance interval characterises the time sensitivity and dynamic properties of the application - relating directly to sensors measuring the application's parameters and to actuators which apply the embedded system's decisions.

A specification, in terms of the Q-model, will be in the form of a network of communicating processes. In such a network it will be possible to distinguish groups of synchronously activated processes - so-called "synchronous clusters" - and within each such cluster, there may exist separate tolerance intervals.

When proceeding from a specification through to design and implementation, the final resulting software must never exceed a specified tolerance interval. In order to be on the safe side, and also to allow for indeterminacies introduced by implementations on real processors (introducing multiprogramming, multitasking, message transfer delays, or possibly random numbers of iterations of algorithms), the adoption of a somewhat shorter tolerance interval is indicated. This interval is called the equivalence interval, and was defined in Chapter 2. The exact, desirable ratio of the equivalence/tolerance intervals, cannot be defined as it depends on the many factors causing the indeterminacy, and also on how really time-critical the application is.

Although the importance of an appropriate equivalence interval lies mainly in the design and implementation stages, it is also very useful during specification. For example, in a sequence of processes which are communicating via semisynchronous channels, the equivalence interval can be used to control the maximum frequency of activation of the process sequence.

An example in the use of the equivalence interval during the design and implementation stages is given below. Assume that two processes, p_1 and p_2, are activated simultaneously by an event e_0 (according to the accepted specification). The dynamic requirements for the embedded system can be satisfied if activation takes place within an equivalence interval τ_e. Assume that the event, e_0, occurs at time instant t_0 and processes p_1 and p_2 are activated at t_1 and t_2, respectively. The requirements will be satisfied if:

$$\max(t_1, t_2) - t_0 < \tau_e.$$

Now, an implementation may result in a configuration in which processes p_1 and p_2 and the event detector are resident on different processors. We can consider two possible cases as follows:

1. The embedded system is implemented in a single processor. In order to estimate the correspondence of the implementation and the specification, we need to know the execution time of processes p_1 and p_2, and that of the event detector. In addition, we will need to estimate the operating system's context switching time, the workload of the processor, and the scheduling discipline of the operating system.

2. The embedded system is implemented in three processors. In this, we assume that one processor detects the event, and the other two processes also execute on dedicated processors. In this case, in order to check if the requirements are satisfied, we will have to consider the time necessary for detecting the event, the maximum message transfer time, and the maximum time needed to activate a process within a processor.

Finally, it should be noted that the equivalence interval, as used in the Q-model, effectively extends that defined in [Macleod and Rodd (1982)], in which the idea was applied to a state-based control architecture for use in a manufacturing environment.

5.2.1 The null channel

We will now move on and investigate problems relating specifically to the use and implementation of the various types of channels. The channels introduced above were defined as logical devices used for point-to-point communication. From the specification point-of-view this is true even for the null channel. However, from an implementation point-of-view, the null channel is particularly interesting as it actually executes a limited "broadcast", which can be referred to as a form of *Multicast* communication, and is often seen to be essential in real-time, distributed systems.

The null channel concept can be used to realise the co-ordinated activation of a group of synchronous processes. To do this it is evident that within this group a broadcast mechanism is necessary to synchronise the processes (which then become a synchronous cluster). To meet this objective, the synchronising event and the start times of processes in the synchronous cluster must all be within a defined equivalence interval.

However, two different delays will, in practice, hinder the instantaneous propagation of the activating signal through a null channel.

- Firstly, there is the time necessary to detect the synchronising event and subsequently warn the processors which support the processes to be activated. This delay is referred to as the *null channel delay.*

- Secondly, there is the time necessary to actually activate a process in a particular processor.

In any practical distributed system we must thus consider the reality, that the start times of processes will be scattered across the equivalence interval. In many applications this might be simply unacceptable, and there might be a demand for synchronised events to be close to each other. A simple example would be a distributed system controlling the independent brakes on each wheel of a car.

It can be seen, therefore, that the equivalence interval specifies the maximum delay which can exist from the occurrence of the synchronising event to the start of the last synchronised process. In many practical cases we will need restrictions on the maximum delay between the starting of the first synchronised process, and the starting of the last. This time interval is called the "simultaneity interval" and was defined in chapter 2.

Provided that each processor in the computing system has access to the global time, it will be possible to make the simultaneity interval significantly shorter than the equivalence interval. For example, having detected the synchronising event, all the members in a synchronous cluster can negotiate an instant in the global time when the synchronised processes should start. This will enable us to eliminate the null channel delay from the simultaneity interval (see Figure 5.6).

These ideas are illustrated in Figure 5.6, which demonstrates the mutual relationships between the time intervals used in guaranteeing the practical correspondence of dynamic requirements in the environment to the dynamic capabilities of the embedded system.

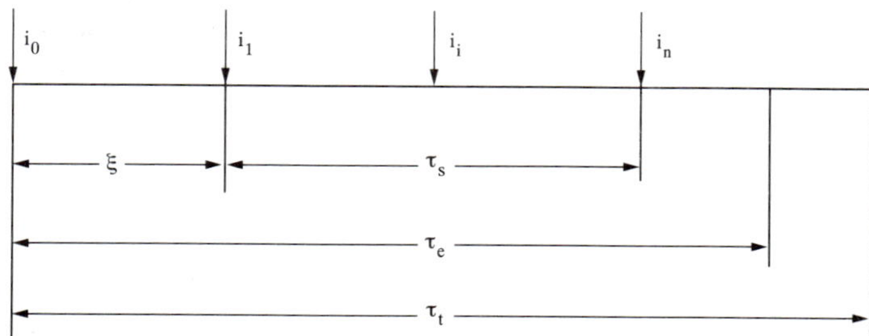

Figure **5.6** Relationships between the tolerance interval (τ_t), equivalence interval (τ_e), simultaneity interval (τ_s) and the null channel delay (ξ)

The same set of intervals discussed above can be used to ensure a successful implementation of the desired system, resulting in specified time parameters being met by the design and its implementation.

5.2.2 The synchronous channel

In order to gain a deeper understanding of the function of a channel, it is useful to consider a channel as being implemented as a separate process. As a result, we can study the interaction of three processes: producer, consumer and channel. The actual communication between these processes is logically realised by simple "**send**" and "**receive**" primitives - as traditionally used in message exchange. On completion of its activity, the producer will send its new state value to the channel process by using the primitive "send". The channel will organise a buffer, and forms from the states of the producer process, a message to be provided to the consumer - in accordance with the channel function required by the consumer process. Whenever the consumer requires data, it will issue a "receive" primitive to the channel. The synchronous activation of the producer and consumer processes is provided by a null channel. (It should be noted that this description is only one possible way of implementing the channel concept, and other mechanisms will be equally successful.)

In this section we are interested only in the channel process. We need to recall that the channel function is given by $K(\sigma_{ij}, t) = [\mu, \nu]$, where μ and ν are integers, and represent time instants in relative time (see chapter 4).

Central to the channel process is a circular buffer which has the following properties:

- The buffer length is determined by the channel function and contains $(\mu + 1)$ elements. Each buffer element can contain exactly one set of value of the processes' state variable, i.e. one message sent by the producer process.

- A "Write" command will shift the content of the buffer by one element, and if the buffer is full, the oldest element is overwritten. A "Read" from the buffer will not change its contents. (This implies that the length of the buffer must be calculated so that overwriting does not cause any problems. There will never be any free space since reading is not destructive.)

- In a single operation, only one element can be written into the buffer. However $(\mu - \nu + 1)$ elements can be read in a single operation, which will correspond to the message requested by the consumer. This concept of reading a multiple element is fundamental to the concept of time-selective communications expanded in the text.

- Reading from the buffer is allowed only when it is full; at system initialisation all buffers must be filled.

These latter points need further explanation. There are two alternative approaches:

1. To make processes more sophisticated by including the required memory necessary to hold the data within the process. This may cause side-effects when modifying the processes at a later stage.

2. To make processes more independent of historical data by placing more data in the external buffer.

However, in either case the data must be available in the system before execution can commence.

It should be noted that the same types of buffers are used for implementing both semisynchronous and asynchronous channels; the only difference will lie in the access discipline. Depending on the specific demands of particular applications, and on the channel type, different access disciplines may be built into the channel process. It might also be reasonable to include exception-handling procedures within the channels.

Returning to the case of synchronous channels, an obvious requirement is that the actions of reading from, and writing to, the buffer must alternate - since the same message cannot be read twice. This implicitly means that the validity time for a message in a synchronous channel cannot be longer than the interval between consecutive activations of the two communicating processes.

The origin of the relative time, which is used to describe communications between the two processes, is at the start time of the consumer-process which will result in the data request. The difficulty is that we have to transfer the origin of this time to the producer-process's timeset. This transfer will be different for each type of channel.

In the case of a synchronous channel, it is intuitively obvious to use the common start instant of the two communicating processes as the origin of the relative time. For example, let $\nu = 0$ denote $t_k \in T(p_j)$, the instant when the consumer-process was activated. In the case of synchronous processes, $T(p_j) = T(p_i)$, the transfer of $\nu = 0$ to the producer process timeset is straight forward. The oldest of the states, accessible through the channel, is, in relative time, denoted as μ. So, in order to determine the corresponding absolute time instant, we have to count μ elements back in the producer-process's timeset.

During specification we will not explicitly fix limits on the channel delay. This is implicitly included in the interval estimates of the process execution time (ζ (p,t)) and in the allowable delay between the start of a process and the request for data (η (σ_{ij}, t)). However, when implementing a system, a careful study will be needed to determine if the actual channel delay satisfies the specification. This actual delay will consist of three components:

- the message transfer time between the producer process and the buffer,
- the message processing time in the buffer, including all the necessary checks and exception handling, and
- the message transfer time occurring between the buffer and the consumer-process.

5.2.3 The semisynchronous channel

The semisynchronous channel may conveniently be implemented by using elements of the null and synchronous channels. The consumer process is started immediately after the producer-process completes its execution. This is, in essence, the synchronisation of two events and can be performed by the same mechanism as that used in the null channel (i.e. a limited broadcast or multicast). The channel function and the buffer will operate in the same way as for a synchronous channel - the only differences occur in the buffer-access discipline and in the interpretation of the origin of relative time, which are parameters of the channel function.

Consider the case in which the consumer process has been started at $t \in T(p_j)$. This will, in turn, determine the origin of relative time ($\nu = 0$). The transfer of this origin of time to the producer process timeset, $T(p_i)$, is not now a trivial matter.

Informally $\nu = 0$ corresponds to the element of $T(p_i)$ which activated the particular execution cycle of p_i and which resulted in regenerating the start instant, $t \in T(p_j)$. Formally, however, this explanation requires more effort!

Assume that the producer process timeset is given as

$$T(p_i) = \{ t_0, t_1 , \ldots, t_k , \ldots, t' , \ldots \}.$$

The semisynchronous channel will generate the consumer process timeset

$$T(p_j) = \{t_0 + \zeta\,(p_i, t_0) + \xi\,(\sigma_{ij}), \ldots ,$$

$$\ldots, t_k + \zeta\,(p_i, t_k) + \xi\,(\sigma_{ij}), \ldots \}$$

where $\zeta\,(p_i, t_k) \in [\alpha\,(p_i), \beta\,(p_i)]$ is the execution time of the producer process, and $\xi\,(\sigma_{ij})$ is the delay in the semisynchronous channel. (As previously defined α and β are lower and upper bounds on execution time). This delay will consist of the same components as the delay in a synchronous channel (see Section 5.2.2 above).

The time instant $t' \in T(p_i)$, which corresponds to $\nu = 0$, can be computed from the following expression:

$$t' = \max_{t''} \{ t'' + \alpha\,(p_i) + \xi\,(\sigma_{ij}) \leq t \,;\, \forall t \in T(p_j), \exists t'' \in T(p_i) \}.$$

It should be noted that a message from a semisynchronous channel can only be read once. The validity time of such a message therefore should not be less than the equivalence interval of the consumer process. One of the peculiarities of a semisynchronous channel is that some activation attempts by the producer process may be neglected: this will depend upon the ratio of the consumer process equivalence interval and the activation period of the producer process.

5.2.4 The asynchronous channel

Asynchronous channels interconnect truly asynchronous processes (see chapter 1). In terms of the definition of a truly asynchronous mode, there is no point in trying to synchronise their associated process interactions. The only control necessary in the case of asynchronous channels will be associated with buffer access since the simultaneous reading from, and writing to, a buffer is not possible. Alternate reading and writing to or from the buffer will not be appropriate here, as the consumer may read the same message many times, or some messages may remain unused.

The delay in an asynchronous channel will arise from two considerations:

- a transport delay, which consists of the time taken for transferring messages from the buffer to the consumer, as well as the time taken for controlling buffer access, and
- a delay caused by differences in activation periods of the producer and consumer processes.

The transport delay may be evaluated by procedures similar to those applied in the case of both synchronous and semisynchronous channels.

However, in order to evaluate the second, non-transport delay, we must proceed as follows.

In this chapter we have only defined the origin of relative time as transformed to the producers timeset. Thus, the time instant $t' \in T(p_i)$ of the producer process timeset, which corresponds to $\upsilon = 0$, (assuming that the request for data was issued during the execution cycle started at $t \in T(p_j)$, may be computed from the expression:

$$t' = \max_{t''} \{ t'' < t + \eta(\sigma_{ij}, t) - \zeta(p_i, t''), \; t'' \in T(p_i), \; t \in T(p_j) \}$$

where $\zeta(p_i, t'')$ is the completion time of the producer process and $\eta(\delta_{ij}, t)$ is the delay between the start of the consumer process and the instant of issuing the request for data.

The actual behaviour of this non-transport delay, $\varphi_n(t) = t - t'$, is analysed in detail in Chapter 7.

5.3 SUMMARY OF ATTRIBUTES OF PROCESSES AND CHANNELS

In this section a summary of the attributes which must be defined for processes and channels is given.

To define a common process p_i, the following attributes must be specified:

- The process timeset, $T(p_i)$,

- The interval estimate for the process execution time

$$\zeta\,(p_i,\, t) \in [\alpha\,(p_i),\, \beta\,(p_i)]$$

- A list of input ports and the channels connected to them. For each channel, an interval estimate of the delay from the start time until the request for data from the channel, is required,

$$\eta\,(\sigma_{ki},\, t) \in [\gamma\,(\sigma_{ki}),\, \delta\,(\sigma_{ki})]$$

- A list of input variables for each channel, which will define the domain of the process,

- A list of output variables which will be defined by the state of the process, and hence define the value range of the output from the process.

It should be noted that the interval estimates introduced actually demonstrate our ignorance of the actual values of essentially random variables. It would have been theoretically more appealing to use probability densities, or estimates based upon them. This approach has not currently been applied because:

- it is extremely difficult to obtain estimates of the corresponding probability densities with any reasonable confidence,

- the analysis of a specification's behaviour, based on probability densities, would very quickly turn into a computational nightmare, and

- in practical embedded systems, the most critical situations are normally caused by minimal and/or maximal values.

Turning to the definition of selector processes, we need the following attributes:

- The conditions for selecting the input channels, if their handling differs from normal. (The point here is that "normal processing" implies that all the data from all the channels would be consumed.)

- The list of alternative states, together with the corresponding list of variables.

- The conditions for selecting alternative states. If probabilities for selecting alternative states are given, the resulting performance analysis will be most informative.

- Finally, the execution times for each alternative state, if they differ from each other.

In defining a channel, we will have to fix:

- the producer process; also, in the case of a selector process, the number of the corresponding state of the producer,
- the consumer process, and the logical number of its input port,
- the channel type, and,
- the channel function.

It should also be noted that in the case of a synchronous cluster, an equivalence interval, and, if necessary, a simultaneity interval needs to be defined. An equivalence interval may also be defined for a single process, if required.

Based on the ideas presented in the last two chapters, in the next chapter we will illustrate their application through a couple of practical examples.

CHAPTER 6

Describing Systems with the Q-Model: Some Examples

This chapter illustrates the use of the Q-model concepts through two simple examples: the practical specification of the software for a direct digital controller and, for academic satisfaction, an interpretation of the classic "five-dining philosophers" problem. This later example might seem out-of-place here! However, it is a classic "reference-example" in the computer science field and does serve to demonstrate the fundamental difference between our approach and that of the traditional computer scientist: the Q-model will **NOT** provide any solution algorithm - rather it will provide a *framework* enabling the use of many possible algorithms; a framework which describes all resulting interactions. A later chapter will give an additional, solid example of an application in an extremely difficult area - the temporal specification of communications software. These examples have been chosen to illustrate the strengths and weaknesses of the approach. Even without knowing at this stage all the formal properties of the Q-model (which will be introduced in Chapter 7), the examples will show that it is possible to obtain a good understanding of a proposed system. At the same time, though, the resulting Q-model-based description does not specify any algorithms for solving the particular problem. As a result of applying the method we get a "framework" which will allow the use of a variety of algorithms, each of which could solve the specific problem. The choice and specification of particular algorithms is deliberately left to the next stage in the development cycle - the logical design stage - which is not covered here. In order to do this logical design, though, we will already have produced well-founded requirements for selecting the appropriate algorithms and, in particular, will have specified all the temporal requirements which, if satisfied, will ensure a reliable, time-correct solution.

Since we have not yet studied the formal properties of the Q-model, the specifications for the examples given here will not involve all the required parameters for processes and channels. Pragmatically, we will use only those parameters which are needed to emphasise important, if informal, features of the Q-model-based approach.

6.1 SOFTWARE FOR A DIRECT DIGITAL CONTROLLER

A direct digital controller is a small, but non-trivial, example of the use of computers in control systems. A simplified description of a controller is as follows: the controller receives, as its input, measured data which characterises the engineering system being controlled. Based on this data, the control algorithm calculates the necessary control actions, and transmits these to an actuator. The actuator applies the control actions to the system under control.

The characteristics of the sensors (which measure the status of the system under control - the control-object) and the actuators (which influence the control object) may be changed, depending on their particular types and, of course, on the physical nature of the measured and output variables.

An additional aspect of the actuator's requirement could be that its output value may normally be altered only in small steps - necessary to cope with the physical properties of the controlled object. For example, suppose that the control action involves closing or opening a valve. Typically, the position of the valve may be changed by, say, only 10% of its total range at any give time. (The delay between two consecutive changes will be determined by the dynamic properties of the application.)

The most important part of the controller's software lies in the control algorithm and this will vary substantially, even for one and the same application. For example, the algorithm may be a digital version of a conventional PI or PID algorithm. It may, though, be a sophisticated adaptive control algorithm, or an algorithm based on fuzzy control concepts. In each case, however, since the controller will be executing its control actions over a real-world, real-time process, there must be a temporal match between the two systems.

6.1.1 Description based on the Q-model

The direct digital controller implements a cascade controller in which one of the controllers (A) computes set-point values and the other (B1, B2) realises the set-point values by controlling the actuator. The logical description of such a controller is shown in Figure 6.1(i), followed by its possible Q-model, Figure 6.1 (ii).

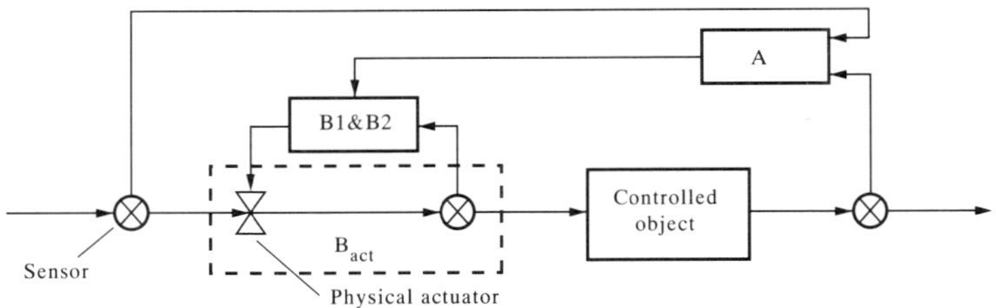

(i) Logical description of a section of a control system

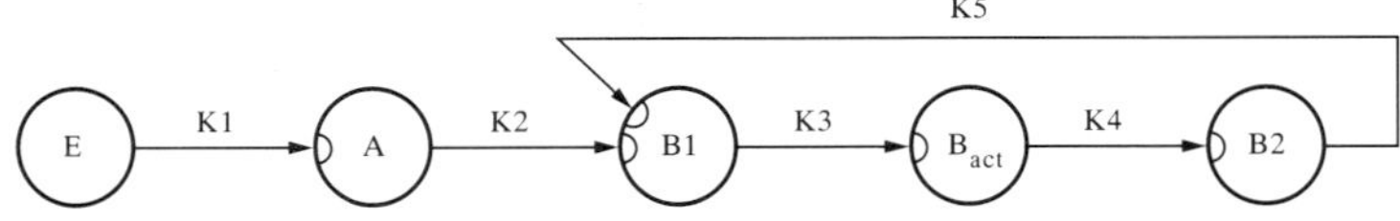

(ii) A Q-model description of the above control system

Figure **6.1** A cascade controller and its Q-model description.

The processes shown in Figure 6.1 have the following functions:

- **Process E** describes the inputs from the controlled object to the controller being designed
- **Process A** implements the control algorithm, and computes new values of the control variable.
- **Process B1** transmits the "allowable" changes in the control variable value to the actuator.
- **Process B2** keeps track of the current position of the actuator (of the current actual value of the control variable)
- **Process B_{ACT}** simulates the actuator. (This process also includes the interface to the environment, and enables the testing and simulation of the controller).

More detailed information about the Q-model processes is presented in Table 6.1 below.

Process name	Execution time	Input channels	Output channels	Timeset	Comments
E	not important	-	K1	T(E)	The process and its timeset are completely determined by the properties of the object
A	4	K1	K2	-	This process is activated as soon as new measurements come from E
B1	2	K2,K5	K3	T(B1)	T(B1) may be generated by T(E) via K1 and K2, or may be determined independently (if required by the actuator and the object)
B2	1	K4	K5	-	May be activated either by B_{ACT} (via K4) or by B1 via (K5)
B_{ACT}	3	K3	K4	-	Is activated by B1

(Note: time units are arbitrary but must be consistent throughout.)

Table **6.1** Q-model processes

It is possible to achieve several different descriptions by changing the interaction patterns of the same set of processes through the use of different channel types. In Table 6.2, 3 possible combinations of channels have been specified, and resulting time diagrams shown in Figure 6.2. To develop the time diagrams, we only need to know the time parameters of the processes and the basic features of the selected channels (see Chapters 4 and 5).

CHANNEL NAME	VERSION ONE		VERSION TWO		VERSION THREE	
	TYPE	FUNCTION	TYPE	FUNCTION	TYPE	FUNCTION
K1	ss	[0,0]	s	[1,1]	s	[0,0]
K2	ss	[0,0]	s	[1,1]	s	[0,0]
K3	ss	[0,0]	s	[1,1]	s	[0,0]
K4	ss	[0,0]	s	[1,1]	s	[0,0]
K5	a	[0,0]	s	[1,1]	s	[0,0]

Table **6.2** 3 possible versions

(i) Time diagram for Version 1

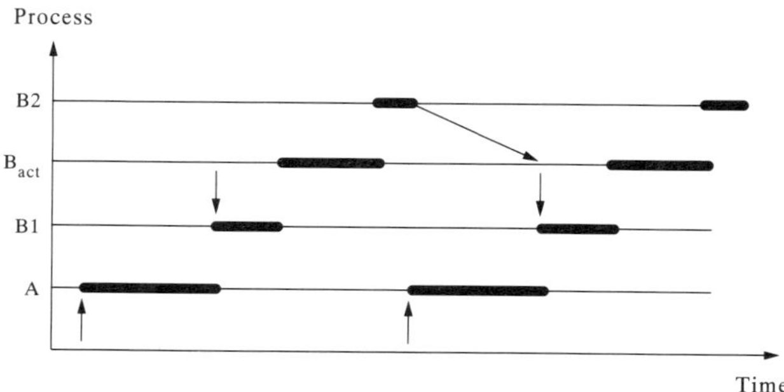

(ii) Time diagram for Version 2

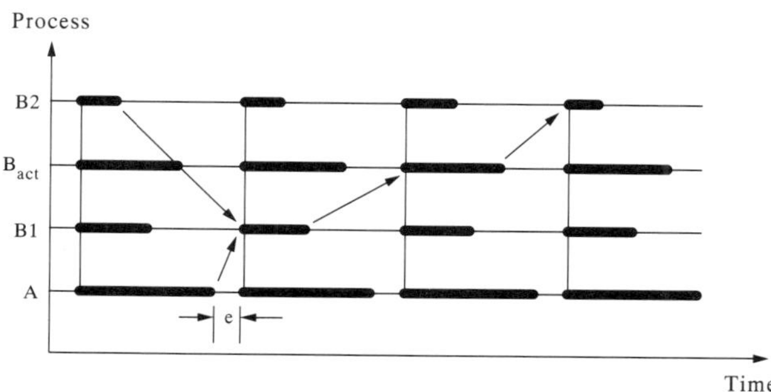

Figure **6.2** Time diagrams for the Q-model of the proposed controller.

Version 1 is a solution based on semisynchronous channels, and is shown in Figure 6.2(i). This has the minimum possible activation period of 6 time units. The total length of an execution cycle will be 10 time units. These results are obtained by considering the process and channel parameters given in Tables 6.1 and 6.2.

It will be possible to implement this version on one processor since there is no process overlap. We should note, however, that in order to make the activation period of the controller shorter than the given limit, parallel processing will be required. From this, note that the feedback signal, which informs the control algorithm about the actual position of the actuator, could be delayed if the activation period is made less than 6 time units.. If the delay in the feedback signal is to be acceptable, then we will have to relax the requirements for channel K5. It is interesting to note that even if we increase the number of processors, the requirements cannot be satisfied if the minimal activation period is shorter than the given limit of 6 time units.

activation period, and we then substitute the actuator by one with a slower characteristic, we will probably face the danger of timing errors. This is because the feedback signal, giving the actual position of the actuator, may occasionally be delayed.

Version 2, whose resulting time diagram is shown in Figure 6.2(ii), is based on synchronous channels, all with channel functions [1,1]; the minimal activation period is $[4 + \varepsilon]$ time units and the total length of an execution cycle is $[16 + 4\varepsilon]$ time units. Here, ε denotes the inevitable delay time which will occur between two consecutive executions of a program on a processor; however, ε is small when compared to the time units of the specification.

This version shows the following peculiarities. Firstly, the feedback signal giving the actual position of the actuator is delayed too much; it is possible, though, to decrease this delay by changing the specified structure. For example, processes B1 and B2 could be aggregated into one; this will eliminate channel K5, and the resulting delay will be the same as in Version 1.

A second feature illustrated is that a number of synchronous processes are easier to implement on a multiprocessor than on a network. This is, of course, intuitively correct.

Version 3 is based on the use of synchronous channels with channel function [0,0]. Here we can see that the design is actually not implementable with the given completion times of processes. If we were allowed to modify the completion times, this version would end up with characteristics similar to those of version 1. A substantial difference to the user, though, will be that the minimal activation period of the resulting controller cannot be less than 10 time units. As will be demonstrated in Chapter 7, this version contains an information deadlock (processes B1, B_{ACT} and B2)

A slightly more sophisticated time diagrams follow if one decides to determine T(B1) independently of T(E), this possibility follows from Table 6.1. This, however, will also need a modification of the corresponding channel types as illustrated in Table 6.3.

Channel name	Version 4	Version 5	Version 6
K1	s	ss	s
K2	a	a	a
K3	ss	ss	ss
K4	ss	a	ss
K5	a	s	s

Table **6.3** Alternate possible versions

The in-depth analysis of the controller versions 4,5 and 6 is left to the reader!

6.1.2 Description based on Petri-nets

In view of the popularity of the Petri-nets technique, we will describe briefly the same direct digital controller in their terms so as to provide a practical comparison. A good survey of Petri-nets and their use in system modelling is given in [Peterson (1981)], and a basic introduction to the knowledge needed to understand Petri-nets is given in Appendix A of this book. This appendix also contains some initial results relating to a formal comparison of Petri-nets and the Q-model.

The direct digital controller may be considered as a modification of the conventional producer - buffer - consumer problem. The control algorithm may be considered as a producer, the consumer is a system consisting of an algorithm for computing the changes to be allowed to the actuator's position, as well as an algorithm for handling the feedback from the actuator, and for completeness, the actuator itself.

A possible Petri-net formulation is shown in Figure 6.3. To aid comparison with the previously described Q-model, activities in the net are described as *places*, and data transmission as *Petri-net transitions.* Transitions fire instantaneously, whilst places will require time to complete their activities.

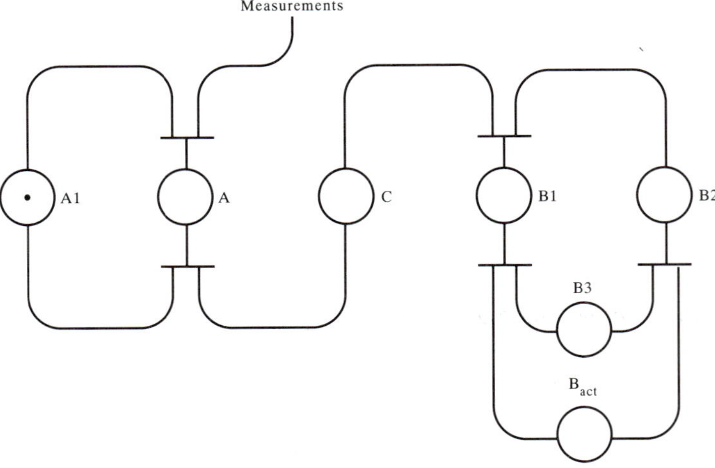

Figure **6.3** The direct digital controller as a Petri-net.

The notation used for processors and their parameters in Figure 6.3 are the same as in Figure 6.1. However, Petri-net functioning, and its necessary synchronisation rules, force the introduction of three additional processes:

- Process A1 is used for handling the dynamic synchronisation of input data.
- Process C is used for handling data transmission.
- Process B3 is used to inform the controller that the actuator has been activated.

The execution time of these additional processes may be neglected. The resulting firing diagram of the corresponding Petri-net is shown in Figure 6.4.

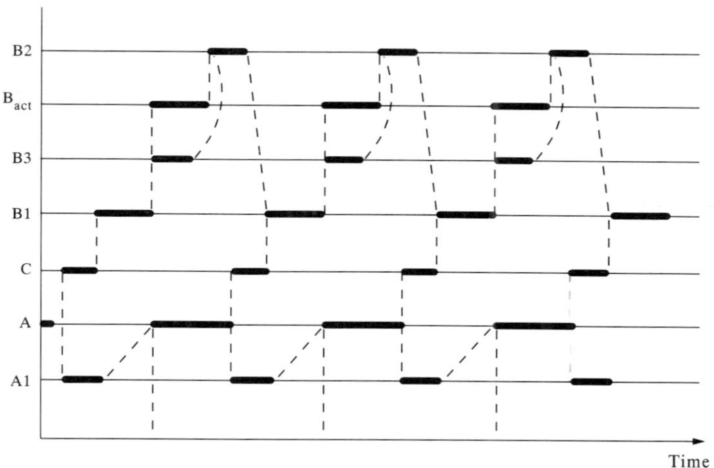

Figure **6.4** The Petri-net based controller's firing diagram

A similar, timed Petri-net was thoroughly analysed by Sifakis (1979). As was shown there, such a Petri-net cannot function faster than its "natural" rate. In our case, the "natural" rate is determined by the minimal possible activation period. For the net shown in Figure 6.3 the minimal possible activation period will be 6 time units, and the total length of the execution cycle is [10 + e] time units. As a result, the integral characteristics of the Petri-net version of the controller correspond closely to those of Version 1 of the Q-model.

It can be seen here that Petri-nets undoubtedly have advantages over the Q-model in some of the features offered, such as the graphical presentation of the control (or data) flow and an explicit description of dynamic synchronisation at different parts of the network.

The Q-model, though, has been developed to aid an analytical study of control and data flow, and also for providing the correctness of dynamic synchronisation. Perhaps, for this reason, the graphical expressiveness of the Q-model is not as well-developed as that of the Petri-nets.

However, let us now look at the application-oriented properties inherent in the two approaches, and focus on some particular issues. One of these relates to the scheduling of the execution of algorithms. The Petri-nets will need substantial changes in order to describe explicitly that the control algorithm might execute less often than the algorithm controlling changes in the outputs to the actuator. To do this we might end up with a subnet which executes with a frequency which is independent of the frequency of the main net, but still receives/demands data from it. In the case of the Q-model representation, all we need is to define a timeset for process B1 and declare that channel K2 is asynchronous.

As another issue, consider the possibility of describing explicitly the necessity to transmit two consecutive values of the producer process's state to the consumer process during each communication exchange. In the controller this may occur in the feedback loop; for example, if B2 has no memory and we need to estimate the speed of changes in the control variables. A similar situation could occur with processes A and B1. In the Q-model, such changes will merely require modifications to the corresponding channel functions. In the Petri-net representation, the explicit demonstration of such new requirements will imply structural changes to the nets.

Based on the above discussion, we suggest that the Q-model description offers the following advantages over one based on Petri-nets.

The first advantage is the simplicity of introducing a subnet with an independent functioning frequency, and of analysing its interactions with the main net. This situation can, be described in Petri-nets, but the available analytical methods are based on studying simulation results.

Secondly, in one and the same model, control and data flow are simultaneously described and both can be modified separately. A Petri-net, in its simplest form, can only describe either data or control flow at any one time.

This brief comparison of the Q-model and Petri-net was deliberately based on trivial observations. For a more detailed comparison see Appendix A. It must be pointed out that since the two methods have been developed with different goals in mind, they are only comparable to a certain degree. For example, one of the most sophisticated problems posed in Petri-nets is the "reachability" problem (i.e. whether certain states or places can be reached through the net). In the case of the Q-model, this problem is not so important because of the autonomy of the interacting processes (many of which have individual timesets). The basic problems tackled by the Q-model relate to consistency of parameter values, correctness in timing and time-selectivity in the communication between processes. Performance evaluation problems are of equal difficulty in both models.

6.2 THE FIVE DINING PHILOSOPHERS

The problem of the five dining philosophers was highlighted by E. Dijkstra (1968) and has since been studied by many authors (see, for example, [Peterson (1981)], [Kerridge (1986)], [Welsh (1981)] and [Jensen (1981)]. The essence of the problem is fundamentally important as it tackles the question of mutual exclusion in a situation of limited resources. Recall here that we are not setting out to find a solution - we are attempting to provide a framework within which various possible algorithms can be explored.

Five philosophers are discussing their philosophical problems. As soon as any of them feel hungry, they go to the dining room. There they find a round table with five dishes of rice on it. Between each two adjacent dishes is a single chop-stick. The philosophers can sit at any place at the table, but whenever one of them starts to eat, needing two chopsticks, they will prevent neighbours from eating! The problem is to develop a fair (in a sense of avoiding starvation) algorithm for synchronising the philosophers' eating.

In this section we will demonstrate the use of the Q-model in *describing, but not solving,* this problem. The difference between the Q-model approach and that of the conventional specification of algorithms, is shown by this example. The Q-model approach starts by building a general framework for the task, and only after a long process of step-wise refinements, will we reach a possible algorithm for solving the problem. As a rule, the Q-model approach tries for as long as possible not to restrict the choice of algorithms. We consider that this results in a more objective investigation of the real requirements of the environment, avoiding the choice of the first (more or less) seemingly suitable, or available, algorithm.

6.2.1 The classical problem

The problem, as stated by Dijkstra, is based on completely known causal relations and does not include any possible timing constraints. In the following, we consider the problem of the co-existence of two parties, the philosophers and the dining room.

Here, the philosophers are in the role of the environment and the dining room is the embedded system. The resulting system is presented in Figure 6.5.

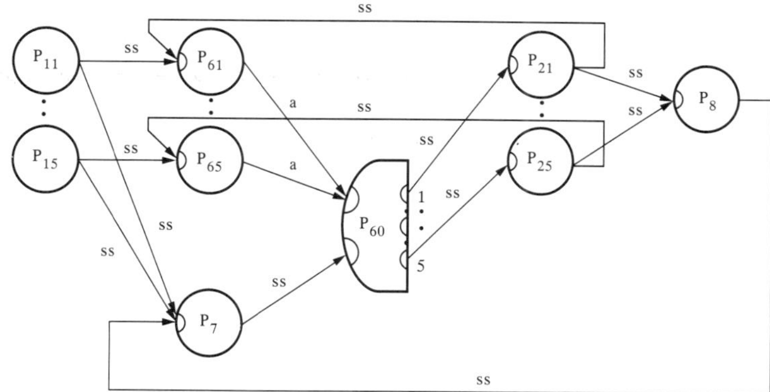

Figure **6.5** The Q-model presentation of five dining philosophers.

The environment interests us only in as much as it is interacting with the embedded system. Consequently it is sufficient to represent a philosopher, i, by only two processes - p_{1i} for getting hungry and p_{2i} when eating. (Note that in Figure 6.5, i ranges from 1 to 5, representing each of the 5 philosophers.)

From our point-of-view, it is immaterial what else happens in the environment. To be able to evaluate the productivity of the dining room, we assume that the process p_{1i} (getting hungry) has a specified timeset.

The embedded system is represented by a reservation book (process p_{6i}) in which each philosopher is checked in as "hungry" or "full", a manager (process p_{60}), who makes decisions, and a procedure for calling the manager, implemented by process p_7 and some help from the philosophers. The only sophisticated process is p_{60}, since synchronisation decisions are made here. Therefore, we need to decompose p_{60}, and reveal more details about it. This is shown in Figure 6.6.

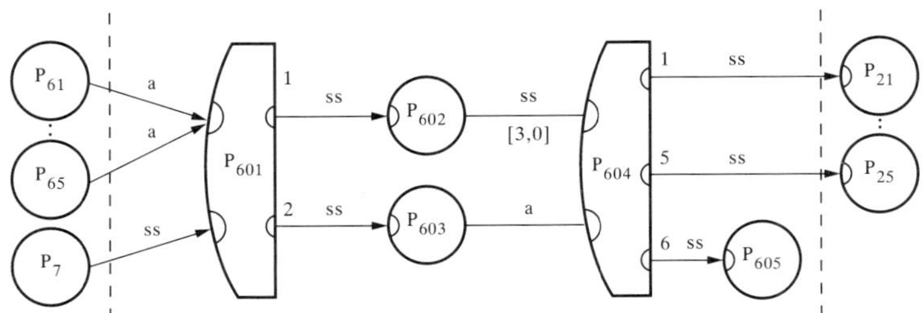

Figure **6.6** A decomposition of p_{60}

We see here that a selector process, p_{601}, is activated as soon as a philosopher "checks in" as "hungry", or "checks-out" as "full". The first state of p_{601} contains a vector describing vacant places at the table, its second state contains a vector, or queue, of hungry philosophers. The values of these states are sorted by processes p_{602} and p_{603} respectively. Whenever a new vacancy appears, process p_{604}, responsible for granting dining permission to the philosophers, is activated. So as to facilitate fairness in the decision, the four previous states of the vacancy vector are transmitted and this will help to avoid possible conspiracy among the philosophers.

The most interesting process is p_{604}, since this is where the decisions are made. We can still employ many different decision-making algorithms here, although we have already restricted the "domain" of operation in defining the algorithms. The freedom of choice for the decision-making algorithm may be further restricted by continuing the decomposition process: each of these decompositions will effectively narrow down the domain, stripping the algorithm to its really essential problem.

6.2.2 Real-time extension of the classical problem

The classical synchronisation problem may be reformulated so as to represent a typical real-time system. Since we have a system which is comprised of two components, the philosophers and the dining room, we can modify both components.

Let us first be so bold as to modify the description of a philosopher! It is only natural that each has a maximum time between two consecutive eating sessions. If this time interval is exceeded and a philosopher has not had access to the dining room, they falls ill, and will not be able to continue philosophical discussions. Also, it is natural (we hope) that each philosopher has the minimal amount of food necessary to avoid illness before the next eating session.

Correspondingly, we can modify the eating regulations in the dining room. Firstly, we assume that each philosopher is given a certain amount of food, which may not necessarily coincide with the amount actually needed. Secondly, to cater for the others, each philosopher is allotted a limited time interval to consume their food. The allotted time, however, is not necessarily sufficient for consuming the given amount of food.

One can argue, as of course the philosophers will, that the constraints introduced are inhuman and not consistent with each other. This may be true, but the criteria for checking the consistency of time restrictions must depend on the overall goal for the joint functioning of the environment and the target system!

It is possible to consider several goals. For example:

- maximising the efficiency of the philosophical discussions, hence satisfying all the requirements of the philosophers,
- maximising the number of clients catered for by the dining room per day, or
- distributing the given, insufficient quantity of food, equally among the philosophers.

In the real-time extension of the philosophers problem, we can no longer describe a philosopher by two simple, implicitly communicating processes, as we did before. Figure 6.7 shows a Q-model description of the "extended philosopher".

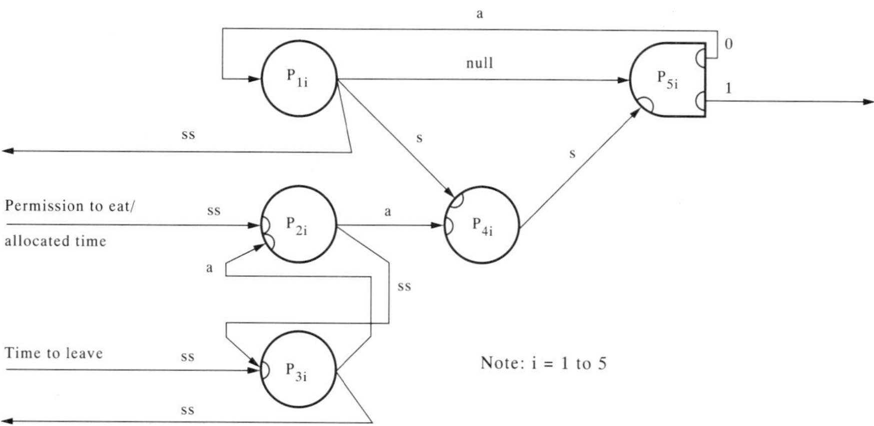

Figure **6.7** A real-time extension of a philosopher

The dining room needs less modification. As shown in Figure 6.8, the only substantial addition is process p_{7i}, which supervises the usage of places at the table by the i-th philosopher. The fact that the manager works independently of the hungry philosophers queue, and of the changes in place vacancies, is not essential.

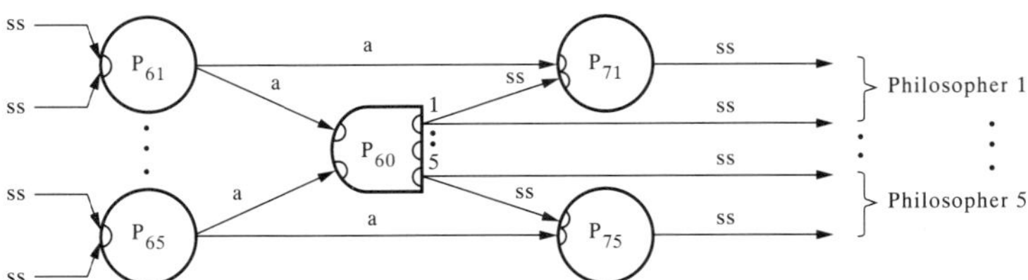

Figure **6.8** A real-time dining room for the philosophers

As in the previous case, the most important part of the system is process p_{60}, which makes decisions about the order of eating. By further decompositions of p_{60}, we can fix more details of the decision-making procedure.

It is not difficult to see that the only way to build a real, lasting, and efficiently-functioning, embedded system will be to build one that satisfies the philosophers' requirements. However., it is still interesting to study the functioning of the system under severe restrictions (e.g., limited time for food consumption, limited amount of food). The important point here is that these different modes of functioning of the system can be studied on the same model, by simply modifying the parameters.

6.3 CONCLUSIONS

This chapter has introduced, in a fairly informal fashion, the use of the Q-model in tackling the descriptions of two different types of time-restricted systems. We have not set out to solve either problem, but have tried, rather, to illustrate how the adoption of the methodology leads, via an evolutionary process, to a system description which restricts and bounds, in-time, subsequent algorithms. In the next chapter we take another step forward and investigate how the methodology leads towards a relatively simple, highly consistent approach to actually analysing the proposed system performance.

CHAPTER 7

Analysis of a System Described by the Q-Model

Experience in applying various software engineering methodologies indicates, not surprisingly, that the productivity of programmers is a function of the selected tools. Most practitioners agree that increased productivity results mainly from the introduction of a strict discipline into the development process, and not so much from the specific tricks and tools offered by the various methodologies.

The same situation is observed in developing embedded software where any systematic approach gives better results than a "trial and error" method. A few authors (e.g. Boehm-Davis (1985)) have compared different design methodologies and discovered that a so-called "mixed approach" gives better results for such applications than a single-minded clean approach, based, for example, specifically on data flow diagrams or functional decomposition.

Now, it is important to re-emphasise that whereas non-real-time applications will usually be based upon a complete knowledge of the causal relations between separate parts of the system, in embedded or real applications the situation is far more sophisticated. We will seldom have complete knowledge of the causal relationships, and the missing information will have to be approximated by timing constraints. The majority of these timing constraints are, in fact, imposed by the environment (e.g. by the controlled object) and largely emphasise its dynamic properties. Some timing constraints, though, which are imposed indirectly upon the processes of the embedded system, are derived from design criteria, or from the assumed properties of algorithms. The latter case is illustrated by time-selective communication.

When specifying an embedded system, the information used usually comes from many sources: expert knowledge from application engineers, simulation results from process models, experiments in the real environment, or, maybe from the designer's subjective decisions. All this multi-source information must, in the final specification, be non-contradictory and consistent.

Looking at current design practice, it appears that problems of ensuring the correctness of basic structural information have been, to some extent anyway, successfully solved in respect of causal information relationships, and information and control flow. However, the analysis of timing correctness (i.e. consistency and lack of conflicts in timing constraints) in a specification and in the subsequent design, have received little attention. This is in spite of the high cost of discovering, localising and eliminating such errors during the testing phase and, even more strangely, in spite of the potential risk of a timing error being present in a functioning, embedded system.

The most popular technique used for studying the timing properties still seems to be simulation. From a programmer's point-of-view, however, simulation is rather like software testing - it can demonstrate that errors exist, but cannot prove that they are absent. Without questioning the necessity for simulation and testing, we suggest that it is vital in embedded systems to prove *analytically* the absence of timing errors - possibly in addition to simulation studies.

We suggest that system specification based on the Q-model allows for such an analysis. In this chapter, several theoretical relationships between parameters in a specification are derived. If the proposed specification parameters satisfy these relationships, the absence of certain timing errors can be guaranteed.

As was proposed by Motus (1984), a specification given in terms of a Q-model, can be analysed through three steps.

- Proving the correctness of separate elements in the specification. (In this step, isolated processes and channels are analysed.)
- Proving the correctness of the interactions between two processes. (Here, a combination of "process-channel-process" is studied.)
- Proving the correctness of the group-wise behaviour of processes.

This chapter provides provisional results relating to proving the timing correctness of a specification. It must be pointed out that these results do not deal with all possible aspects of a specification, and do not cover all potential timing errors. This area is still open for further research, especially in proving a complete set of tests. We would also like to point out, due to the abstract nature of the Q-model, exactly the same tests, inequalities and propositions will be valid whether we are analysing a design or an implemented system.

7.1 CHECKING SEPARATE ELEMENTS OF A SPECIFICATION

During this phase, the correctness of the parameters of an element which do not depend on the parameters of other elements are checked. In many cases, this analysis can be reduced to the trivial checks that are present in the majority of CASE tools - mainly ensuring the completeness of all necessary information. There are, however, several specific items which need to be carefully investigated. These are spelt out below.

1. The *execution-time of a process* is essentially, at this time, a random variable $\zeta(p,t)$, since algorithms are not known and code has not been produced. However, as explained in chapter 4, we use interval estimates for this random variable, and from pragmatic considerations, avoid the use of probability densities. Thus, we interpret the interval as an indication of our ignorance; as a result, the less-precise our knowledge, the larger we must make the interval! However, in practice, and emphasising the value of hindsight, we can often make educated guesses at possible, realistic execution times.

   Being pragmatic, though, and despite the claims made for the virtue of top-down design, we all know in practice that very rarely do we not have some idea of our target processes! Increasingly we are striving for code-reuse, and in most real engineering design situations, we always have a good insight into potential execution times. (Note, also, that for simplicity, we always express time as having an integer value).

   The cyclic execution of a process will be possible if the interval estimate of the execution time satisfies the following relationship:

$$0 < \alpha(p) \leq \beta(p) < \Psi < \infty,$$

   where Ψ is a sufficiently large integer, depending upon the dynamic properties of the environment.

2. The *allowable delay in data consumption from a channel* $\eta(\sigma ij,t)$ is another, essentially random variable, which denotes the delay which can, and normally will, exist between the activation of a process and a request for data from the channel. Traditionally, though, this delay has been assumed to be zero, implying that input data must be available at the instant when a process is activated. In the Q-model, however, we have allowed more freedom in describing a process.

   As explained in Chapter 5, the allowable delay is also specified as an interval estimate, and we have assumed that the following relationship must be satisfied:

$$0 \leq \gamma(\sigma ij) \leq \delta(\sigma ij) < \alpha(pj).$$

3. A *process-timeset* may be specified for each process. Consequently, it is necessary to check that each process has an individual timeset, or, at least, has a pointer to an existing, defined timeset via, say, a channel. If the results of the existence check are positive, then we can proceed to check the properties of the timesets themselves.

To simplify the behavioural analysis of a specification, we assume that all processes are executed periodically. Strictly speaking, of course, this is not true; however, it is true that all processes are executed repeatedly. This assumption follows from the fact that we can allow deterministic (regular), as well as random (aperiodic), execution. Thus, even a boot-strap routine will be executed repeatedly - every time the embedded system is started up!

In order to determine a process timeset, it will be necessary to specify two attributes.

Firstly, the average period of process activation (for aperiodic processes), or the exact required period (for regular processes), is denoted $t_a(p)$ and will be referred to as the "average period".

Secondly, an estimate of (or allowable) fluctuations in process start times must be made! This is necessary because of the random behaviour of the environment, or because of indeterminacies in the computing system. The fluctuation is specified as a fluctuation interval of length $t_r(p)$, which is placed symmetrically around a start time (see Figure 7.1).

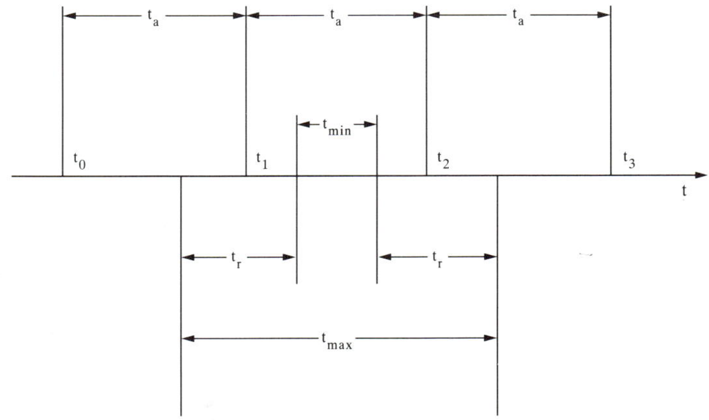

Figure **7.1** Definition of a process timeset

The fluctuation interval $t_r(p)$ may, again, be regarded as an indication of our inability to define the average period. In practice, however, most designers prefer to define minimum and maximum periods (in other words, the distances between two consecutive activations of a process) in defining a timeset. The two different sets of possible parameters are related as follows:

- the minimum distance between two consecutive activations of a process is

$$t_{min}(p) = t_a(p) - t_r(p), \text{ and}$$

- the maximum distance between two consecutive activations of a process

$$t_{max}(p) = t_a(p) + t_r(p).$$

The values of $t_a(p)$ and $t_r(p)$ (or $t_{min}(p)$ and $t_{max}(p)$) depend upon the dynamic properties of the environment. It is, therefore, impossible to check formally their selected values, except the mutual relationship:

$$0 < t_{min}(p) \leq t_{max}(p) < \infty$$

4. *Correct ordering of process copies.* In order to achieve the desired throughput of a system, it is often necessary to reactivate a process before it has completed its previous execution. This will be necessary as soon as $\zeta\,(p,t) \geq t_{min}(p)$.

   In practice, it will not be complicated to do this, since we will just need additional computing power, and an appropriate technique for handling such concurrent processes. These are implementation issues, so the fact that the need for multiple copies occurs during specification is not serious. Such occurrences, i.e., when more than one copy of the same process is being executed simultaneously, are called "creating copies" of that process, and certain properties will have to be checked. It is natural to expect that the earliest activated copy of a process will also terminate first. However, this may well not happen, simply because the completion time of a process, and hence of each of its copies, is specified as an interval.

   Quirk (1977) provided two propositions which give sufficient conditions for the correct ordering of such process copies, and we reproduce these here.

Proposition 1:
Let $t_1, t_2 \in T(p)$ be any two consecutive elements of T(p), and let $t_1 < t_2$. Process copy $p(t_1)$ terminates before the copy, $p(t_2)$, if

$$\beta\,(p) - \alpha\,(p) < t_{min}(p).$$

(As before, α and β are lower and upper bounds on process execution times). Quirk's second proposition gives a sufficient condition for the ordering of access to a channel by the copies of a process.

Proposition 2:
Assume that we have a channel, $\sigma ij \in \Sigma$, a producer-process $p_i \in P$, and a consumer-process, $p_j \in P$. Let the consumer-process be activated at any two consecutive elements in its timeset, t_1 and t_2, where $t_1 < t_2$. A demand for data from the channel comes earlier from the copy $p_j(t_1)$, if

$$\delta(\sigma_{ij}) - \gamma(\sigma_{ij}) < t_{min}(p_j).$$

(Proofs of these propositions are given in Appendix B).

5. *Domain of definition and value range for a common process.* Conventional tools for specifying algorithms concentrate on the description of the actual mapping from the domain to the value range. The Q-model approach leaves the algorithm for mapping open and only imposes some timing constraints on its mapping. Nevertheless, the Q-model approach is somewhat pedantic in specifying domain and value range.

   In the case of a common process, the value range is completely defined by the process state and a list of its state variables. At the specification stage it is usually too early to fix actual data structures, although it must be admitted that the presence of such data structures would facilitate an in-depth analysis! The same information is also required for defining the domain.

At this stage in the analysis, we can only check the presence of the information, the variable list, and correspondence to each other - for both the value range and domain.

6. *Domain of definition and value range for a selector process.* In practice, a selector process can be conveniently considered as a collection of common processes. Therefore, the same checks as for a common process can be applied to each state of the selector process and to its domain. Additional tests are required, however, for checking the presence of conditions for the output selector mechanism and the predicates for fixing input selection.

   The performance evaluation of a specified system becomes substantially simpler if each state of a selector process is given a probability with which it may be assigned a new value, resulting from an execution. If such probabilities are specified, their values must pass trivial tests for mutual conformity.

7. *A channel function* is usually specified as an interval in relative backward time. All that we can formally check here is that

$$0 \leq \nu \leq \mu < \infty.$$

   where the values of ν and m will depend on the intrinsic properties of the application.

7.2 CHECKING COMMUNICATIONS BETWEEN TWO PROCESSES

Interprocess communication in embedded software is inherently complex, primarily because of the time-selective nature of the communication, but also because of the many time restrictions imposed on the processes. Therefore, emphasis in the following analysis will be on checking the consistency of imposed timing constraints, and on evaluating achievable timing characteristics, given specified parameters.

Before proceeding to tackle these problems, there are two trivial checks to be made:

Firstly, it is necessary to check for the absence of isolated elements in the specification. Such isolated elements may occur in the following situations:

- processes being specified which have non-empty lists of input and/or output variables, but which do not have input and/or output channels, or

- channels being specified which have neither producer nor consumer processes.

Secondly, we need to ensure that there is a correspondence in data at the channel termination points. This test must check for correspondence between the elements in the state variable list of the producer-process, and the elements in the list of input variables expected to be obtained from this channel by the consumer-process. It is obviously acceptable that the state variable list for the producer-process should contain all the input variables of the associated consumer-process.

Following these basic tests, the following tests will be specific to the selected channel types, and are therefore appropriately grouped.

7.2.1 Synchronous processes

Processes are activated synchronously if they are connected by synchronous channels or null channels; these channels imply that they have a common timeset. Synchronous activation requires that corresponding start times lie within an appropriate equivalence interval, as was discussed in Chapter 5.

A synchronous cluster indicates a group of communicating processes in which all members are activated synchronously and, therefore, will have identical timesets.

The notion of a synchronous cluster helps a designer to formulate explicitly the requirements applying to the precision of synchronisation. This synchronisation requirement becomes important as we proceed from the specification to the design stage, and especially on into implementation. The precision required will help us to select communication primitives for the operating system, and will also directly assist in allocating processes between processors. In order, physically, to create a synchronous cluster, it will be necessary either for the processes to have one and the same timeset, or to ensure that the processes are all connected with synchronous, or null, channels. Having identified a synchronous cluster, it can be given a simultaneity, and/or equivalence, interval; both of these intervals are determined from the dynamic properties of the implementation.

To analyse communications between pairs of synchronous processes, it will be necessary to consider the factors discussed in the following paragraphs.

> *1. The maximum allowable waiting time for data from a synchronous channel.* In an ideal synchronous computing system, it may be possible to schedule tasks so that they function without the need to wait for data. In a realistic computing system, however, this is difficult because of a variety of random factors. In an embedded system this is even more difficult because the environment is neither fully controllable, nor completely observable by the computing system. As a result, the environment will significantly influence the functioning of the computing system.

As a rule in an embedded system, we are not able to avoid waiting for data, and we will only be able to guarantee that the system functions correctly if we allow for this waiting.

Proposition 3:
Let $p_i, p_j \in P$, be two synchronous processes which communicate via a synchronous channel, $\sigma_{ij} \in \Sigma$. Communication via this channel will not change the specified time parameters of the consumer-process, if

$$\beta(p_i) < \gamma(\sigma_{ij}) + \nu\, t_{min}(p_i).$$

(The proof of this proposition is given in Appendix B.)

This proposition gives us a condition to ensure that the specified time parameters will never be violated through waiting for data to be received from a synchronous channel. This condition can be relaxed in two ways.

Firstly, based on a rather ad hoc idea, and only for large values of ν, we can substitute $t_{min}(p_i)$ by $t_a(p_i)$, assuming that the actual activation interval will, in practice, be averaged over a long time.

A second approach, and one which can be justified theoretically, is based on an improved usage of the time between two consecutive activations of the consumer-process. In many cases it will be found that the maximum execution time for a process is less than the minimum activation period of this same process. This "vacant" time can then be used (during the implementation) for the system's internal requirements, such as the processing of queues or the exchange of process status words. As a result, the execution time for the consumer-process will be violated in an acceptable way. This relaxation is stated in Proposition 4.

Proposition 4:
Let $p_i, p_j \in p$ be two synchronous processes communicating via a synchronous channel, $\sigma_{ij} \in \Sigma$. The communication may increase the specified execution time of the consumer-process, but will not change the next scheduled activation of that process if the following inequality holds:

$$\beta(p_i) < \gamma(\sigma_{ij}) + \nu\, t_{min}(p_i) + [\, t_{min}(p_j) - \beta(p_j)\,].$$

(This proposition may be proved using a similar argument to that used when proving Proposition 3.)

2. *A process consuming its own state values*. The situation in which a process consumes its own state variable values often occurs in practice. Problems will appear in this case only if the process has to wait for its own state value obtained from its previous execution; in other words, if the process has more than one copy. The following proposition, again, has been provided by Quirk (1977).

Proposition 5:
Suppose that a process $p_k \in P$ consumes its own previous state value via a synchronous channel, $\sigma_{kk} \in \Sigma$, where the channel function is $K(\sigma_{kk}, t) = [\mu, 1]$ and $\mu \geq 1$. Let the execution time for

the process, without any waiting time, be $\overline{\zeta}(p_k)$. The actual execution time for the process has a finite upper bound if

$$t + h(\sigma_{kk}, t) > \overline{\zeta}(p_k) + t', \; t \in T(p_k)$$

and

$$t' = \max_{t''} \{ t'' : t'' \in K(\sigma_{kk}, t) \}$$

(Proof of this proposition is given in Appendix B.)

This proposition demonstrates how small disturbances, such as a negligible waiting time, which occur often, say because a process is being executed a significant number of time, may result in a non-trivial change in the system's behaviour.

7.2.2 Semisynchronous processes

The analysis of processes interacting via semisynchronous channels is complicated because the consumer process's timeset is generated by the producer process. In Section 5.2.3, the generated timeset was derived using the producer process's parameters and the delay in the semisynchronous channel.

In a real specification, any consumer process may have several producers connected to it via semisynchronous channels. In such a situation, activation attempts may occur which will be neglected by the consumer; for example, if the consumer is executing at the time of the corresponding attempt and parallel copies of this process are not allowed.

A neglected activation attempt can be explained simply by considering the equivalence interval. If two activation attempts fall into the same equivalence interval, they are considered to be a single event.

Now, let us consider a consumer process p_j and producer processes, $p_i, p_k, \ldots, p_m$, - each of which communicates with the consumer through semisynchronous channels. Any element of this consumer process' timeset, $t_r \in T(p_j)$, is determined by the following two conditions.

1. A candidate for $t_r \in T(p_j)$ may be any of the time instants

   $$t_{rn} = t_{nv} + \zeta(p_n, t_{nv}) + \xi(\sigma_{nj}),$$

   where n can take the values i, k, ... ,m (in other words, indices of all the producer-processes), and where t_{nv} denotes an start time, $t_{nv} \in T(p_n)$, such that the resulting execution completes at a time instant, $t'_{nv} > t_{(r-1)}$, with $t_{(r-1)} \in T(p_j)$ as the immediately previous start time of the consumer process.

2. The rule for selecting $t_r \in T(p_j)$ from the possible candidates is given by

$$t_r = \min_n [t_{rn} : t_{rn} - t_{(r-1)} \geq \tau_e(p_j)],$$ where $\tau_e(p_j)$ is the equivalence interval defined for the consumer process.

There do not appear to be any other major problems which need to be checked during the pairwise analysis of processes interaction via semisynchronous channels.

7.2.3 Asynchronous processes

The communication of processes through asynchronous channels is the most liberal, flexible form of interaction, and therefore the only interesting question which appears to arise lies in the analysis of the delays which occur during communication.

Any channel naturally causes some delay in the delivered message. This delay may be caused, for example, by the physical propagation speed of the signal, by competition for the communication line, or in the conversion of data caused by the formats required by the sending and receiving processes. This composite delay is normally called a "transport delay" and cannot be avoided in real communications.

In addition to this transport delay, in a truly asynchronous mode of process execution, a non-transport delay in communications appears. This delay is caused by the activation of the interacting processes at independent time instants.

The non-transport delay of data is effectively the delay in activating the producer process (which results in the acceptance of the most recent state value available at the moment when the consumer process demands the data) in respect of the activation of the consumer process requiring the data.

Suppose that we have a producer process, p_i, and a consumer process, p_j, communicating via an asynchronous channel. The corresponding timesets, $T(p_i)$ and $T(p_j)$, are, by definition, independent of each other and no synchronisation takes place (except for reading and writing to and from the buffer). Let $t \in T(p_j)$ be a start time resulting in a demand for data from the channel. Assume that the start time of the producer process, resulting in the production of the most recent state value of the producer process available to the consumer, is $t' \in T(p_i)$.

Since the timesets $T(p_i)$ and $T(p_j)$ are independent of each other (and, in the general case, also of different powers), the difference $(t - t')$ will vary, depending upon which element in the consumer process's timeset has been considered (see Section 5.2.4).

In this chapter we are interested in estimating the maximum non-transport delay, which is given by,

$$\varphi^*(p_i,p_j) = \max_t (t-t'). \quad t' \in T(p_i),\ t \in T(p_j),$$

where t' is selected according to the rule given in Section 5.2.4.

Now let us model time by a sequence of non-negative integers, and assume, for simplicity, that all the processes involved are periodic.

If the average periods of p_i and p_j are $t_a(p_i)$ and $t_a(p_j)$ respectively, then any element in the corresponding timesets can be determined as $t = n\,t_a(p_j)$ and $t' = m\,t_a(p_i)$. Here, $m,n,t_a(p_i)$ and $t_a(p_j)$ are non-negative integers.

Thus, calculations based on the properties of an asynchronous channel give us an expression determining the absolute upper bound of the non-transport delay as

$$\varphi_{n'} = t_a(p_i) + \varsigma(p_i,t') - \eta(\sigma_{ij},t).$$

Consider, now, only the interval estimates for time parameters, we have

$$\varphi_{n'} \leq \varphi_n = t_{max}(p_i) + \beta(p_i) - \gamma(\sigma_{ij}).$$

Another, more sophisticated way of determining an estimate of the upper bound of the non-transport delay, is to formulate a problem in integer programming:

For any instant, $nt_a(p_j)$, of the consumer-process activation, the corresponding non-transport delay may be expressed as

$$nt_a(p_j)-mt_a(p_i),$$

provided that m is selected properly. The task of searching for the maximum of the above expression, as a function of n and m, is formulated in Proposition 6 contained in Appendix B. As one may expect, the upper bound of the non-transport delay will have the following form:

$$\varphi_n^* \leq t_{max}(p_i) + \beta(p_i) - \gamma(\sigma_{ij}) - 1.$$

This upper bound estimate is rather pessimistic and is seldom reached in practice.

Example of non-transport delay calculation: Consider a system of two processes, p_i and p_j, communicating via two asynchronous channels, σ_{ij} and σ_{ji}, (see Figure 7.2.). The average periods given are $t_a(p_i)=50$, $t_a(p_j)=110$, and the maximum periods are $t_{max}(p_i)=54$, and $t_{max}(p_j)=114$, respectively. The maximum execution times of processes are $\beta(p_i)=40$, $\beta(p_j)=80$, and the minimum delay in demanding data with respect to the start time are $\gamma(\sigma_{ij})=20$ and $\gamma(\sigma_{ji})=30$, respectively. In Figure 7.2, the table contains the average start times, and the corresponding non-transport delays. On the corresponding graphs, the upper bounds of the non-transport delay are also marked.

As one can see, the graph of φ_n behaves in a saw-tooth fashion. If time is modelled by non-negative integers, the graph of non-transport delay will be periodic.

The saw-tooth format of the non-transport delay explains the seemingly random nature of some of the timing errors which occur, making them extremely difficult to isolate and eliminate.

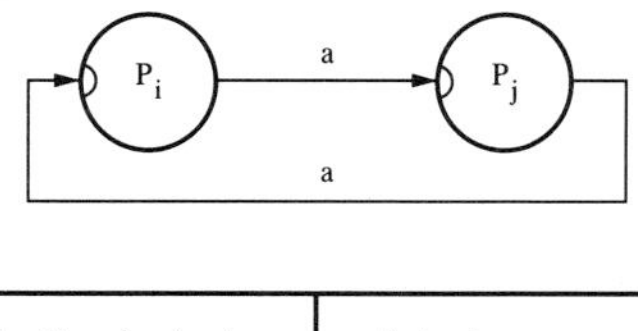

Activation instants		Actual average delay	
$T(p_i)$	$T(p_j)$	$\varphi_n(\delta_{ij})$	$\varphi_n(\delta_{ji})$
0	0	–	–
50	–	–	–
100	–	–	100
150	110	10	150
200	–	–	90
250	220	20	140
300	–	–	80
350	330	30	130
400	–	–	70
450	440	40	120
500	–	–	50
550	550	50	110
600	–	–	160
650	660	10	100
700	–	–	150
750	770	20	90
800	–	–	140
850	880	30	80

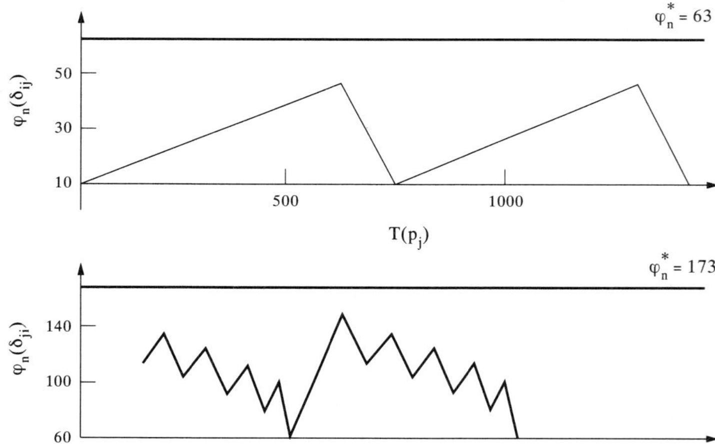

Figure **7.2** The behaviour of the non-transport delay

7.3 CHECKING GROUPS OF COMMUNICATING PROCESSES

In this section we will consider the analysis of the evaluation of subsystems, specific groups of processes (such as synchronous clusters) and a completely specified system. At the specification stage, the Q-model enables a designer to detect potential information deadlocks, and it is possible to evaluate some performance measures analytically; for example, the time required for a message to pass through a network from one process to another. This latter task is not as trivial as it might seem because of the different channel functions and the potentially autonomous functioning of some processes, which will introduce irregular delays.

7.3.1 Information deadlocks in a Q-model

A deadlock denotes a situation in which some processes in a system are not able to proceed as specified because of erroneous co-ordination between them. If a deadlock has occurred, the system cannot extract itself from the deadlock, and an additional, special anti-deadlock function will be required.

A deadlock can typically be caused by the lack of required information or the unavailability of a physical resource. The second cause becomes acute, and more relevant, at the stage of physical design and implementation. A deadlock caused by an insufficiency in physical resources may appear dynamically during the functioning of the system - thus an absence of such a possible situation should be checked dynamically. If dynamic process migration and dynamic creation and deletion of processes are not allowed, such dynamic deadlock may be avoided at the physical design stage by the correct design of schedulers.

To cope successfully with an analysis for such potential dynamic deadlocks, one has to specify deadlock-detection subsystems as part of the final application. The problem is well understood, and the majority of deadlock-related publications are devoted to the detection of, and recovery from, dynamic deadlocks (see, for example, [Kohler (1981)] and [Halang (1983)]).

On the other hand, an information deadlock can occur dynamically in a correct system only if something unexpected happens, such as a hardware failure, or a software error. By their nature, information deadlocks are static, and only a specific, erroneous structure in the system can lead to one.

At the specification stage it will only be possible to detect static deadlocks which have been built into the system's inherent structure. A static deadlock can thus be permanently present, but the moment at which its presence becomes explicit will depend upon the functioning of the system.

In a specification described in terms of the Q-model, therefore, the only possible deadlock type is static, and this may be caused by a lack of information resources. The only common resources in a Q-model which are shared by processes, are messages. Consequently, the only cause of a deadlock will be a "circular" message-waiting condition.

The most obvious cause for such a circular wait condition will be missing channels - and this will be discovered by tests for isolated elements (see Section 7.2). So, provided that all channel types are correctly specified, and that all the necessary channels are present, the only reason for a circular wait condition will be erroneous channel functions. We therefore need to investigate how these could arise.

Firstly, null channels cannot cause a circular wait since they do not transmit any messages. Also, in the case of asynchronous channels, any associated consumer-process will never wait since it consumes the message that happens to be available in the channel at the time. Recall, also, that a message from an asynchronous channel does not disappear after reading, so the same message can be read several times; therefore, a message will always be available.

So we are left with two types of channels, synchronous and semisynchronous, and both can cause dangerous conditions. It is therefore important to investigate various possible substructures which may be formed when using these two channel types. We start by defining some typical structures:

- *A simple semisynchronous chain* is a sequence of common processes, $p_1, p_2, \ldots, p_n \in P$, communicating via synchronous and semisynchronous channels. Here, we assume that no process in the sequence may have more than one input semisynchronous channel, as shown in Figure 7.3(a). (We should recall that, by definition of the Q-model, a common process may not have both synchronous and semisynchronous input channels at the same time.)

- *A complex semisynchronous chain* is a sequence of common processes, $p_1, p_2, \cdots, p_n \in P$, communicating via synchronous and semisynchronous channels, in which at least one process has more than one semisynchronous input channel, as shown in Figure 7.3(b).

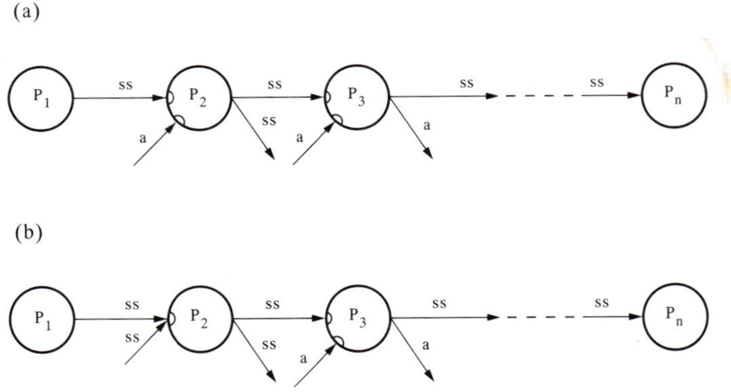

Figure **7.3** Simple (a) and complex (b) semisynchronous chains

- *A synchronous chain* is a sequence of common processes, $p_1, p_2, \ldots, p_n \in P$, communicating via synchronous channels.

Any synchronous chain has its own timeset. Any semisynchronous chain can be represented as a sequence of synchronous chains connected to each other via semisynchronous channels. In a simple semisynchronous chain, the timeset for a synchronous sub-chain is determined by the process which activates the synchronous sub-chain. Because of this, all simple semisynchronous chains will function at their natural rate (which can be compared to the natural rate of Petri-nets, see [Sifakis (1979)]).

Consider, as an example, a simple semisynchronous chain comprising three processes, as shown in Figure 7.4

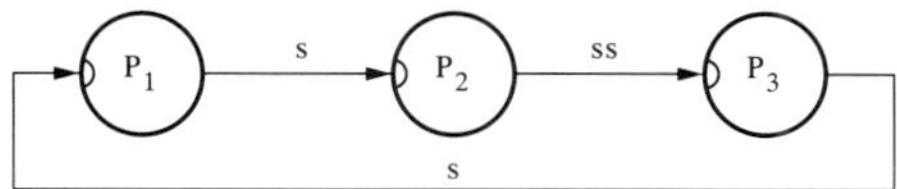

Figure **7.4** A simple semisynchronous chain.

All the processes in this chain are executed synchronously and the frequency of the repeated start times of the processes is determined by the characteristics of the processes themselves. From the definition of the Q-model, at the system's initial, or cold, start, all the channels have to be filled with data. All that is needed, then, is for an initial start signal to be received from the outside by process p_3; after this initial activation, the cycle starts executing at its own natural rate.

The timeset for the processes in this chain, functioning at its natural rate, is:

$$T(p_1) = T(p_2) = T(p_3) = \{\ 0;\ t_1 = \zeta\ (p_2,0) + \xi\ (\sigma_{23});$$

$$;\ t_2 = t_1 + \zeta\ (p_2,t_1) + \xi\ (\sigma_{23});\ \ldots\ ;$$

$$;\ t_i = t_{(i-1)} + \zeta\ (p_2,t_{(i-1)}) + \xi\ (\sigma_{23});\ \ldots\ \}.$$

In the case of a complex semisynchronous chain the timeset is determined by combining the natural rate with additional activation frequencies received from outside the chain through semisynchronous channels. The resulting frequency is determined according to the rules given in Section 7.2.2.

It must be pointed out that specified parameters of the processes in semisynchronous chains may be inconsistent. This, of course, can result in erroneous functioning of the specified system. The majority of these inconsistencies will be discovered through the systematic application of all the tests which have been described so far. As long as we are permitted to alter the parameters in a semisynchronous chain, then we can achieve a correctly-functioning system.

However, there is at least one important exception. Real information deadlocks, which cannot be detected, and hence eliminated, by applying the tests previously described, can occur in a so-called "synchronous loop".

A synchronous loop is a synchronous chain in which $p_1 = p_n$, and in which the channel functions of all the channels in the loop are given as $K(\sigma_{i,(i+1)}, t) = [\mu, 0]$, where μ may be different for different channels.

In Appendix B a proposition (Proposition 7) is presented which proves that a synchronous loop presents sufficient conditions for the occurrence of an information deadlock. This proof relies on a deadlock definition given in [Coffman and Denning (1973)].

It is appropriate here to discuss briefly practical deadlock-detection methods. As we have seen, the Q-model description can be viewed as a directed graph, and so deadlock detection may be reduced to the problem of investigating the properties of chains in the corresponding graphs. We need to find all chains which satisfy the definition of the synchronous loop. Still, it must be said that in theory the task is, in the general case, NP-complete (see, for example, [Reingold (1977)]).

A well-known method of handling complexity is through decomposition, and since deadlocks can only be situated inside a synchronous cluster, we are led to a need to decompose the whole network. A detailed search for possible deadlock conditions can then be undertaken inside each detected synchronous cluster.

Figure 7.5 illustrates how a deadlock in one synchronous cluster may induce disturbances in the functioning of other synchronous clusters. This is a very fundamental point which indicates that even once synchronous clusters have been detected, they cannot be handled in complete isolation. Many algorithms exist for searching for such chains in directed graphs. Here we suggest, for example, [Chachra (1979)] and [Reingold (1977)], for a more-detailed study of such algorithms.

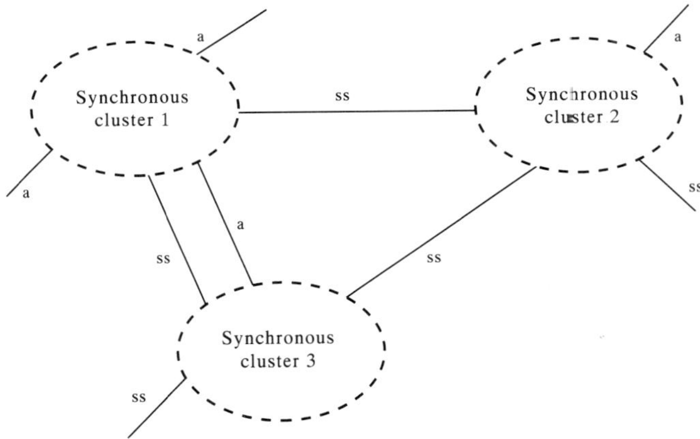

Figure **7.5** A deadlock in a synchronous cluster may induce disturbances all over the whole system

7.3.2 The paths of message transfer

The full description of an embedded system, in terms of the Q-model, may consist of several thousands of processes and channels. When investigating or analysing a particular problem, however, we often do not need the whole description of the system. Thus, the necessity for separating a group of processes, $P' \subset P$, together with the corresponding sub-set of channels, from the complete description of the system (P, Σ), will occur many times during the development of a practical system. For example, having described an embedded system and the interface to its environment, we might decide to reduce the functionality of the embedded system. As a result, the part that will be implemented on the computing system might be reduced. However, it will be useful to retain the rest of the Q-model description as a detailed interface to the environment.

In order to separate a group of processes, $P' \subset P$, together with the corresponding sub-set of channels, from the total system (P, Σ) we will have to go through the following steps:

1. Compile a list of the required processes, P'.

2. If some of the processes belonging to P' are activated indirectly by timesets whose origins have been omitted from P', the corresponding timesets should be transferred to the processes that belong to P'.

3. Remove all processes not included in P' and not directly (or, immediately) connected via channels to processes from P'.

4. Remove all isolated channels and complete, where necessary, the description of processes so that they will be able to work without information from outside of P'.

As a result of these actions, we will have separated out a sub-system (P', Σ') from the system (P, Σ), and will also have formulated its interface with the environment (i.e. with the system (P, Σ)) which now, in turn, includes the new system (P', Σ').

The Q-model presentation (P', Σ') can be transformed into a directed graph $\wp$ whose set of vertices (a vertex being a point on a graph) coincides with the set of processes P'. Common and selector processes are transformed into the same types of vertices. Each vertex has two attributes, completion time and timeset, which are known from the Q-model definition. The arcs of the directed graph correspond to the channels of the Q-model and the set of arcs coincides with Σ'. Each arc has a "weight". Those arcs which correspond to output channels of common processes have weight 1, whilst those which correspond to the output channels of selector processes have weights which equal the probability of obtaining a new state value. In addition to their weights, each arc has two attributes: channel type and function.

The movement of a reaction across a network of processes in response to an input message is determined by the sequence of process activations and the corresponding channel functions. Usually, we are interested in the time required by the reaction to move from the initial process to a specific terminating process. Both these processes must be defined by the user when stating the problem to be addressed.

The vertices of the directed graph which correspond to the initial and terminating processes, determine the set of all possible paths which can be used for transmitting a reaction to the original message.

A path $\pi(p_s, p_t)$ from vertex p_s to vertex p_t is determined by a sequence of vertices and arcs from the initial vertex to the termination vertex. The set of all paths from p_s to p_t is denoted by $w(p_s, p_t)$.

Now, if a directed graph, $\wp$, contains cycles, the set of all possible paths $w(p_s, p_t)$ is infinite. In our particular case, however, the situation is not quite as hopeless as it might seem; although our graph might contain cycles, we have two reasons why we will not have to deal with an infinite number of paths.

Firstly, the memory in the channels and in the attributes of the arcs respectively, is finite. Thus, the channel function will determine the necessary number of times a cycle must be traversed. If we pass along the arc more times than is allowed by the channel function, the message being passed along will not explicitly contain any reaction to the original message. (There is a minor complication to this, which occurs when dealing with a sequence of channel functions.) However, in all cases, the total number of times we have to pass through a cycle will be finite. This is not in contradiction to graph theory, but is a result of the mechanisms used to implement our model.

Secondly, we can deliberately limit the number of times a particular cycle is passed through. This can be done by fixing a "path expression" which must be satisfied by each path of the set. This expression characterises the details of paths which are of interest. It can specify, for example, an acceptable sequence of processes, how many times one process may be passed through, or which process(es) should not be passed through. Additionally, we may fix a "threshold probability". If the probability of passing along a particular path is less than the given threshold, the path will not be included in the set of all possible paths. (The threshold probability is only of value in handling cycles which contain at least one selector process.)

When evaluating the time taken in passing through a particular path, we assume that a delay in a particular process is determined only by the attributes of that process and does not depend on the path taken to reach this particular point. This assumption is based on the fact that the corresponding Q-model description (P', Σ') has been checked for consistency and non-contradiction of time parameters, and also that deadlock detection has been undertaken. We also assume that processes and channels function correctly and that no failures occur.

As an example, let us consider a very simplified procedure for frame transfer in a communication system, as shown in Figure 7.6.

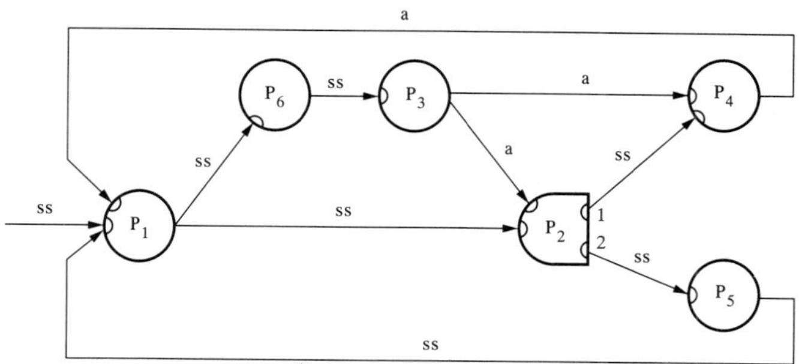

Figure **7.6** Frame transfer in a communications system

In this model, the receiver is represented by process p_6 and all the other processes belong to the sender. Process p_1 accepts a message to be transferred, forms the frames, transfers them, and finally checks the results. Process p_3 accepts an acknowledge signal from the receiver, and sends a message to the watchdog timer (p_2), and also to p_4 which counts the frames successfully sent. If an acknowledge signal is not received in time, the watchdog timer signals this (state 2 of process p_2), and the frame is transferred again.

In this example, two elementary paths π (p_1,p_1), can be distinguished:

$$p_1(p_1p_6)p_6(p_6p_3)p_3(p_3p_2)p_2(p_2p_4)p_4(p_4p_1)p_1 \text{ and}$$

$$p_1(p_1p_2)p_2(p_2p_5)p_5(p_5p_1)p_1.$$

Only the first of these is used in transferring a frame, and all other possible paths are combinations of these two.

We can further limit the number of paths by introducing a "path expression". In this example, we could use two different path expressions (depending on what we are interested in examining):

$$A1(\pi(p_1,p_1)) = p_4 \quad \text{or} \quad A2(\pi(p_1,p_1)) = p_4 \vee 2p_5 \wedge p_4.$$

When applying A1, we include all paths which are used for transferring the frame. When we apply A2, we allow only two unsuccessful attempts to be included, but ultimately require final success.

7.3.3 Time required to pass through a path

The complexity in the definitions of processes and channels make it impossible to evaluate the time to pass through a path by the simple summation of process execution times. Things are also made worse when there are truly asynchronously executed processes in a path. As was demonstrated in [Motus (1986)], the time required to pass along a path which contains a truly asynchronously executed process depends on the start times of the starting process.

Now, for each particular start time it is possible to compile an equation for calculating the time to pass along a path. We might end up with an almost infinite number of complex formulae; therefore, we will continue to adopt a pragmatic approach and derive formulae for evaluating the lower and upper bounds on such times.

Each path is partitioned into homogeneous legs, each of which consists of a sequence of processes, communicating through channels of the same type. Consequently, we have three types of legs: synchronous, semisynchronous and asynchronous. The following formulae are used for evaluating lower and upper bounds of the time taken for passing along each type of leg. Having evaluated the time taken for a homogeneous leg, the processes of this leg can be aggregated into a single entity. Such a manipulation will be repeated until the whole path is transformed into one equivalent process, with a known execution time.

Synchronous leg of path: Let us consider the leg of a path with processes p_k, $p_{(k+1)}$, ... , p_r, which are communicating via synchronous channels. The channel functions are given as follows

$$K(\sigma_{k(k+1)}, t) = [\mu_{(k+1)}, \nu_{(k+1)}], \dots,$$
$$, K(\sigma_{(r-1)r}, t) = [\mu_r, \nu_r].$$

It is always possible to renumber processes so that the processes, in a selected leg, will form a subsequence of consecutive integers [k,r]. Now, since all the processes are synchronous, their common timeset is $T(p) = \{t_0, t_1, \dots, t_m \dots\}$.

It is also known that, for any two consecutive start times, $t_{min}(p) \le t' - t \le t_{max}(p)$, the execution times are given as $\zeta(p_i) \in [\alpha(p_i), \beta(p_i)]$, $k \le i \le r$.

Proposition 8:
Assume that the assumptions of Propositions 1 and 2 are satisfied. Assume also that assumptions of Propositions 3 or 4 are satisfied, and $\nu_j > 0$, $k \le j \le r$. Then, the upper and lower bounds of time required to pass through a synchronous leg of a path are determined by the following:

a) Upper bound of path passing time

$$D_{sync}(\pi(p_k, p_r)) = t_a(p) \sum_{j=k+1}^{r} (\nu_j - 1) + (r-k)\, t_{max}(p) + \beta(p_r)$$

b) Lower bound of passing time

$$d_{sync}(\pi(p_k, p_r)) = t_a(p) \sum_{j=k+1}^{r} (\nu_j - 1) + (r-k)\, t_{min}(p) + \alpha(p_r)$$

(The proof of Proposition 8 is given in Appendix B.)

Semisynchronous leg of a path: We use here the same notation as we did for a synchronous leg. The processes in the leg are communicating via semisynchronous channels, but only the first process has an independent timeset. The timesets for all the other processes in the leg are generated within the leg.

Proposition 9:
Assume that the assumptions of Propositions 1 and 2 are satisfied.

Let $v_j > 0$ for $k \le j \le r$, and

$$t_{min}(p_k) \ge \max(\tau_{e(pk)}, \tau_{e(p(k+1))}, \dots, \tau_{e(pr)}).$$

Then the upper and lower bounds of time required to pass through the semisynchronous leg of a path are determined by the following:

a) Upper bound of path passing time

$$D_{semisync}(\pi(p_k, p_r)) = t_a(p_k) \sum_{j=k+1}^{r} (v_j - 1) + (r-k)\, t_{max}(p_k) + \sum_{j=k}^{r} \beta(p_j)$$

b) Lower bound of passing time

$$d_{semisync}(\pi(p_k, p_r)) = t_a(p_k) \sum_{j=k+1}^{r} (v_j - 1) + (r-k)\, t_{min}(p_k) + \sum_{j=k}^{r} \alpha(p_j)$$

(The proof of Proposition 9 is given in Appendix B.)

Asynchronous leg of a path: A characteristic property of an asynchronous leg will be that each process of this leg has its own timeset, independent of those of other processes in the leg. When transferring information through an asynchronous channel, we will also have to deal with the non-transport delay. Earlier in this chapter it was shown that the graph of a non-transport delay will have the form of a saw-tooth function. The lower bound of this function equals 0 and the upper bound is given by Proposition 6 (see Appendix B). Practical experience has indicated that the lower bound is too optimistic, and likewise, the upper bound is too pessimistic.

Proposition 10:
Assume that the condition of Propositions 1 and 2 are satisfied. Let $v_j > 0$ for $k \le j \le r$, and time is modelled by non-negative integers. Then, the upper and lower bounds of time required to pass through an asynchronous leg of a path will be determined by the following:

a) Upper bound of path passing time

$$D_{async}(\pi(p_k, p_r)) = \sum_{j=k}^{r-1} \varphi_n^*(p_j, p_{(j+1)}) + (r-k)t_{min}(p_k)$$
$$+ \sum_{j=k}^{r-1}(t_{max}(p_j) + t_a(p_j).(\nu_{(j+1)} - 1)) + \beta(p_r)$$

b) Lower bound of path passing time

$$d_{async}(\pi(p_k, p_r)) = \sum_{j=k}^{r-1}(t_{min}(p_j) + t_a(p_j).(\nu_{(j+1)} - 1)) + \alpha(p_r)$$

(The proof of Proposition 10 is given in Appendix B.)

7.4 CONCLUSIONS

In this chapter we have discussed the current situation relating to the analysis of the formal correctness of a specification described in terms of the Q-model. The methods presented do not cover all the possible (and necessary) aspects for formal correctness, but form a collection which has proved to be of practical value, and from which good results are being achieved.

There are, however, important areas which are not covered by the methods presented, especially in the rules for the formal decomposition and aggregation of processes and for the handling of more-advanced problems in semisynchronous chains. The study of these methods is not yet completed and the results will be published in the next edition of this book.

Also, new aspects of the formal analysis will be required when the application of the Q-model is fully extended into the logical and physical design stages. Some of these problems have been touched on by Haavel (1987) and Motus (1982), and these include the following points:

- evaluating the intensity of the interactions between groups of processes, and
- evaluating the time characteristics of a message passing through a given physical medium, with a known, given workload and stated communication protocols.

However, in summary, the current situation is that the analysis of a specification developed using the Q-model approach is at an advanced stage, and the results obtained are extremely valuable. The next chapter will describe how a practical CASE tool can be based on these methodologies, and Appendix C provides a full investigation into the theory underlying the Q-model approach.

CHAPTER 8

Towards A Case Environment based on the Q-Model

Software engineering environments were introduced to enhance the integrated use of tools which supported certain aspects of specification, design, programming *or* software management. Before this, separate environments were necessary for specification, for design and for implementation, and the only unifying link between them was the user. Surveys of existing environments, in addition to that given in Chapter 3, can be found in the papers by Hausen (1982) and Hesse (1984).

According to an expert forecast [Riddle (1986)], commercial interest in the so-called "integrated environments" increased remarkably in the 1990s. It is important to see that because of hardware developments such integrated environments no longer require to execute on an extensive host system, often with a mainframe architecture. The ideal now is seen to be a set of workstations, each possibly dedicated to specific life-cycle stages, working in an integrated environment which automatically handles the exchange of information between the individual users.

Since the market for embedded software has been relatively small when compared to that for data-processing products, the temptation has been to consider tools for embedded software as special cases of those required in data processing. This view is supported in most of the surveys previously referred to.

This book takes the opposite point of view! For the sake of argument, we suggest that it would be more fruitful to consider data-processing software as a special case of embedded software! This seemingly radical approach can be justified by considering the number of additional problems which must be solved when developing embedded software. Such problems include the essential parallelism; the strict timing-constraints on the frequency of repeated activations of processes; the time-selectiveness of communications; incomplete knowledge of causal relations; and the need for increased attention to the fault-tolerance, reliability and maintainability of the system. One can extend this list by mentioning the highly dedicated nature of embedded software and hardware as compared to the high level of standardisation in the data-processing field. The ability to handle these many and varied problems will make the development environment rugged and reliable -

characteristics desirable in any supporting system. Likewise, any product developed in such an environment should be very efficient and effective.

As a result, a software engineering environment which can meet our embedded-system needs will be in a good position to handle the relatively trivial requirements of the data-processing, or scientific computing, industry!

In this chapter the design of a software engineering environment, developed specifically for embedded software, is described. A significant part of this environment has already been implemented and is in regular use. Although the major emphasis of the environment is on the analysis of timing behaviour, we can also use it to describe common data-processing applications, as specific cases of hard real-time software.

8.1 GOALS OF THE PROPOSED ENVIRONMENT

A software engineering environment should provide support for all the activities involved in software development, including documentation and management of the activities which occur. At different stages in the life-cycle we will normally require different sets of tools. Whilst the tools for one particular activity can normally communicate amongst themselves, communication and co-ordination between different sets, typically used at different times, are normally less well-integrated and transparent, and co-operation becomes almost impossible (see [Kuo (1986)]).

Whilst such co-ordination is a central factor, especially in terms of software development management, the most useful role of an environment is, in practice, to introduce a *discipline* for the users. This discipline could typically involve rules for tackling problems, the ordering and auditing of activities, and often, the automatic storing of products, progress and results.

The necessity of applying formal methods at each life-cycle stage has become far more urgent in the area of embedded software than in the other areas. This is, as we have previously suggested, because of the specific properties of embedded systems and their resultant software. This introduces another important role for a development environment - to conceal any formalism from the end-user of the environment. Whilst the majority of users agree that formal methods are of value in software development, very few are willing to learn how to use a formal method properly. Asking a control engineer to use a first-order predicate calculus will cause an immediate and violent reaction!

Another peculiarity of an embedded software engineering environment is the strong need for "openness". This follows directly from the multidisciplinary nature of embedded systems, which requires intensive co-operation between specialists from different subject areas, including hardware experts, process and control engineers, programmers and managers. This will be necessary practically throughout all the software life-cycle stages. Increasingly, many of these specialists will have their own computer-aided tools, and so the ability to provide automatic information exchange between tools from different application domains, is an important goal. This goal will be difficult to achieve, however - especially when we consider how difficult it is to get any human specialists to communicate.

Amongst the many features which characterise the difference between humans and computers is one which is of particular interest in the present context. When people develop solutions for similar applications more than once, they are almost invariably much more productive when developing their third system than their first. This is human nature, since we are always gathering experience without even noticing it. The acquisition and reuse of such experience are naturally amongst the most intriguing topics in artificial intelligence, but, as yet, little has been achieved which is of practical value in the design of large-scale systems. It certainly would be very attractive to have an experience-collection and -reuse capability in a software engineering environment!

These speculations, relating to the desired properties of a software engineering environment for embedded software systems need to be transformed into guiding principles for environment designers. It is useful in this context to refer to the historic paper by Balzer and Goldman (1979), in which eight principles for specification systems were spelt out, and also to a more recent paper by Magel (1984), which gave fifteen principles for software environments.

For our own guidance, though, we have managed with only three basic principles, since we believe that their proper understanding reveals all the necessary fundamental keys to developing an acceptable environment!

Principle 1: Autonomous functioning of separate tools
Considering the total number of man-years required to develop a complete software engineering environment, it is economically pragmatic to use an individual tool as soon as it is functional. The danger here is that we end up having a set of separately functioning tools, and only a shell of an environment! The issue of integrating separately-functioning tools into a unified whole is an eternal problem in engineering. (Just recall the battles to get the OSI reference model for communication systems accepted.) A possible interpretation of the integration problem in the computer-aided software engineering (CASE) context was presented by Kaplan (1986), who suggested, in essence, that the tools themselves cannot be integrated, but that it is vital that they can exchange information in a consistent fashion. The previous reference to the OSI principles is appropriate here as well. The various layers of protocols represent independently functioning, self-contained entities, which only communicate and co-ordinate via the exchange of information. The information, in turn, contains both data and control, representing instructions and results.

In the environment which is described in this book, the different tools communicate via data bases, and, when required, an appropriate transformation of input and output data is provided. This approach corresponds to Kaplan's ideas in that the various tools are exchanging information and not operating together.

Principle 2: Compatible information structures
If different tools have the same information structures, then their integration into a unified system will not be very difficult. In practice, though, the complete unification of information structures

invariably leads to inefficient processing algorithms - at least in some of the tools. Therefore, this principle must be applied carefully.

Techniques facilitating the compatibility of information structures can be traced in two directions.

Firstly, the principle can be directly applied to developing a dedicated database (information- or knowledge-base) which captures all necessary data structures, and answers all enquiries. Such an approach is described in [Kuo (1986)]. This approach is especially feasible in closed computer systems, since the outsider's influence will be weak.

Secondly, the principle will be supported by the adoption of common formal methods as the basis for tools developed for different life-cycle stages. As a direct by-product, common formalisms in the tools will decrease possible errors and misconceptions caused by changing from one tool to another, or from one life-cycle stage to the next. An additional by-product will be that a common formalism will greatly enhance the re-use of software modules, since it will impose a unified description on the various modules' properties.

A danger, though, in adopting a too-widely applicable formalism is that whilst we might gain from its universality, we could lose (as we often do with general solutions) in effectiveness and analytic power. Therefore, we will need to make a reasonable compromise. For example, whilst the Q-model approach can be used for describing and analysing structural and behavioural properties in all the life-cycle stages, it has limited descriptive abilities. Thus, we will need to adopt other methods for detailed algorithm specification.

Principle 3: Accumulation and re-use of experience
At the present time this principle is the hardest to apply, primarily because we have little idea of where to begin. It leads us to many insufficiently studied problems, such as the problem of finding similarities between two different samples of a specification and the problem of reasoning with incomplete information.

Another consequence of this principle is the necessity to increase the importance of the database, which, in fact, must be replaced by a knowledge base. As we know only too well, the appropriate structuring of the information needed by a software engineering environment is still a difficult problem, and this is only the first step necessary towards a true knowledge base (see, for example, [Kuo (1986)]).

As a result, most conventional environments are used for a single (or several, independent) projects, and currently accumulate little experience, except in holding details of the modules developed.

In this book we present the design of a software engineering environment which confirms the first two principles, and provides a test-bed for developing methods which could potentially satisfy the third.

8.2 A SOFTWARE DEVELOPMENT METHODOLOGY

Our goal is to cover with our proposed environment, with minimal effort, as large a portion of the software life-cycle as we possibly can. Previous chapters have set out to back our suggestion that we can adopt the Q-model approach as the basic formalism used in our environment. As we have demonstrated, the Q-model has the following advantages:

- The abstract notion of a "process" is close to the concept of an "object"; this will enable the use of the same notion in describing several life-cycle stages.

- The Q-model's processes and channels require only characteristics, such as input/output variable lists and time parameters, which can be obtained either from the environment (when specifying a system) or from measurements on existing software (when analysing an existing system). The latter will also be needed for conformance tests, software proving, etc.

- The Q-model has a sufficiently strict mathematical basis to permit the analysis of the formal correctness of a system's structure and its behaviour in time.

- The Q-model contains enough intrinsic information about the target application to enable an informal analysis, based mainly on information contained in the Q-model, by the use of simulation on an automatically-generated prototype version of a proposed system.

- The Q-model supports, in principle, the step-wise development of a system. For practical support of step-wise refinement, we have introduced the idea of an "**heredity tree**", which is used for storing the steps involved of the evolutionary process of creating a hierarchical description.

Drawbacks to the adoption of the Q-model follow directly from its abstract nature, its structural orientation and its ability to handle only behavioural characteristics. This leads us to the necessity of using other formalisms for handling more-detailed information, in particular, for algorithm development. However, bearing in mind the overall and, in particular, the temporal, complexity of embedded software, such partitioning of the problem solutions will inherently decrease the complexity of each particular step. Our own experience has been that after overcoming a natural tendency to rush into algorithms, users quickly realise the advantage gained by adopting the proposed approach, particularly as it isolates the real problems.

In summary, the suggested methodology offers the following major features:

1. The software life-cycle is divided into stages, each with clearly distinguishable problems and fixed interfaces between each stage.

2. The essential problems of each stage are presented and analysed by use of the selected formal method - in our case, the Q-model. For auxiliary problems, other formalisms may have to be adopted.

3. The resulting description of the future software system must pass formal analysis at each stage. In the ideal case, the underlying set of analytical tools is the same for different stages.

4. Recognising the limited capabilities of any formalism when used for the description and analysis of real-world phenomena, we introduce at each stage the possibility of the automatic creation of a prototype version of the future system (based on current knowledge). Simulation studies can then be undertaken on this prototype.

In the rest of this chapter, each step in the methodology will be discussed.

8.2.1 Partitioning the software life-cycle

The basis of our methodology is the division of the software life-cycle into five stages (see also Figure 8.1):

- *The specification stage* includes the specification of both functional and non-functional requirements, as well as the behavioural requirements.

- *The logical design stage* includes the specification of algorithms and the formation of software or hardware modules.

- *The physical design stage* includes the mapping of the logical design onto a physical network of processes, and the forming of tasks to be controlled (where required) by the operating system. This stage will therefore also involve tailoring the operating systems - in particular their scheduling algorithms.

- *The implementation stage* includes the coding, debugging, testing of modules and also, finally, system testing.

- *The maintenance stage* includes modifications and improvements, as well as searches for any remaining errors.

The output of each particular stage is a Q-model-based description of the corresponding results. From the physical design stage, the Q-model will be accompanied by information relating to the physical location of Q-model elements.

The objective is to ensure that at the end of the specification stage (provided we have a good specification, that is), the corresponding Q-model should contain a very detailed description of the future system's structure and behaviour. The development of this specification, of course, usually starts with a set of rather vague ideas, which are extended and enhanced during the evolutionary process by the use of common-sense and theoretical knowledge about the application (so-called, "deep" knowledge), empirical facts about the application (so-called "shallow" knowledge), and guidance given by results obtained from the formal analysis of the properties of the evolving Q-model. An overview of this methodology is shown in Figure 8.1.

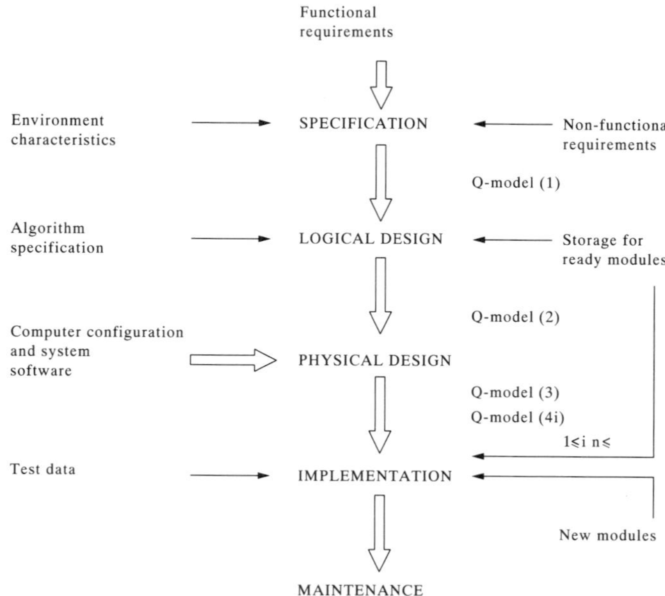

Figure **8.1** A methodology for embedded software development
[Note that cyclic activities are not described here]

At the specification level, the typical approach to the problem of obtaining a description of the future system is essentially a top-down one. We start with a few vague ideas and end up with a detailed representation of the structure of the future system. It is important here to ensure, though, that reliability and fault-tolerance requirements are included in the specification at this stage. In practice, these are often added much later, and can often change the time behaviour of the system, hence introducing additional timing problems.

It is interesting to note here, and as will be shown in Chapter 9, a useful and intuitive approach is, in fact, to start with simple data flow models - which provide a good insight into the basic functioning of the proposed system. Having developed such data flow models, expressed say as data flow diagrams, the introduction of timing parameters is a simple and meaningful step. Indeed, many real-time software engineering practitioners have wondered why such an obvious step was not introduced before - especially as the conventional next step has normally been the introduction of the somewhat-limited and uncomfortable "state transition diagrams", the use of which tends to be foreign to most engineers.

The resulting Q-model description of the specification (which is the output of the specification stage) will serve as the input to the logical design stage. At this next stage, the specified processes and channels of the Q-model are re-arranged into modules which, formally-speaking, are also processes in the Q-model, communicating via channels. In most cases, a module will consist of several processes described in the specification.

Before forming the modules, though, we have to determine the algorithm for each process inherited from the previous design stage. The selection of algorithms is easier now, since we have limited their definitions and value ranges. Also, the major time constraints which must be imposed on the algorithms, have been fixed. These features all help to restrict the range of possible algorithms. We still do not, in theory, assume anything about the implementation of the algorithms, as the modules could be implemented in either hardware or software. In practice, though, at this stage we will be calling upon our designers' experience to help make the decisions.

In forming a module, we will consider the algorithms of the processes involved, and in addition, the configuration and availability of potential off-the-shelf modules.

At the end of the logical design stage we have, again formally, a Q-model which has now been obtained by a bottom-up modification to the output of the specification stage.

A particular difficulty in the logical design stage is that we have to provide for the possibility of having to use another tool for algorithm specification. Also, we might have to obtain information about ready-made modules - typically those used in previously implemented projects, or available from vendors. (Our system should, of course, be able to suggest possible candidates to the user!)

The output of the logical design stage will serve as one of the two major inputs to the physical design stage. Another major input will be a description of the various available computing systems and their system software. At the end of the logical design stage we will have a system which is described in terms of hardware or software modules. The modules, though, have not yet been allocated to physical processors, and allowable physical migration rules have not yet been fixed.

The output of the physical design stage will take the form of tasks, essentially software modules, controlled by operating systems (or, at least, operating systems' executives), allocated to physical processors.

At the physical design stage, the manipulations which will take place on the available Q-model will typically have a bottom-up nature - since the resulting Q-model will contain less detail than the original one. In order to undertake effective physical design, many complementary problems need to be solved. We have, for example, to develop schedulers to ensure the required activation of processes, and also to evaluate interprocessor communications. It is interesting to note that in practice, module coding, testing and verification can actually start after the logical design stage - just as soon as we fix the computer configuration, i.e. early in the physical design.

At the output of the physical design stage, we will have more than one Q-model. Q-model (3) see Figure 8.1, will give an overall description of the network in which each station, or each processor, is represented by a small number of processes. This model is used mainly for interprocessor communication evaluation. The sequence of Q-models (4i), $1 < i < n$ (see Figure 8.1), will describe the system processor-wise, and is used for studying the behaviour of a particular processor under its allocated workload.

The major problem in the maintenance stage is caused by the necessity for modification. Practical experience has indicated that a significant amount of the total effort required in modifying a system is actually spent on identifying and understanding existing software and its structures. [Belady (1982)]. This is quite understandable if we remember that the logical physical and implementation stages have traditionally been documented from a programmer's point-of-view. The only overall structure of the system that we ever had was at the specification stage. In practice, at the end of the implementation stage there is usually only a vague reflection of the original, specified system! It might happen, for example, that a process, carefully defined at the specification level, ends up being located in many places in the final configuration, with nobody really understanding its basic functions.

However, the use of the suggested programming methodology should automatically result in a series of Q-model-based descriptions, produced as the system evolves. It is, therefore, not difficult to backtrack, when making suggested modifications, from the final implemented version to the originally specified version. We must insist, though, that we introduce modifications only at the specification level; by doing this, we can check, and then guarantee, that a modification will not have any undesirable side-effects, and that it does not violate any specified behavioural pattern.

8.2.2 Formal analysis at life-cycle stages

Each particular life-cycle stage has its own specific problems. Concentrating on these problems is important when developing appropriate support tools to cater for each decision stage. Thus, when designing an environment which attempts to cover more than one life-cycle stage, we have to concentrate on problems which are common to several stages.

In the previous section it was mentioned that a Q-model description of a system is applicable at each life-cycle stage. Such a description is also useful in ensuring a smooth transition from one life-cycle stage to another. Naturally, however, when comparing the Q-model descriptions for different stages, we can assume that they will capture only a few characteristics common to every life-cycle stage. These characteristics represent the essential structure and behaviour of the system.

It is intuitively clear that certain aspects of a system's structure and behaviour must remain invariant throughout the development process. Data and control-signal communications between structural units of a system must, for example, follow the same pattern at every life-cycle stage. The pattern, though, may change slightly as a result of process decomposition or aggregation, and the correctness of such changes will need special verification. Another example of evolutionary change will be that the majority of imposed time restrictions cannot be loosened; in many cases, the opposite will occur!

We suggest that the methods adopted for the formal analysis of structural and behavioural properties of a system, as described by the Q-model, are applicable, without modification, at all life-cycle stages. Consequently, the same will be true for the formal tools based on these techniques. The properties that can be analysed by the same tools at each life-cycle stage will include:

- *Structural correctness* of a description, including the absence of deadlocks.

- *Correspondence* of the data sent by producers to that required by consumers, and the absence of retarder processes in semisynchronous chains and cycles.

- *Behavioural correctness* of a description, including analysis for the correct order of simultaneously executed copies of the same process; allowable waiting time for messages during synchronous communication, and acceptable non-transport delays during the truly asynchronous mode of communication. Behavioural correctness also includes verification of the consistency of timing constraints imposed on activation frequencies, execution times and data consumption-times of the processes involved; also, guaranteed correctness of time-selective data communication.

Another group of properties which can be analysed by essentially the same set of tools at any stage, is connected with actual performance evaluation and analysis. The methods which can be used for undertaking this are described in Section 7.3.3.

We will not, however, discuss in detail here questions related to the analysis of properties specific to a particular life-cycle stage. However, there is at least one group of problems which lies between the two extremes, i.e. those required at every stage, versus separate tools for separate stages. These problems arise from a principal drawback in the use of formal methods whenever we deal with real-world phenomena, especially those which are as complex as embedded systems. No one formalism can provide a full coverage for all the problems. The mapping of a real-world phenomenon into a formal description is never unique, and as a rule we have to make use of simplifications, assumptions and approximations, especially in causal relationships. These are normally necessary in order to bridge the semantic gap which always seems to exist between a real-world phenomenon and its formal description.

As a result we seem to require our human expertise in checking the correspondence between the two systems - that is, the real system and our model - and simulation techniques are usually adopted. A key point to the spiral life-cycle model suggested by Boehm (1986) is the development of a sequence of prototypes, which will enable the study of the intrinsic properties of each prototype. At different life-cycle stages, the prototypes will naturally differ from each other because of their evolutionary nature. Consequently, the properties accessible through simulation studies will also be different.

In our approach, a common, formal representation of a system's description at different life-cycle stages will allow the use of the same prototype generator for each different stage.

In summary, then, in our approach, three groups of tools may be seen as usable in more than one life-cycle stage. These are:

- a set of tools for the formal analysis of structural and behavioural correctness,
- a set of tools for performance evaluation and estimation, and
- a set of tools for prototype generation and subsequent simulation support.

8.3 OVERALL STRUCTURE OF THE NEW ENVIRONMENT

We will first discuss the structure of an ideal software engineering environment, as this will serve as a reference when discussing our own approach. A large portion of the environment discussed is not yet backed with sufficiently tested theory and efficiently implemented methods. As a result, unsolved problems are highlighted at the end of this chapter, and the actually implemented portions of the environment are emphasised.

Based on the previous section, we can conclude that any embedded software engineering environment which will cover more than one life-cycle stage will need, at least, the following:

- the availability of two types of tools: those necessarily applicable to only one life-cycle stage, and those applicable to several life-cycle stages, and
- an interactive connection to other environments, such as Computer-Aided Control Systems Design tools, and tools for algorithm specification, implementation and testing.

The inherent complexity of the real world must influence the embedded software development process at the very first stage, specification, and subsequently at the last two stages, implementation and maintenance. The central stages in a project's evolution are relatively well-insulated from the direct influence of the surrounding world. At the implementation stage, though, we will have to deal with a variety of existing computing configurations, whereas at the specification and maintenance stages, we have to deal with a variety of applications and the problems of interfacing them to the computing system. This indirectly implies that whenever there is a need to change an embedded system (because of changes required by the application), modifications must be initiated right back at the specification stage.

This implies that we have to keep a full record of the evolution of a specific project throughout the whole of its development life-cycle. At each stage we need to record a formal description of the software, the results of any formal analysis of the description, automatically generated prototypes of the software, and results from any informal analysis - which are normally obtained through simulations on the prototypes.

In an ideal software engineering environment we will also need another feature. In order to aid the accumulation of experience from previous projects, we will need to store reusable elements of completed embedded systems, together with their formal and informal characteristics.

The above factors lead to the following structuring of the environment (Figure 8.2).

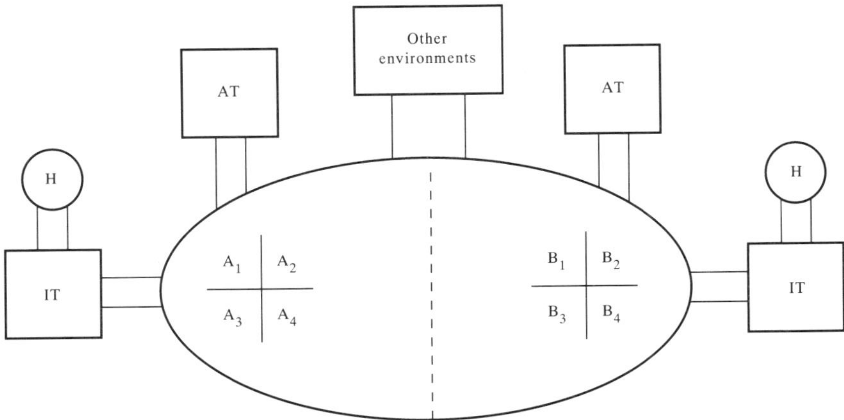

Figure **8.2** The overall structure of an embedded software engineering environment
AT - automatic tool
IT - interactive tool
H - human user

From the figure it can be seen that the software engineering environment is built around a knowledge base, which has two domains:

Domain A:
This contains information about the projects currently in hand; thus the information contained here is organised on a project-wise basis.

Domain B:
This contains information applicable to future projects. Thus, information here relates to existing software and hardware products, their characteristics, and experience obtained in their usage.

Each of these domains can be further split into sub-domains. For each project (i.e. domain A), we will have four subdomains.

Subdomain A1:
This will contain information about the dynamic specifications, such as functional, non-functional and behavioural specifications, as required by the Q-model. More specifically, it will contain:

- The system's heredity tree, which reflects the process of obtaining a specification. The tree is based on relations "is-part-of" and "has-part", and thus reflects the step-wise refinement process (see section 8.3.1. for details).

- A formally-correct specification, which is a cross-section of the heredity tree. One may, in principle, have several different specifications defined at the same time, on the same heredity tree. Only one of them, though, can be studied (i.e. formally analysed or simulated) at a time.

- A prototype, automatically generated from the formally-correct specification, together with defined simulation games and the results obtained for this particular prototype. (It is possible to modify the time parameters of the prototype to allow for different simulation games.)

- One or more semi-manually created documents, describing the activities and results of a particular life-cycle stage.

Previously-obtained experience can be used by substituting into the current project large components of previously implemented projects. In practice, one can always find components which are more or less the same in many applications. For example, a chemical reactor loading task can be found in the majority of batch chemical processes. The difficulty is to do this knowledge inclusion automatically - and, as we mentioned previously, this is still an unresolved problem.

Subdomain A2:
This will contain information about the current logical design, and will be based on the formally-correct specification stored in subdomain A1. This specification has been automatically reorganised so that the elementary structural units of the Q-model correspond to software or hardware modules in a traditional sense.

In order to understand such a logical design, we will have to specify algorithms for each process in subdomain A1, and decompose or aggregate processes, depending on their functions and specified algorithms. We will thus create an heredity tree for the logical design.

As with the previous subdomain, we will store the heredity tree, its formally-correct cross-section (in other words, a logical design in terms of the Q-model), and the corresponding prototype and resulting simulation results. The subdomain will also contain appropriate documentation.

When undertaking a logical design, it is important to consider modules which are already available. This information is, or should be, stored in domain B of the knowledge base.

Subdomain A3:
This will contain the physical design, which is, of course, based on the logical design. In fact, it is actually the logical design which is mapped onto an available computing configuration. The critical aspect here is this mapping, and past experience (obtained from domain B) will be of great help. The results of this stage are then stored as:

- An heredity tree, obtained from mapping modules into tasks.

- A cross-section of that heredity tree, which is a Q-model in which a process will correspond semantically to a task.

- This latter Q-model, further partitioned according to the given physical configuration, so that each processor has a separate Q-model. There will also be a model which describes the co-operation between processors.

- A set of prototypes, one for each processor and one for studying interprocessor communication.

- Corresponding documentation.

Subdomain A4:
This will contain the fully-implemented system which will be used by the end-user. The subdomain will contain all source and object code of the software, user's and programmer's documentation, and test and evaluation results which are required for system maintenance. In addition, this subdomain will contain pointers used in backtracking during modifications at the specification stage - recall that this is the only stage where a modification is allowed to be introduced.

Domain B will contain information applicable to future projects which are to be based on experience obtained from previous work. This domain can also be split into subdomains.

Subdomain B1:
This will store elementary processes, and groups of elementary processes, together with references to their applications and to the typical situations in which they have been used. The environment, when recognising an appropriately similar situation, should be able to propose an available, already-used, solution. The final decision whether to accept the proposal is made by the designer. (This aspect of the proposed environment has not yet been implemented, and will need much additional consideration (see, for example, [Maiden (1991)] and [Prieditis (1988)]).

Subdomain B2:
This will contain algorithms which implement processes from subdomain B1. One process may have more than one possible algorithm - the differences may lie, for example, in the calculation precision, the required memory space, or in actual performance. Likewise, an algorithm may have more than one implementation, such as the use of different languages or execution on different processors.

Subdomain B3:
This is used for storing implemented software modules, with links to the contents of subdomains B1 and B2. Each module must have a list of characteristics, corresponding to those required by the Q-model formalism, and a list of physical requirements, such as memory space and processor type. These attributes are also linked to the following subdomain, B4.

Subdomain B4:
This stores information about off-the-shelf software and hardware modules - such as available controllers, LAN interfaces and protocols, and operator stations. Again, the modules must have associated with them the characteristics necessary for inclusion into a Q-model.

All the tools included within this ideal environment, together with tools from other CASE systems (such as those used for algorithm specification) and from associated CAD systems (say, for algorithm development) interact with each other only through the knowledge base. This gives us freedom in the development of tools, provided that we maintain well-understood conventions relating to human/computer interfacing.

A set of tools which partly supports the specification stage has already been implemented. The corresponding embedded software environment has been called CONRAD, and the tools which implement the previously mentioned concepts are briefly described in the following sections.

8.3.1 The heredity tree and its cross-sections

In Chapter 4 we introduced the Q-model description of an embedded system which has served as the basis for all the further work. The task of obtaining a Q-model description, like any system description in any formalism, is not trivial. Many methodologies and tools have been developed to support such system modelling (see, for example, [Mellor and Ward (1986)]). Usually, only the final model is considered to be of interest, and interim results are discarded as not being useful. We consider that such an approach is not pragmatic because of the following points.

Firstly, modelling is a cognitive process having as its main goal the understanding and determination of how a system functions, or should function. We must concentrate on this goal, and should not try to solve other problems at the same time; in other words, we should disregard attempts to implement the model.

Secondly, having obtained a detailed description of the system, and started to consider the next problem (such as physical design or implementation), we will often require access to some of the interim results which were obtained during modelling. For example, as we move ahead we might need a less-detailed description from some earlier stage.

The *heredity tree* will serve as a controlling mechanism for storing all interim results obtained during modelling. A *particular* model of the system will be a cross-section of this heredity tree (see Figure 8.3).

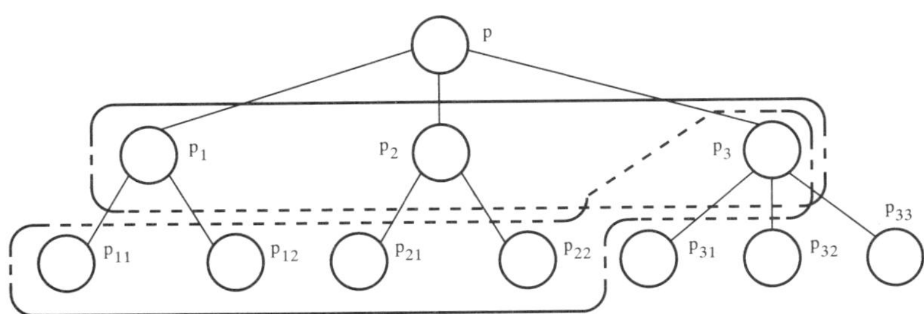

Figure **8.3** A heredity tree and its cross-sections

In Figure 8.3, a process p has been refined by decomposing it into a network of more detailed processes. The heredity tree explicitly indicates the relationships "is-part-of" and "has-part". All the information connections between processes are implicitly presented by the process descriptions. As an example, one of the marked cross-sections, consisting of p1, p2, p3 has the information connections described in Figure 8.4. For each process in a cross-section, all the parameters required by the Q-model must be specified.

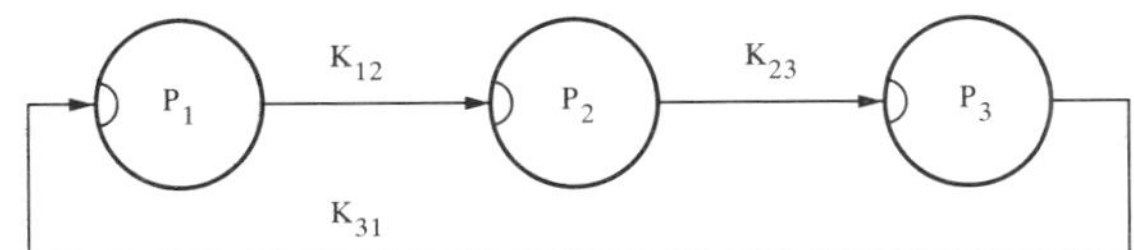

Figure **8.4** A cross-section of the heredity tree as a Q-model (compare to Figure 8.3)

By "marking" processes in the heredity tree, we can fix a particular cross-section. In order to be a true Q-model representation of the system, the selected cross-section must have representatives from all branches of the tree. The majority of the tests described in Chapter 7 must be carried out during the heredity tree's development, and during the specification of its components (i.e. processes). Only tests for checking the behavioural and structural correctness of process groups can be postponed until a cross-section has been defined.

Two operations are necessary for building and modifying the heredity tree: the decomposition of a process, and the aggregation of several processes belonging to the same level of the tree.

The *decomposition* of an existing process creates new branches in the tree by substituting one process by a network of interacting processes. By definition, the process which was substituted will remain in the tree, as the parent of the new processes. A decomposition of process p3 (see also Figures 8.3 and 8.4) is illustrated in Figure 8.5. One of the major problems of decomposing a process is maintaining the interface to its communication partners, since these partners should not notice that the process being decomposed (say, in the example p3) has been substituted by a more-detailed description. Usually, special data-transformation processes, called *dummy processes*, are required; in our example, p_{in} and p_{out}, shown in Figure 8.5. In an ideal case, dummy processes will not be visible to the user, and they should be added and deleted automatically where necessary.

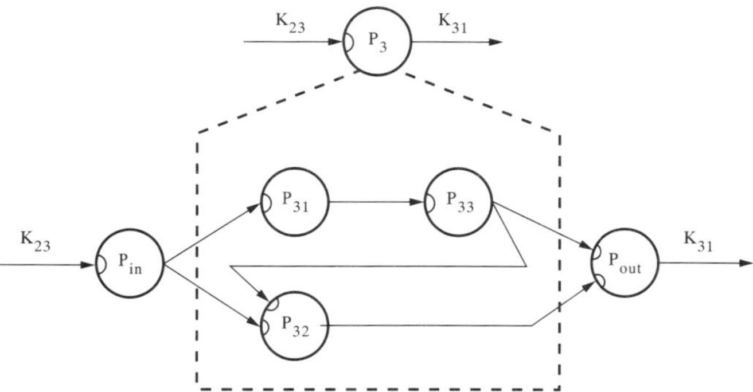

Figure **8.5** A process p_3 is decomposed into p_{31}, p_{32}, p_{33}; two dummy processes (p_{in} and p_{out}) are added to maintain the I/O interface of p_3.

Another requirement in decomposition is that it should not cause a deterioration in the time parameters specified for the parent process. This can be guaranteed by applying methods given in Chapter 7, but in some cases help will be needed from the user.

So often, too, after decomposing a process, the user will want to change channels or time parameters in the upper-level processes of the heredity tree. This will clearly require interactions to ensure consistency.

An *aggregation* is the second operation required in building and modifying a heredity tree. By applying aggregation, one can unite several processes which are situated at the same level in the heredity tree. As a result, a new level in the tree is created. For example, in Figure 8.3, process p_2 may be regarded as a process obtained by aggregating processes p_{21} and p_{22}. Thus, aggregation may be considered as an inverse operation to decomposition.

Again, as in decomposition, the major problem in aggregation lies in maintaining the interface to the communication partners, and in ensuring that there is no deterioration in the applicable timing parameters.

In the context of the different life-cycle stages, the strategy for applying decomposition and aggregation will differ. At the specification stage, a top-down approach is inevitable - therefore the heredity tree is usually built here by starting at the root, and applying decomposition. The inverse operation, aggregation, is used occasionally for achieving local improvements.

At the logical design stage, for example, we will normally start with the cross-section of the heredity tree which was obtained at the specification stage - the goal being to map processes into reasonably-sized modules. As a rule, though, a module, will be larger than a process, which will normally be the final result of specification. By applying a bottom-up approach, we will build a new heredity tree for this life-cycle stage, mainly by applying aggregation.

The theoretical results which have been described in this book have proved to be sufficient for building tools for the semi-automatic support of decomposition and aggregation. However, some difficult problems exist which still require the intervention of the user. In order to automate those operations fully, further research is needed to address specifically the difficulties connected to the invariant interface problem.

8.4 CONRAD: AN EMBEDDED SOFTWARE SPECIFICATION ENVIRONMENT

In this section a pilot project, named CONRAD (CONtrol software Requirements, Analysis and Design), is described. This is an embedded software specification environment which currently supports the first stage of the software life-cycle. As will be shown in the application case study given in the next chapter, CONRAD has proved to be useful throughout the whole life-cycle - even if, at the present time, design and implementation aspects have largely to be undertaken manually. It must be explicitly stated that CONRAD currently concentrates on the development of software specifications, and on proving the correctness of their structure and time behaviour.

The goals set for the CONRAD project include the following:

- Developing a research vehicle for testing theoretical results (as discussed in this book) and for facilitating detailed statements of any new problems which would arise.

- Developing a laboratory tool for students which would provide them with a sound insight into the intrinsic properties and problems of embedded software. In particular, the tool should expose timing problems and time-selective, interprocess communication difficulties.

- Providing a prototype system for ultimately building an industrially-acceptable software engineering environment to support the specification stage in the software life-cycle, concentrating on consistency in handling imposed timing constraints and on evaluating the behavioural and structural correctness of specifications.

In its current form, CONRAD enables its users to discover timing inconsistencies and errors before physical design and implementation starts. The common practice has been that such timing properties are properly checked only at the implementation stage, and even then, this is mainly accomplished by simulation and not by analytical proofs. We have found that the early discovery of timing inconsistencies reduces error elimination costs very significantly. We have also shown that, whilst the use of older techniques makes it almost impossible to discover the non-transport delays which occur during the interaction of truly asynchronously executed processes, these can now be determined.

CONRAD has currently been implemented on an advanced PC, for machines with a minimum of 4Mbytes of main memory. Most of the code has been written in LPA Prolog Professional, but the dedicated database, and some components of the user interface, are written in "C" and in assembler.

Compared to the ideal environment, domain B of the knowledge base, intended for the re-use of design experience and software/hardware products, has not yet been implemented. Consequently CONRAD is, at the moment, a project-oriented environment. It can, however, support several concurrent projects, each of which may have several versions at different levels of development. CONRAD also does not support algorithm specification; for this we use existing tools. CONRAD concentrates specifically on functional (or operational) and non-functional (e.g., reliability and fault-tolerance) requirements, and the emphasis is firmly on proving the consistency of the imposed timing constraints, and on verifying behavioural and structural correctness.

CONRAD, which is built around a dedicated database, offers the user four integrated tools - the Governor, Editor, Animator, and Evaluator.

The Governor:
This is a set of tools for controlling access rights to selected projects, or versions of projects. It is also used for basic book-keeping. Limiting access to projects, or project versions, is important when many are under development at the same time. It is currently possible to have different classes of projects, as follows:

- Open projects, in which any user can study and modify specifications.
- Unclassified projects, in which any user can look at existing specifications, but where modification is not automatically permitted. To be able to make modifications to an unclassified project, or to organise simulation sessions on the corresponding prototypes, a password is required.
- Classified projects, which are accessible only to authorised users, via password control.

The potential users of CONRAD fall into three categories:

- A system manager, who has access to all details in the CONRAD database. Only a system manager can introduce new projects and project managers.
- Project managers, who are users who have access to all versions of a particular project. Project managers can introduce new users on to particular projects.
- Users, who are developing applications using CONRAD. Users have access to CONRAD data and tools within limits defined by the project managers. Open projects are accessible to all users.

It is possible to add book-keeping functions to the Governor, such as "who did what and when", as well as to produce simple user statistics.

The Editor:
This consists of a set of tools for eliciting the specification for a selected project version. The Editor's user interface has a menu-driven, fill-in-the-blanks format, which is used in the evolutionary

building of a specification. All the answers given by a user must pass the formal tests described in Chapter 7. Decomposition and aggregation operations are built into the Editor. However, the insertion and deletion of dummy processes is not fully automated in the current version of CONRAD, as certain problems still need to be overcome. The procedures currently adopted require guidance by the user.

In the process of step-wise refinement, an heredity tree for the specific project version will be automatically created. Each process included in the heredity tree must satisfy the tests for individual elements (both processes and channels), as well as tests for the pair-wise interaction of processes (see Chapter 7).

A cross-section of the heredity tree is defined by marking the processes suitably, so that there is a representative from each branch of the tree. The tests for group behaviour may be executed only after a cross-section has been defined. When all the tests have been successfully passed, the chosen cross-section is available for further processing as a formally-correct specification.

The Animator:
This consists of a set of tools which are usually applied to a formally-correct specification for further, informal analysis. The aim of such analysis is usually to ensure that the formal description corresponds to the actual needs of the application. Quite often, too, this will be the right time for going through "what-if" scenarios. Examples of this could be "What happens if a failure in this part occurs?" or "What if I change the value of these parameters?"

Based on the Editor's output, a system prototype will be automatically generated. Whilst the prototype can only fully simulate the time behaviour of the specified system, it can also simulate control- and data-flow from a formal point of view. This means that we can follow the activation of processes (not just their sequence, but also the corresponding time delays), as well as interprocess message-exchange patterns. This latter aspect will include the identification of transferred generations of data, and their correspondence to specified channel functions. Any violations of the Q-model rules will be detected by the Animator.

It should be noted that the Animator cannot handle (and hence, simulate) the semantic contents of data, since the specification provided by the Editor does not include algorithms to implement processes. The user of the Animator may also, if he chooses, simulate separately only part of the specification. In this case, the interface to the rest of the specification is normally built automatically, but often some critical events will have to be generated manually. The possibility of simulating only part of the specification is important, particularly when we are dealing with a large specification, since simulation is time-consuming.

During simulation a selector process's state selection can be controlled manually so that specific selection mechanisms have no access to actually computed data (the algorithms have not yet been specified). As an alternative, a user may choose to use specified state selection probabilities in an automatic mode.

The results of a simulation are always presented as a list of events which are stored in the database. This list can then be used for post-mortem analysis; users may write their own routines for this, depending on what features are being investigated. Also, as a quick, superficial overview of the simulation results, a time-diagram option is provided. Since the number of processes displayed in such a diagram will be limited by the screen size, the user may select the specific processes required on the display.

A useful feature is that it is possible to modify the time parameters of processes before any simulation. These prototypes, with modified time parameters, may be declared as "new S-versions", usable only for simulation study. S-versions may be stored in the database and used at a later time.

The Evaluator:
This consists of a set of tools used for analytical performance evaluation at the extreme modes of a system's functioning. The evaluation will give minimum and maximum time estimates for the passing of a message between two selected processes in the specification. (The evaluation is based on formulae derived in Chapter 7.)

The tasks solved by the Evaluator are essentially based on graph theory, since they involve the searching of paths from a stated, initial process through to a terminating process. In each case, the length of a path is measured in terms of time units. Three specific problems, however, complicate the execution of this rather classical graph technique:

- graphs in the Q-model often contain cycles,
- local delays are caused by process-timesets and completion-times in vertices and by channel functions in arcs, and
- local delays will have different characteristics, depending upon the attributes of an arc which interconnects two vertices (in other words, the channel type).

To assist the Evaluator, path expressions, path-passing threshold probabilities and the various related formulae derived in Section 7.3.3, are used to suppress the infinite number of paths, and to handle non-deterministic delays.

The Evaluator works with a transformed, formally-correct specification obtained from the Editor. It can be seen that one can receive similar performance estimates by using the Animator. However, there will be a basic difference between the estimates obtained from the Evaluator and those obtained by using the Animator. The performance estimates obtained when using the Animator are measurements based on a single occurrence of a random variable; however, using the Evaluator, results are comparable to minimum/maximum estimates obtained for the same random variable.

Finally, it is possible to modify the time parameters of a specification which is used by the Evaluator. A specification with modified parameter values may be declared as a new version for the Evaluator (called a "new E-version", similar to the "new S-version" in the Animator). Similarly, several E-versions may be stored in the database. However, a single run of the Evaluator can handle only a single E-version. So, as an option, it is possible just to scan the given range of time parameters for a specific E-version. This means that evaluation can be cyclically undertaken on a given set of automatically modified parameter values.

8.5 CONCLUSIONS

The chapter started by outlining an ideal software engineering environment, based firmly on the use of the selected Q-model formalism. On the basis of this, CONRAD, a pilot version of part of such a CASE tool, has been introduced. CONRAD has been under development and evaluation for some years, and its practical use will be described in the next chapter, where a specific, temporally-critical software development will be described.

CHAPTER 9

A Case Study: Specifying a Communications Protocol

Previous chapters suggested the Q-Model as an appropriate approach to specifying embedded systems, and introduced CONRAD as a tool which supports requirement specification and analysis, with a strong emphasis on the timing characteristics of the proposed system. Earlier chapters have also suggested that communication systems facilitating distributed computing systems should also possess well-defined timing characteristics.

In the communications arena, the march towards genuine internationally-accepted standards-based products is well and truly underway. The key to these products lies in the work undertaken by the International Standards Organisation (ISO) which resulted in their now fully-accepted Open Systems Interconnect (OSI) model - an abstract model which describes in a layered architecture, all the processes necessary to effect reliable communication between distributed computers and their associated devices, such as terminals. Of importance to embedded, distributed computing systems is the fact that OSI-based standards have been adopted in industry-specific communication protocol profiles, such as the General Motors-inspired MAP (Manufacturing Automation Protocol) exercise and the Boeing-inspired TOP (Technical Office Protocol) development.

In both cases, however, whilst the target applications will typically exhibit time awareness, and while, in the case of MAP, the developers publicly proclaim deterministic temporal performance, in practice the OSI protocols are not, and never have been, designed to operate in such time-dependent fashions.

It is suggested, therefore, that in future the design of communication protocol-handling devices, which normally consist of several embedded microprocessor devices, must not only be undertaken on the basis of logical conformance with the international standards, but must also take into consideration temporal performance.

In this light, a well-established and well-defined protocol of the OSI profile, the Logical Link Control of the Data Link Layer has been chosen to evaluate its temporal performance using the CONRAD environment. The objective here is twofold; firstly to demonstrate the validity of the Q-Model and illustrate the operation of CONRAD. Secondly, the results of the exercise will indicate the effectiveness and reliability of the approach in specifying, modelling and testing a practical, complex system in the time domain.

9.1 THE LLC PROTOCOL - A BRIEF INTRODUCTION

The OSI model divides a communications system into a hierarchy of seven independent, supportive and interacting, functional layers, and specifies the abstract functions for each of these layers. The second layer of the OSI model is the Data Link Layer, which specifies the "rules" of how the network is to be accessed. The ISO standards for this layer and also for the lower, Physical Layer, have been largely adopted from the IEEE suite of standards for Local Area Networks.

The Data Link Layer is divided into two sub-layers, the Logical Link Control (LLC) sub-layer, which controls the actual mode of message transmission between two or more participating stations on the network, and the Medium Access Control (MAC) sub-layer, which controls the station access to the physical medium for data transmission (see Figure 9.1).

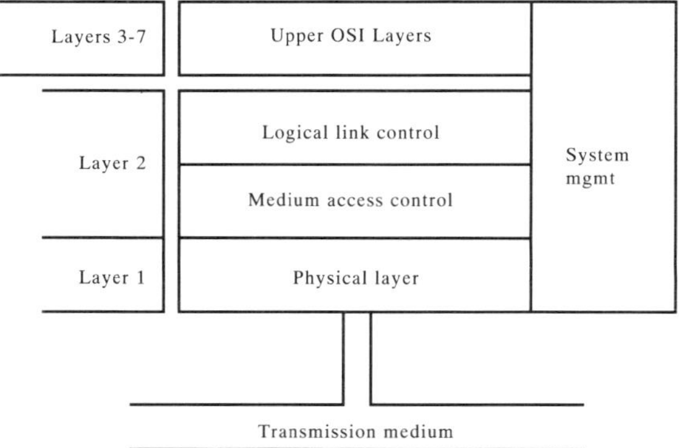

Figure **9.1** LLC sub-layer in relation to the OSI model

Three types of LLC are defined by the IEEE 802 standards, and two of them (Type-1 and Type-3) have been selected for inclusion in the MAP 3.0 specification [Rodd (1989)]. Type-1 LLC is really a 'transmit and forget' protocol, which is the basic service provided by the LLC conforming to the standard, whilst Type-3 is an acknowledged connectionless service which has been chosen for the industrial LANs concerned with "real time", and has been adopted in reduced protocol profiles, such as in MiniMAP [Rodd (1989].

It is appropriate at this juncture to introduce the main functionality of the Type-3 LLC, for a full description see [IEEE (1987)]. This "Type" offers a point-to-point data transfer mode which allows data to be transferred with an acknowledgement, and the polling of data without the need for data-link establishment. The confirmation of the transmission of a frame is generated for an LLC user only when the acknowledgement frame, for the transmitted one, is received from the destination LLC. This confirmation includes information relating to the message reception at the remote site, including the reporting of errors, or that no reception has occurred.

In the next section, a description is given of the Type-3 LLC services specification and protocol structure, drawn largely from the ISO documentation [ISO (1988)]. As most standard documents are complicated to comprehend, the LLC will be presented here in a highly simplified manner, and we shall avoid details in the specification which are felt irrelevant to this current exercise. Since the objective is to investigate the temporal characteristic of the protocol, its description will be mainly restricted to the definition of the Type-3 working procedures. The chapter then proceeds to formalise these procedures using the Q-model, and then examines the temporal characteristics by executing the model using the CONRAD environment.

9.2 THE TYPE-3 STANDARD

When describing the protocol standards of the LLC sub-layer, it is important to differentiate between the services provided by the layer, the internal operation of the layer (that is, the protocol) and the services used by the layer. The ISO Reference Model uses the layer concept, where a protocol layer, in this case the LLC sub-layer, uses the services of the underlying layer, here the MAC sub-layer, to provide a set of defined services to the User. In this case the "User" is the Network Layer.

The specification of the LLC sub-layer [ISO (1988)] consists of two main sections: *a service definition section* and a *protocol definition section*. The services provided by the LLC sub-layer (the *user services*) to the upper layer are given in the service definition section. Normally, these are in the form of a defined set of *service primitives*, each with an associated set of *service parameters*. It is through these service parameters that the user layer initiates the transfer of information to a similar LLC sub-layer in a remote system on the network.

The protocol specification, on the other hand, contains a precise description of the *protocol data units (PDUs)* used by the LLC to communicate with a similar (peer) LLC entity in a remote station. It also contains the specification of the MAC services used by the LLC to transfer each PDU type to the remote LLC. A description of the Type-3 procedures is the final part of the protocol specification. This formalises the internal operation of the LLC entity in order to provide the set of defined services to the Network Layer, which includes procedures for addressing, controlling information transfer (which includes sending PDUs) and responding to incoming PDUs.

9.2.1 The services

The Acknowledged Connectionless Services provided by the Type-3 LLC are specified by three sets of service primitives:

(a) Data Unit Transmission primitives:

L_DATA_ACK.request passed from the User to the LLC,

L_DATA_ACK.indicate passed from the remote LLC to the peer User

L_DATA_ACK_STATUS.indicate passed from the originating LLC to the User

(b) Data Unit Exchange primitives:

L_REPLY.request passed from the User to the LLC,

L_REPLY_STATUS.indicate passed from the LLC to the User.

(c) Reply Data Unit primitives:

L_REPLY_UPDATE.request passed from the User to the LLC in the remote station, and

L_REPLY_UPDATE_STATUS.indicate passed from the LLC to the User, also in the remote station.

These three sets of primitives and their interrelationship are employed by the LLC to provide two kinds of Acknowledged Connectionless services;

- *Send Data with Acknowledgement (SDA)*, which is a one-way data unit transmission service provided by invoking primitives from set (a) above, and

- *Request Data with Reply (RDR)*, which is a bilateral transmission service between two participating LLCs, or a polling for data service, provided by employing primitives from both sets (b) and (c) above.

The primitives and their interrelationships in the Type-3 services are all depicted in the time-sequence diagram of Figure 9.2.

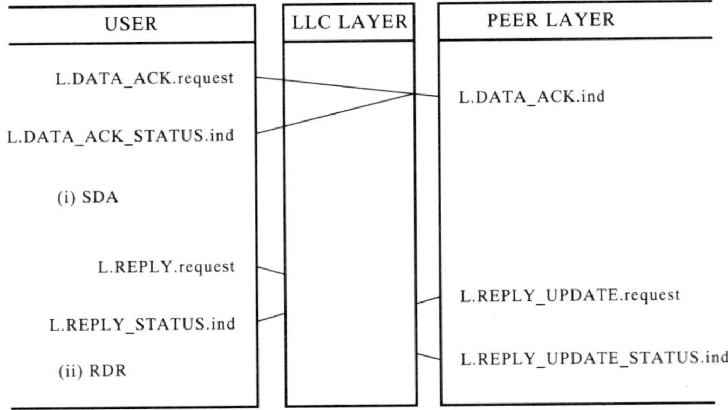

Figure **9.2** LLC Type-3 user primitives

Each of the primitives illustrated in Figure 9.2 has a defined set of parameters associated with it. It is through these parameters that adjacent layers within the same system pass information, and that two peer layers, in different systems, exchange PDUs. These parameters include the source (local) and destination (remote) addresses, the SDU (service data unit), and priority and status information. Depending on the type of primitive, some, if not all, of these parameters will be present.

The LLC sub-layer is provided by the underlying MAC layer with a standard set of user services for use - irrespective of the mode of operation of the MAC - in transferring LLC-PDUs to a corresponding layer. These user primitives are:

- MA_DATA.request,
- MA_DATA.indicate, and
- MA_DATA.confirm.

Each of the service primitives has parameters associated with it. The MA_DATA.request primitive includes: the destination address, a service data unit (containing the LLC-PDU) and the required class of service applicable (when used with a token ring or token bus medium access control, which are prioritised protocols). The success or failure of the associated MA_DATA.request primitive is specified in the status parameter of the MA_DATA.confirm primitive. However, the confirmation is generated by the local MAC entity and not by the LLC layer. The confirmation carries only information about the MAC's success in transmitting the message onto the medium, or indicates the reason if the attempt has failed. Figure 9.3 illustrates the time-sequence diagram of these primitives.

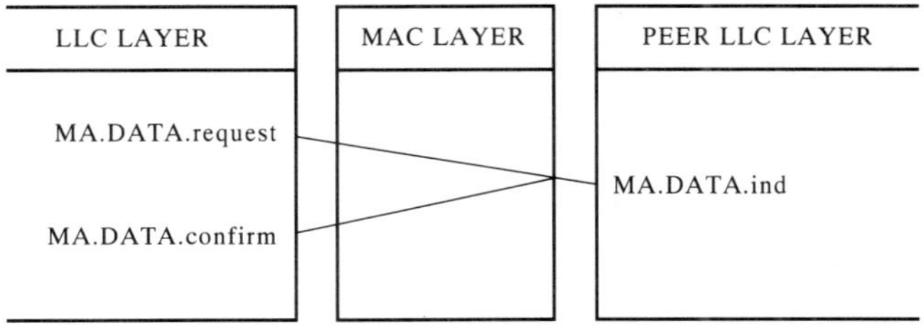

Figure **9.3** MAC sub-layer user primitives

9.2.2 The protocol activity

The Type-3 protocol supports four kinds of PDUs; namely, the AC0 command, AC0 response, AC1 command and AC1 response. These ACn PDUs (the term ACn refers to both AC0 and AC1) will be used to send information to remote LLCs, or to request information from remote LLCs without the prior need for a permanent data link connection between two LLC entities. When a station receives an ACn Command PDU, it is acknowledged by returning to the source LLC, an ACn response PDU; this contains information regarding the reception status of the associated command PDU. This PDU must be transmitted by the receiving station at the earliest opportunity and may, or may not, bear user information. A station will not send a new command PDU with a similar address (and priority) to the same station whilst waiting for an acknowledgement of the receipt of a previous PDU.

A mechanism of alternating code-points in successive PDUs provides a one-bit sequence number capability, which allows the LLC receiving a command PDU to differentiate between a new PDU and a second copy of a previously received one. Further, with this mechanism the LLC can match an acknowledgement PDU to the appropriately sent command PDU, and ignore excessively delayed acknowledgement PDUs. The protocol also defines the structure of the PDU and the use of the control bits which regulate it. For a detailed description of the PDU structure, refer to Reference [ISO (1988)].

9.2.3 Description of procedures

In this section the operational procedures of the Type-3 LLC protocol within the OSI stack will be presented. This will be based on current understanding of the specification of the Type-3 procedures contained in ISO (1988). As mentioned earlier, we will concentrate on the procedures for information transfer, which will show the internal workings of the LLC when activated by a user request primitive, in sending and receiving a PDU. The discussion is divided into three main areas: description of the logical link parameters, the procedures for sending an ACn command PDU and the procedure involved when receiving an ACn response PDU - which includes sending a response PDU. Where appropriate, diagrammatic illustrations will be included to enhance the understanding of complex, and rather abstract, concepts.

1. The logical link parameters:

A number of logical link parameters for the Type-3 operation are defined as follows:

- *Maximum Number of Transmission, N4*: This parameter essentially determines the maximum number of retries the sending LLC makes for each command PDU, in trying to accomplish a successful information exchange. N4 is usually set to be large enough to overcome the loss of a PDU due to erroneous link conditions.

- *Acknowledgement Timer, T1*: This determines the length of time the source LLC should wait for a response ACn PDU as an acknowledgement for the associated command PDU, from the destination LLC.

- *Receive Variable Lifetime, T2*: This is the maximum validity time for all the 1-bit receive sequence variables stored. T2 should be longer, by a margin of safety, than the time for the first transmission of a valid command, PDU plus T1.

- *Transmit Variable Timer, T3*: This time determines the minimum lifetime of the 1-bit transmit sequence state variables. T3 must be longer, by a margin of safety, than T2 of the destination station and the longest possible transmission round-trip time of a command-response PDU pair.

2. Sending an ACn command PDU:

The LLC is activated by a request primitive from the User layer. An ACn command PDU is constructed and sent to the corresponding LLC layer as soon as possible. The ACn command PDU can be set to perform various functions, including a logical resynchronisation for the bilateral exchange of information. These functions will depend on the type of request primitive, and the P/F bit of the control byte will be set according to Table 9.1.

When a new ACn is to be sent, and a transmit sequence state variable, V(SI), associated with the addresses and priority of the PDU, exists, the value of the V(SI) variable (a single bit held within the control frame), will determine the code-point of the command PDU according to

Table 9.2. If no V(SI) variable exists, a new variable will be created and assigned a value of 0, and hence, an AC0 command PDU will be sent.

Primitive Type	P/F bit	LSDU	Command PDU functions
L_DATA_ACK.request	0	null	Logical resynchronisation
L_DATA_ACK.request	0	non-null	Sending data
L_DATA_REPLY.request	1	null	Polling for data
L_DATA_REPLY.request	1	non-null	Bilateral exchanging of data

Table **9.1** Possible functionalities of ACn command PDUs
(Note: P/F is also held as a single bit in the control frame)

When the LLC sends an ACn command PDU, the LLC should start the acknowledgement timer, T1, for that particular transmission, and should also increment the internal retransmission counter. If no response PDU is received before time T1 expires, the LLC retransmits the ACn PDU, increments the counter variable, and resets the acknowledgement timer T1. This resending procedure is repeated until a valid response is received, or until the counter variable equals the number of maximum retries allowed, N4; at this time an unsuccessful status condition is reported back to the data link user.

V(SI)	Command PDU type
O	AC0
1	AC1

Table **9.2** ACn command PDU assignment

3. Receiving a command PDU

On receipt of an ACn command PDU, the LLC checks to determine whether the PDU is a valid, new PDU, or a duplicate of the last PDU received. If the PDU is a non-duplicate, the LLC takes a series of actions - depending on the type of the PDU and whether it is carrying any user information. The summary of the actions is given in the flow diagram in Figure 9.4. Upon receipt of a duplicate ACn command PDU, the LLC actions are the same as those for the non-duplicate PDU, with the following exceptions. Firstly, the one-bit state variables and their associated timer remain unchanged. Secondly, no indication primitives are issued, regardless of the P bit in the command PDU. Any LSDU (Logical-link Service Data Unit) present will also be discarded. Finally, an ACn response is sent in the same manner, except that the status code in the status subfield reflects the reception status of the previously accepted PDU, instead of reflecting the status of the current duplicate PDU.

An AC0 (or AC1) response PDU is sent upon receipt of an AC0 (or AC1) command PDU respectively, and this will be sent to the source LLC. The status subfield in the response PDU will indicate the reception status of the associated command PDU to which this PDU is responding.

Upon receipt of an ACn response PDU, the LLC will first check to determine whether the PDU is a valid response PDU. If it is not, the PDU will be discarded and no further actions will be taken. If a valid response PDU is received, the actions taken by the LLC are summarised in the flow diagram of Figure 9.5.

In summary, the LLC sub-layer protocol defines receiving and sending components. The former handles the processing of command PDUs from remote stations and provides the appropriate response PDUs. The latter, as a consequence of upper-layer or system-management requests, prepares and sends out appropriate ACn command PDUs to the corresponding LLC stations, and receives response PDUs. In the rest of the chapter, the LLC protocol will be modelled in accordance with the Q-Model, and the specification derived will be analysed in the CONRAD environment.

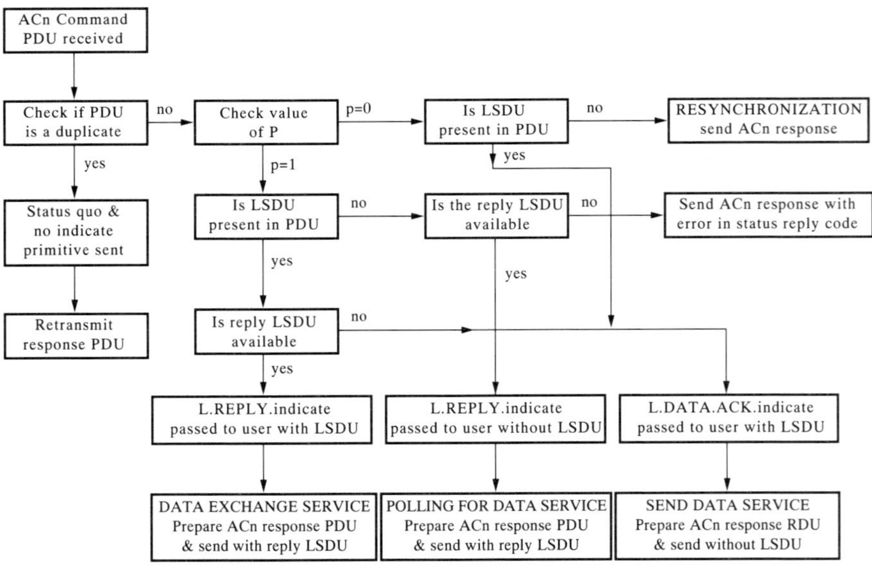

Figure **9.4** Summary of LLC actions on receiving an ACn command PDU

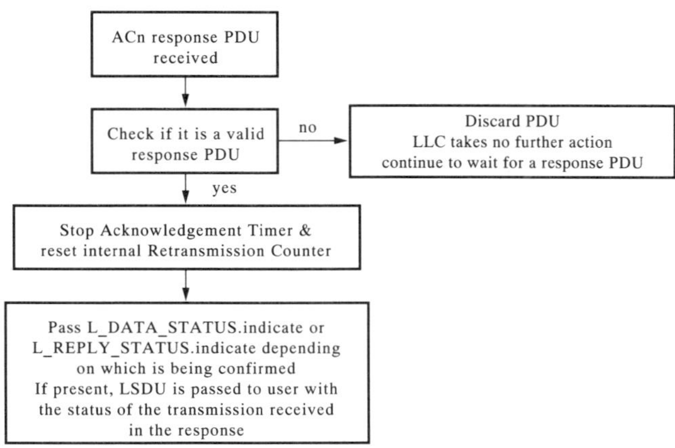

Figure **9.5** Summary of LLC actions to an ACn response PDU

9.3 SPECIFYING LLC WITH CONRAD

As was mentioned in Chapter 8, the current version of CONRAD requires the user to have a good working knowledge of the Q-Model, especially in the initial stages of specifying a potential system in the formalism. A structural design error introduced at this stage cannot be recovered easily in the later stages of the specification analysis. In the Type-3 LLC case, a considerable amount of time has to be spent at this stage on making sure that the LLC specification is as close a representation of the conceptual model defined in the standards as possible. This is, in fact, not a simple matter, given that the ISO specifications, are, themselves, abstract with little clue given as to their interpretation.

9.3.1 The Q-Model representation

For the Type-3 LLC procedures, the modelling task has been divided, for convenience, into three separate areas; i) the User/LLC interface, ii) the LLC sending and receiving components and, iii) the MAC sub-layer, Physical Layer, Transmission medium and the remote LLC station components. This is shown in Figure 9.6.

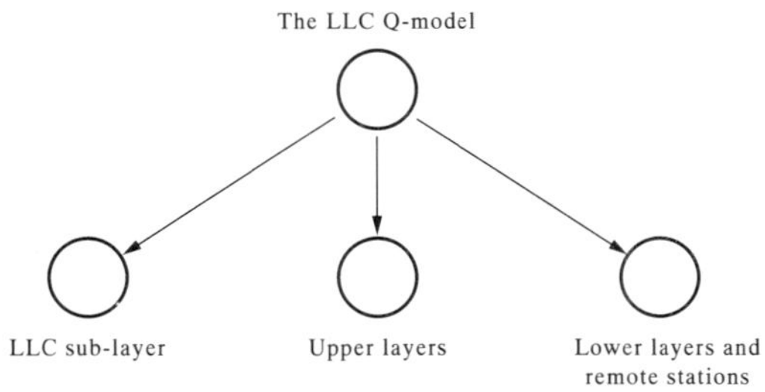

Figure **9.6** The LLC Q-model main components

The three processes, representing the main parts of the LLC Q-model, are further refined in a step-wise fashion by decomposing the processes into their appropriate sub-processes. At this stage, the LLC sub-layer is divided into two main sub-processes - the sending component (i.e. that component dealing with the transmission of ACn command PDUs), and the receiving component (which deals with analysing response PDUs from correspondent LLC stations). The processes at the lowest level of decomposition have been assigned unique numbers. These numbers are just "markings" which will correspond to the processes in the Q-model of the system, which will be shown later. The arrangement is illustrated diagramatically in Figure 9.7. The technique of step-wise decomposition is in itself a useful approach, especially when dealing with complex systems, where the procedure will assist the designer to avoid overlooking any important parts of the proposed system.

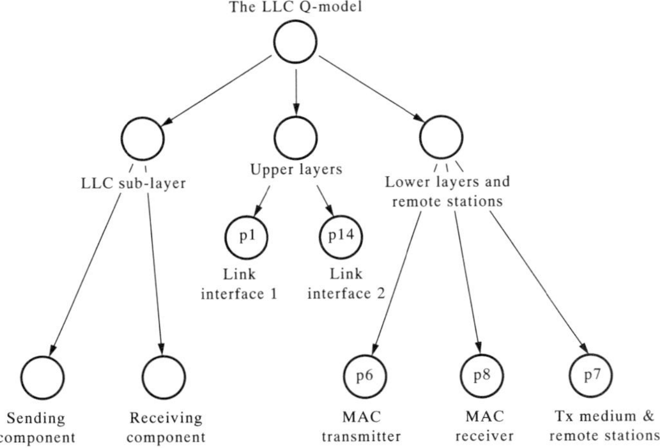

Figure **9.7** Second-stage decomposition of the model

Finally, the model is taken a step further by decomposing the two parts of the LLC sub-layer into sub-processes, representing the protocol standard of the Type-3 procedures. This is shown in Figure 9.8.

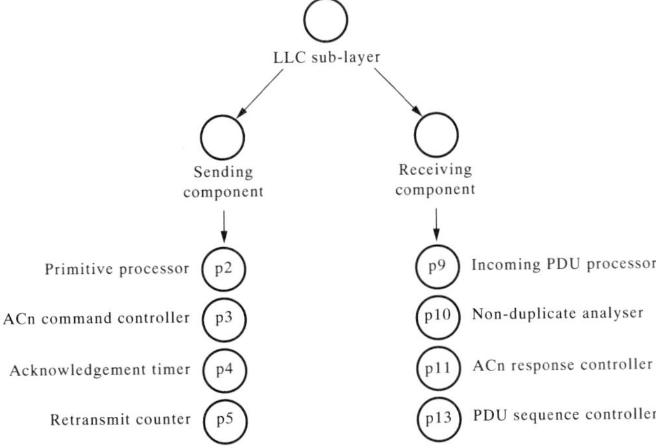

Figure **9.8** Sub-processes of the LLC Type-3 protocol

Once the final decomposition is reached, the next task is to model the logical structure of the LLC Type-3. This is shown as interprocess interactions between the subprocesses of the LLC's model. The accuracy of the stage rests entirely on the designer's interpretation of the system's ultimate implementation structure. This is incorporated into the model by linking up the individual sub-processes representing the LLC sub-layer by use of the appropriate channels, according to the logical structure of the LLC. The resulting model is called the Q-model of the candidate system. Figure 9.9 shows the Q-model of the LLC Acknowledged Connectionless protocol. Different line types have been used in the graph to represent the different channels of the Q-model. The input and output variables have also been indicated to differentiate between common and selector processes. It must be stressed that in most cases, the choice of channel type is determined by the designer at the later implementation stage, and allocation might have to be modified to realise specific solutions.

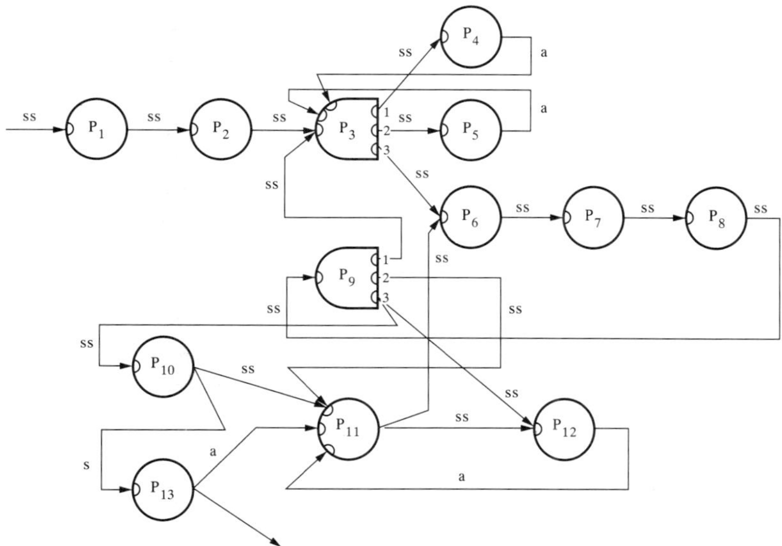

Figure **9.9** Q-model of the LLC Type-3 protocol

From the Q-model in Figure 9.9, it is evident that most of the inter-process interactions of the Type-3 LLC protocol have been accomplished by the use of semisynchronous channels. This is because the bulk of the protocol activities are "execute and trigger" type functions which are essentially sequential. Use of asynchronous channels, which model the feedback of information for status updates, have also been included. Some of the specified channels have also been left out of the model, shown in Figure 9.9, for clarity. With the Q-model representing the candidate system, the stage will have been reached where the designer is ready to investigate the timing and structural characteristic of the LLC protocol model.

9.3.2 The Editor

It is important to mention at this juncture the manner in which this chapter will proceed. To illustrate the procedure involved, the exercise will go on as one would when invoking CONRAD, and key points will be explained along the way. Where it is necessary to show the results obtained graphically, these will be reproduced and the reader assisted with appropriate explanations. The bulk of the routine CONRAD processing, which bears little significance to the discussion, has been omitted - for example, the initial set-up routines using the Governor, etc.

1. The Heredity Tree:

In this simple example, the LLC Type-3 description has been limited to a heredity tree with a single branch, as shown in Figure 9.10.

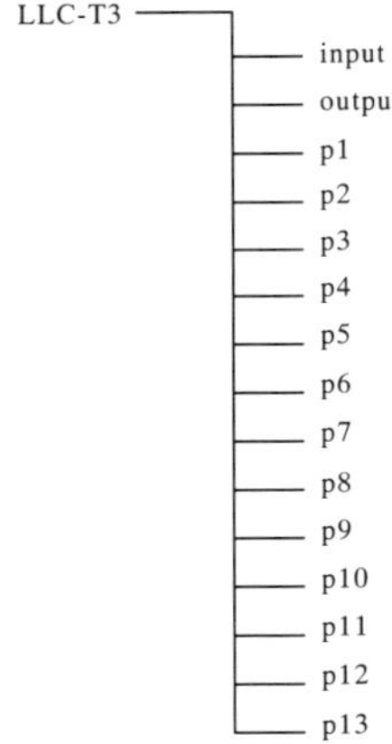

Figure **9.10** Heredity Tree of project LLC-T3

2. Temporal Specification and Formal Checks:

The task is entered into CONRAD together with all the timing information for the processes in the tree. The System Editor allows the user to select processes and, at each request, all the necessary information must be provided. This information will include the type of process, list of input arguments and their consumption intervals, channel types and functions, and a list of output states and their computing times

With the LLC model, it is not an easy task to assign the appropriate timing units accurately for all the processes. Best judgement has to be used in comparing the process execution times for assigning timing parameters. In any case, the timings are relative, and can be interactively changed during the animation games in order to study various arrangements and their effects on the overall performance of the model. An initial attempt at specifying the parameters is shown in Table 9.9. For the selector processes, p3 and p9, a probability distribution will also have to be assigned at the outputs to portray the most likely output behaviour.

Process	Execution Time	Consumption Time	Equivalence Interval
input	[0.0001]		-
p_1	[2,3]	[1,1]	-
p_2	[2,3]	[1,1]	-
p_3	[3,4]	[1,1]	-
p_4	[2,2]	[1,1]	-
p_5	[2,2]	[1,1]	-
p_6	[3,5]	[1,1]	-
p_7	[10,12]	[1,1]	-
p_8	[4,6]	[1,1]	-
p_9	[2,4]	[1,1]	-
p_{10}	[3,4]	[1,1]	-
p_{11}	[4,5]	[1,1]	-
p_{12}	[3,5]	[1,1]	-
p_{13}	[2,2]	[1,1]	-
output	[0.0001]	-	-

Table **9.3** Initial temporal specifications for the LLC Type-3 processes

3. Section Transformation:
At the end of each process definition, the Editor runs a series of checks on that process. These tests look for simple structural and timing inconsistencies within each process definition. When all the processes of the LLC model are defined and tested, a "section" (see Chapter 8) is created by "marking" the appropriate processes in the heredity tree. This is normally shown by a square block at the end of the tree branch. In this current exercise, for simplicity, only one section (the entire Q-model) has been created, and this includes all the sub-processes in the heredity tree. The "section" can then be analysed for group behaviour according to the specification, and more formal tests can be run. At the end of the analysis, the formally tested section is ready for a data structure transformation. This restructures the data of the formally tested LLC model and produces an "S-model", necessary for the Animator, and an "E-model", required by the Evaluator. It should be emphasised that these operations are merely data transformations, necessary because of the nature of the processing to be undertaken subsequently. The operations do not change the inherent characteristics of the system modelled.

9.3.3 The Animator

All the timing information within the LLC specification is now available for modification to study 'what if' scenarios of the protocol behaviour. Some of these scenarios will be discussed below. The specification elements of main interest here are the execution and data-consumption timing intervals of the processes, and the channel functions which control the data flow within the specification. The logical structure of the LLC specification cannot be modified using the Animator because such changes will need formal testing, which the Animator does not provide. The results are displayed graphically, using a time diagram showing the processes' execution times, data and control information.

1. The LLC games:

Part of the timing specification given to the Editor is a special function called the *start time*. It is necessary to specify this time interval when a process is passive (say, without any triggering events) in the Q-model, i.e., where no semisynchronous or synchronous channels are connected to it. During the LLC animation, this functionality is employed as a cyclic trigger, enabling the entire model to be executed at random periods. A start time is assigned to the main process, LLC-T3, at the top of the heredity tree. This models the frequency of messages arriving (essentially request primitives) from the upper layers. By changing the intervals of this time specification, the effect on the overall temporal performance of the entire protocol layer can be animated.

With this flexibility of time interval modifications, another interesting element of the LLC protocol animation is that of process p7, which cumulatively models the execution of the physical layer - the medium propagation delay, the remote station MAC and correspondent LLC sub-layer. Hence, by modifying the execution time interval of process p7, it is possible to study immediately the effect of the round-trip delay of each command PDU transmitted by the originating LLC sub-layer. In fact, p7 can be further decomposed into several processes. One of these processes can then model the actual frame transmission time over the physical medium of the communication network. Then, manipulation of the execution time of this process will allow the user to determine the maximum round-trip propagation delay that is required to achieve a specified LLC Type-3 sub-layer performance - assuming that all other processes in the specification have been similarly optimised.

2. The Animation results:

Several animation runs have been made here to investigate the timing performance of the acknowledged connectionless protocol. Each LLC game was executed for 40 *animation time units* (atu): in Figure 9.11 the system ran with all processes executing at the minimum execution times. In Figure 9.12, however, execution times were varied randomly between their respective upper and lower limits. With a start time interval of [7,7], the protocol description showed the need for second copies of the main processes to be introduced, after just 4 or 5 user requests. This factor displayed by the animation time diagram is significant, as it arises when a process has not completed calculating the current values of its output variable(s), but receives a new request to recalculate its output variable through one of its input channel(s). This effect is shown on the time diagram as a *second copy* of the process execution running, overlapping the first one. When this situation arises, two copies of the same processes are running in parallel for a specific period of time, as shown in the timing diagrams.

In the run shown in Figure 9.11 the request primitive from the User is set to arrive, on average, every 7 atu. The second User request is already causing p7 to run a second copy of itself. However, this is acceptable, since p7 is a cumulative process and the second copy only starts at the final stages of the first. In practice, this could represent a frame being transmitted by the MAC layer, whilst at the same time the same MAC receiver is processing a response frame, i.e. a valid situation because these are two isolated processes. A slightly different situation occurs when p9 analyses the first response PDU, and request p3 to transmit an ACn command PDU. This request causes p3 to run a second copy of its process. This can only be valid if p3 can, in fact, operate in parallel - but otherwise the specification must be modified to overcome the problem. For example, an equivalence interval [7.5] can be defined for process p3. This specifies the period of time during which only a single activation of the process is considered valid, in that any new activation, occurring within this interval, will be considered part of the first execution and hence will not cause a second copy of the process to be executed.

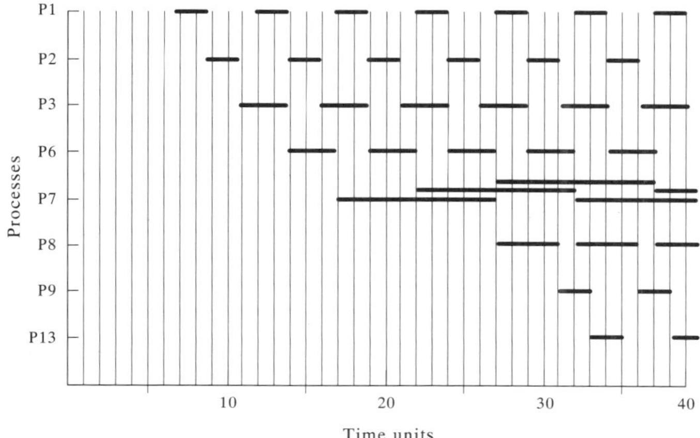

Figure **9.11** Animation time diagram: all processes running at minimum execution times

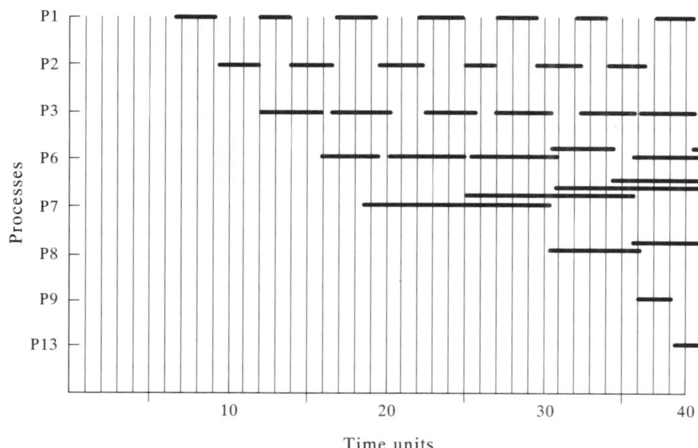

Figure **9.12** Animation time diagram: processes running with random execution times

9.3.4 The Evaluator

Use of this tool completes the second part of the non-formal analysis of the specification. The Animator gives the designer an overview of the timing behaviour of the specification, whilst the Evaluator provides the user with the possibility of evaluating the "data-passing" performance of specific paths in the model. The system allows us to study the length of time occurring between a pair of specified events in the Q-Model of the proposed system. In the case studied here of the Acknowledged Connectionless protocol, a specific path can be specified, starting with the request primitive from an Upper layer (the activation of process p1), and ending with the corresponding status indication primitive from the originating LLC to the upper layer (i.e. the termination of process p13 - referring to the Q-model of Figure 9.9). It is clear from the graph that between the starting (p1) and ending events (p13), there are many possible routes that the data can take, and hence the Evaluator allows us either to define a specific data route of interest during a particular evaluation, or to study all the possible routes and their passing time estimates between a pair of specific intervals.

There are possible cyclic loops which can occur within the intervals of a specified path; again, referring to the Q-model of the LLC-T3 model, process p9 provides a return loop to process p3 - the retransmission of a PDU request and this is an example of a possible cyclic loop in the p1 to p13 path. The user must therefore define the number of loops to consider in the evaluation, i.e. how many retransmissions to consider during a single transmission of a command PDU until a valid correspondent response PDU is received at the originating LLC sub-layer. A defined path can then be handled for estimating the timing parameters. A completely specified evaluation interval is defined as a "task" in the Evaluator. The task is then processed by the tool, and will produce all the possible paths within the intervals, with their respective data-passing time estimates. In the case of the LLC evaluation, the result gives the minimum, average and maximum time units needed to pass the data from the point of activating process p1 till the termination of process p13, including the specified number of retransmissions.

9.4 CONCLUSIONS

This chapter has illustrated how the Q-model and its CONRAD implementation can be used to specify a complex interacting system, which will ultimately be deeply embedded within a communications unit. The case study selected is important, not only as it illustrates the power of the proposed techniques, but equally relevantly, it shows how a seemingly logical specification, defined by an international committee, can be handled in terms of its potential temporal behaviour.

In an atmosphere in which the pressure is on engineers to produce control systems which not only operate as efficiently as possible, but are also safe and reliable, the need for correct specification has become of the utmost importance. As we realise that systems not only need to operate in a logically correct fashion, but that they must also match their dynamic requirements, the need for adequate computer-based tools has become very evident. Such tools are not freely available, and even when they are, are not being used by anybody other than their own experts!

This text has suggested an approach to satisfy this need.

APPENDIX A

A Brief comparison of Petri-nets and the Q-model

Petri-net theory surfaced in 1962, essentially based on the dissertation by C.A. Petri. Since this time, Petri-nets have become a popular tool for modelling and designing systems containing asynchronous (in the classical sense) and concurrent working components (see, for example, [Peterson (1981)]). Petri-nets now appear to offer the most widely-studied, well-understood, single formalism [Advances, (1984)], with a general theory that has grown out of the original ideas. A significant number of extensions have been suggested, and the theory has recently been linked to other formalisms (see [Jensen and Rozenberg (1991)]). An example of this is the "theoretical-net" approach which has been used for interpreting temporal logic formulae (see, for example, [Queille (1982)]).

In this section we aim to introduce the basic notions used in elementary Petri-nets, and to survey some initial results, comparing their modelling powers to those of the Q-model.

A.1 BASIC CONCEPTS

For full details, see [Peterson (1981)]. In essence, a Petri-net consists of a set of *places*, a set of *transitions* and *two functions* determining the connections between places and transitions (see Figure A-1). *An input function* maps a collection of places to a transition, and an *output function* maps a transition to a collection of places. The input function defines the input places of a transition, whilst the output function defines the output places of a transition.

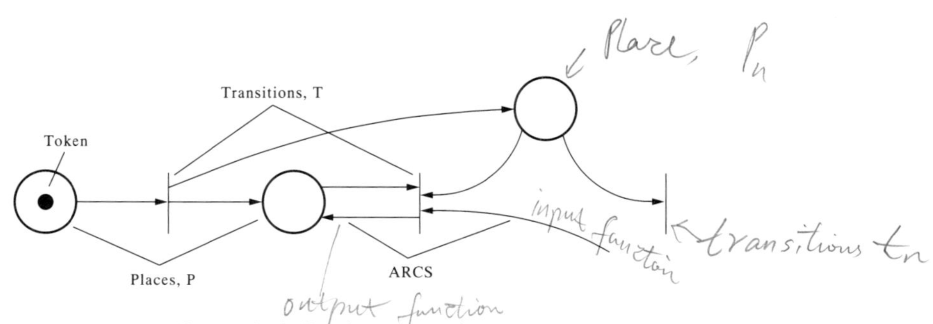

Figure **A-1** Petri-net notation

Here, a Petri-net is seen to consist of 4 components:

- a set of places, p_n, represented by circles,
- a set of transitions, t_n, represented by bars,
- the input functions, represented by directed arcs to the transitions, and,
- the output functions, represented by directed arcs from the transitions.

When describing a system, places and transitions correspond to *events* and *conditions*. In Petri-net theory this duality is important - in one net an event may correspond to a place, whilst in its dual, the same event may correspond to a transition.

Places, transitions, and input and output functions can be graphically represented as *bipartite directed multigraphs*. An example of this is shown in Figure 6.3 in Section 6.1.2.

A *token* is an important concept in Petri-nets. A *marking* is an assignment of tokens to places and this marking may change during the *execution of a net*. A Petri-net *executes* by the *firing of a transition*; in this, tokens are moved from their input places, and new ones are created at the output places. The actual firing of a transition takes place when certain execution rules are satisfied.

The *state of a Petri-net* is defined by its marking; thus, firing a transition will represent a change in the state. The execution of a net results in a *sequence of transitions* which have been fired. The set of all the possible sequences of transitions characterises the Petri-net. This set of sequences is often referred to as a *Petri-net language*, the obvious usage of which can be in proving the equivalent behaviour of two nets.

A.2 SOME PETRI-NET PROPERTIES

- *Safeness* A place in a Petri-net is "safe" if the number of tokens in that place never exceeds a fixed number. Thus, a Petri-net is safe if all the places in the net are safe. For example, a "1-safe" Petri-net is one in which each place contains no more than one token.

- *Conservation* A Petri-net is conservative if the total number of tokens during its execution remains constant.

- *Liveness* of a Petri-net is associated with the concept of deadlock. A transition is *live* if it is not deadlocked, if, in other words, it can be enabled. A transition is *dead* if it can never be fired. It is clearly possible to distinguish several intermediate stages between live and dead transitions. A Petri-net is *live* when all its transitions are live.

In order to prove the presence or absence of the above properties, it is necessary to solve the so-called *reachability* problem. This problem essentially involves ensuring that a specific marking is reachable from its initial marking. For readers interested in more advanced developments in Petri-nets, we suggest a paper by Jensen (1990).

A.3 THE Q-MODEL AND PETRI-NETS

Considering the popularity of net theory and the extensive amount of work being undertaken in the Petri-net area, it is inevitable that any new formalism will be compared with them.

The "conservative" approach, used by Peterson (1981), seems to be a reasonable basis for comparing the structural and behavioural characteristics of the two formalisms.

The Q-model class of computational models can be said to be less than, or equal to, the modelling power of a class of Petri-net based models if, for any instance of the Q-model, there is an algorithm which creates an instance of a Petri-net such that the following apply:

- Each structural component of the Q-model is represented by a collection of Petri-net components. The number of components may differ by a constant multiple, which is determined by the two classes of models, and not by the particular instances.

- Any sequence of actions in the Q-model can be simulated by a sequence of actions in the Petri-net.

- The Petri-net deadlocks only when the Q-model does.

The two classes of model are equivalent if each includes the other.

The comparison, according to this conservative approach, pays no attention to quantitative time constraints, and the behaviour is fully determined by the sequence of actions only. In the following comparison, therefore, we have ignored some of the properties of the Q-model.

Structural correspondence:
As demonstrated by Vain (1987), a Q-model process may be represented by a collection of non-trivial transitions of a Petri-net. In order to do so, the following restrictions are introduced:

- A Q-model process is executed a finite number of times. (In other words, we permit only a finite timeset). This is necessary since Petri-net expressions are not closed under infinite concatenation.

- To decrease the dependency of the non-trivial transitions upon their surroundings, only explicitly defined timesets are permitted, or only simple semisynchronous chains and cycles are allowed, in the Q-model structure.

- Selector processes are not allowed.

A Petri-net representation of a Q-model process will consist of several, non-trivial, transitions; these are used for modelling process timesets, process completion-times and data-consumption times. All the non-trivial transitions use a simple comparison to zero, and the number of elements will depend upon the value of the corresponding time parameters.

A Q-model channel is represented by a subnet of a Petri-net which will depend upon the channel type and function. The structural complexity of the subnet will depend upon the value of the channel's function parameters.

In summary, it is possible to represent Q-model components by using Petri-net components. Guaranteeing the constant multiple difference in the number of components is difficult, as the number of components depends upon the value of the Q-model time parameters.

Behavioural correspondence:
A Petri-net inherently describes completely known causal relationships, and the net's behaviour is determined by the sequence of transitions fired and, of course, the initial marking. These permitted transition sequences form the Petri-net "language". However, in the case of real-time embedded applications, the causal relationships are seldom completely known, and, as a rule, they are approximated by time constraints. Also, the qualitative order of events does not always adequately describe a system's behaviour, and quantitative time delays between events are often important.

Nevertheless, it is possible to compare the qualitative behaviour of a Q-model and a Petri-net. The "language" of a Petri-net, corresponding to a Q-model, can be described by using finite substitutions, concatenations, unions and concurrent compositions - which are all legal operations for Petri-net languages [Vain (1987)].

In [Tekko (1988)], an alternative comparison of the behaviour is suggested. A language of the Q-model is defined; its alphabet consists of process names, and each word of the language represents a sequence of processes that have completed. After introducing certain restrictions, a mapping is defined which maps the restricted class of Q-models into marked graphs. After this, it is proved that the Q-model language and the language of the corresponding Petri-net are equivalent. From Vain (1987) and Tekko (1988) we may conclude that for a subset of Q-models, it is possible to define Petri-nets such that their qualitative behaviours are equivalent.

Error correspondence:
One of the relatively few comparable errors which can be discovered by both a Q-model and a Petri-net, is deadlock. Both Vain (1987) and Tekko (1988) prove, using different methods, that the absence of deadlock in a Q-model, and the liveness of the corresponding Petri-net, can be maintained by suitable mappings from one formalism to the other.

Vain (1987) has also extended the theorems which ensure a proper order in the handling of simultaneous copies of Q-model processes in the Petri-net domain.

In summary, it is reasonable to conclude that Petri-nets and the Q-model are not disparate, although they have been developed for studying different properties of the modelled phenomena. A comparison of the Q-model with timed and coloured Petri-nets would be very useful, as it would give a good insight into the potential handling of complex timing issues in these Petri-net extensions. This needs to be done, since the real strength of the Q-model approach lies in these features.

APPENDIX B

Proofs of Propositions

Proposition 1: [(Quirk (1977)]

Let t_1, t_2 $\in$ T(p) be any two consecutive elements of T(p), $t_1 < t_2$. Process copy $p(t_1)$ terminates before the copy $p(t_2)$ if

$$\beta(p) - \alpha(p) < t_{min}(p).$$

Proof:

The latest possible termination instant of copy $p(t_1)$ is determined by the expression $t_1 + \beta(p)$. The earliest termination of copy $p(t_2)$ takes place at $t_2 + \alpha(p)$. We require that the actual termination of $p(t_2)$ be later than that of $p(t_1)$, hence

$$[t_2 + \alpha\,(p,t_2)] - [t_1 + \beta\,(p,t_1)] \;>\; 0.$$

Based on the Q-model definitions we have

$$[t_2 + \zeta\,(p,t_2)] - [t_1 + \zeta\,(p,t_1)] \geq$$

$$\geq\; [t_2 + \alpha\,(p)] - [t_1 + \beta\,(p)] \geq$$

$$\geq t_{min}(p) - [\,\beta\,(p) - \alpha\,(p)] > 0,$$

which proves the assertion.

Proposition 2: [(Quirk (1977)]

Assume that we have a channel σ_{ij}, a producer-process $p_i \in P$ and a consumer-process $p_j \in P$. Let the consumer-process be activated at any two consecutive elements of its timeset t_1, t_2, where $t_1 < t_2$. A demand for data from the channel comes earlier from the copy $p_j(t_1)$, if

$$\delta(\sigma_{ij}) - \gamma(\sigma_{ij}) < t_{min}(p_j).$$

Proof:

Using the same argument as in Proposition 1, we have

$$[t_2 + \eta(\sigma_{ij}, t_2)] - [t_1 + \eta(\sigma_{ij}, t_1) \geq$$

$$\geq [t_2 + \gamma(\sigma_{ij})] - [t_1 + \delta(\sigma_{ij})] \geq$$

$$\geq t_{min}(p_j) - [\delta(\sigma_{ij}) - \gamma(\sigma_{ij})] > 0$$

which proves the assertion.

Proposition 3: [(Motus (1990)]

Let p_i, $p_j \in P$ be two synchronous processes communicating via a synchronous channel, $\sigma_{ij} \in \Sigma$. Communication via the channel will not change specified time parameters of the consumer-process, if

$$\beta(p_i) < \gamma(\sigma_{ij}) + \nu\, t_{min}(p_i).$$

Proof:

(i) Case for $\nu = 0$

The producer-process terminates not later than $t + \beta(p_i)$, where t is a common activation instant of the two synchronous processes. The consumer-process does not expect data from the channel σ_{ij} before $t + \gamma(\sigma_{ij})$. The specified item parameters will not change if

$$[t + \eta(\sigma_{ij},t)] - [t + \zeta(p_i,t)] > 0.$$

By substituting the above maximum termination time, and minimum data demand time, we have, after simplification, the inequality

$$\beta(p_i) < \gamma(\sigma_{ij}).$$

(ii) Case for $\nu \neq 0$.

The consumer-process is activated at $t_0 \in T(p_j)$. The producer-process activation that is of interest in this context, takes place ν elements earlier, at $t_\nu \in T(p_i)$. Note that $T(p_i)$ is a well-ordered set, and $T(p_i) = T(p_j)$. In the same way as in the previous case, we can write

$$[t_0 + \eta(\sigma_{ij}, t_0)] - [t_\nu + \zeta(p_i, t)] > 0$$

and after simplification

$$\beta(p_i) < \gamma(\sigma_{ij}) + (t_0 - t_\nu)$$

The minimal allowable value of $(t_0 - t_\nu)$ can be estimated by using the timeset properties. So we have $t_0 - t_\nu \geq \nu \,.\, t_{min}(p_i)$, which proves the assertion.

Proposition 4:

Let $p_i, p_j \in P$ be two synchronous processes communicating via a synchronous channel $\sigma_{ij} \in \Sigma$. Communication via the channel may increase the specified completion time of the consumer-process but will not change the next scheduled activation of the consumer-process if

$$\beta(p_i) < \gamma(\sigma_{ij}) + \nu.\, t_{min}(p_i) + [t_{min}(p_j) - \beta(p_j)].$$

Proof:

The proof is similar to the proof of proposition 3.

Proposition 5: [(Quirk (1977)]

Suppose that a process $p_k \in P$ consumes its own previous state value via a synchronous channel, $\sigma_{kk} \in \Sigma$, whereas the channel function is $K(\sigma_{kk}, t) = [\mu, 1]$ and $\mu \geq 1$. Let the completion time of the process, without any waiting time, be $\bar{\zeta}(p_k)$. The actual completion time of the process has a finite upper bound if

$$t + \eta(\sigma_{kk}, t) > \bar{\zeta}(p_k) + t', \qquad (*)$$

where $t \in T(p_k)$ and $t' = \max_{t''} \{ t'' : t'' \in K(\sigma_{kk}, t) \}$.

Proof:

Suppose that inequality (*) does not hold. Then, there exists $\varepsilon \geq 0$ such that

$$t_{(i+1)} + \eta(\sigma_{kk}, t_{(i+1)}) + \varepsilon = t_i + \zeta\, p_k) \qquad (**)$$

where t_i, $t_{(i+1)} \in T(p_k)$ are two consecutive elements in the timeset. Without considering the possibility of waiting for data, a process p_k, which has been activated at $t_{(i+1)}$, completes at $t_{(i+1)} + \overline{\zeta}(p_k)$. Considering also the possibility of waiting for its previous state value, the completion time may be found as

$$t_{(i+1)} + \zeta(p_k, t_i) + \overline{\zeta}(p_k) - \eta(\sigma_{kk}, t_{(i+1)}).$$

The actual time of completion of p_k, activated at $t_{(i+1)}$, is given by the expression

$$t_{(i+1)} + \zeta(p_k, t_{(i+1)}) = \max\{t_{(i+1)} + \overline{\zeta}(p_k)\,;$$
$$;\ t_i + \zeta(p_k, t_i) + \overline{\zeta}(p_k) - \eta(\sigma_{kk}, t_{(i+1)})\}.$$

Considering (**) above, we have

$$t_{(i+1)} + \zeta(p_k, t_{(i+1)}) = \max\{t_{(i+1)} + \overline{\zeta}(p_k)\,;$$
$$;\ t_{(i+1)} + \zeta(p_k, t_i) + \varepsilon\}.$$

By definition, $\overline{\zeta}(p_k) \leq \zeta(p_k, t_i)$ and $\varepsilon \geq 0$, therefore

$$t_{(i+1)} + \zeta(p_k, t_{(i+1)}) = t_{(i+1)} + \zeta(p_k, t_i) + \varepsilon,$$

and consequently

$$\zeta(p_k, t_{(i+1)}) - \zeta(p_k, t_i) = \varepsilon.$$

At a system's initial start-up, initial data is provided without any waiting, therefore

$$\zeta(p_k, t_1) = \overline{\zeta}(p_k).$$

Going step-by-step further through the elements of $T(p_k)$, we have an upper bound for the (i+1)-th activation.

$$\zeta(p_k, t_{(i+1)}) = \zeta(p_k) + (i-1)\,\varepsilon$$

Since i may increase without limit, $\zeta(p_k, t_i)$ may also increase without a limit.

Let us now assume that inequality (*) holds. In that case there exists $\varepsilon \geq 0$ such that

$$t_{(i+1)} + \eta(\sigma_{kk}, t_{(i+1)}) = t_i + \overline{\zeta}(p_k) + \varepsilon.$$

Using a similar argument to that used in the first part of the proof, we have

$$t_{(i+1)} + \zeta(p_k, t_{(i+1)}) = \max \{t_{(i+1)} + \overline{\zeta}(p_k) ; \; t_{(i+1)} + \zeta(p_k, t_i) + \varepsilon\}$$

and

$$\zeta(p_k, t_{(i+1)}) - \zeta(p_k, t_i) = \max \{\overline{\zeta}(p_k) - \zeta(p_k, t_i) ; -\varepsilon\}.$$

As before, we have $\zeta(p_k,t_1) = \overline{\zeta}(p_k)$ and consequently $\zeta(p_k, t_i) = \zeta(p_k, t_{(i+1)}) = \overline{\zeta}(p_k)$, which leads us to assertion (*).

Proposition 5 is based on an implicit assumption that between the completion of a copy which produces data and activation of a copy consuming this data, there is no idle time.

Corollary 5.1:

The assumptions of Proposition 3 include assumptions of the Proposition 5.

Proposition 6: [Motus (1990)]

The upper bound for the solution of the integer programming task

$$\varphi_n^* = \max_{n,m} (n\, t_a(p_j) - m\, t_a(p_i))$$

with the constraint $0 \leq (n\, t_a(p_j) - m\, t_a(p_i) < \varphi_n$, is given by the expression

$$\varphi_n^* \leq t_{max}(p_i) + \beta(p_i) - \gamma(\sigma_{ij}) - 1$$

provided that the parameters concerned satisfy the inequality

$$\beta(p_i) > \gamma(\sigma_{ij}) - 1 - (t_{max}(p_i) - t_a(p_i)).$$

Proof:

Let us first introduce new notations for convenience: t_j instead of $t_a(p_j)$, t_i instead of $t_a(p_i)$, β instead of $\beta(p_i)$, γ instead of $\gamma(\sigma_{ij})$, and t_{mi} instead of $t_{max}(p_i)$.

The task expressed in these new notations is thus

$$\max_{n,m} ((n\,t_j - m t_i) : 0 \le n\,t_j - m\,t_i < t_{mi} + \beta - \gamma$$

and in its equivalent form

$$t_i \left(\max_n \max_m \left((n \frac{t_j}{t_i} - m \right) : 0 \le n \frac{t_j}{t_i} - m < \frac{t_{mi}}{t_i} + \frac{\beta - \gamma}{t_i})) \qquad (*)$$

For any fixed n, we can find m* maximising the expression (*), with respect to m, by solving a system of inequalities

$$\left\{ \begin{array}{l} m^* > n \frac{t_j}{t_i} - \frac{t_{mi}}{t_i} - \frac{\beta - \gamma}{t_i} \\ m^* \le n \frac{t_j}{t_i} \end{array} \right\} \qquad (**)$$

A rational number, $n \frac{t_j}{t_i}$, can be represented as the sum of its integer [.] and fraction { . } parts.

$$n \frac{t_j}{t_i} = [n \frac{t_j}{t_i}] + \{n \frac{t_j}{t_i}\}.$$

If $\{n \frac{t_j}{t_i}\} - \frac{t_{mi}}{t_i} - \frac{\beta - \gamma}{t_i} \ge 0.$ then the system of inequalities in (**) has no solution. Informally, this means that the parameters of interacting processes are such that the non-transport delay is negative, i.e. the computation of the state values available through an asynchronous channel starts after the activation of the consumer-process. (**) will have a solution if

$$\{n \frac{t_j}{t_i}\} - \frac{t_{mi}}{t_i} - \frac{\beta - \gamma}{t_i} < 0.$$

or, equivalently, $\beta > \gamma - 1 - (t_{mi} - t_j)$.

The solution to (**) which satisfies these constraints is

$$m^* = [n \frac{t_j}{t_i}] - [(\frac{t_{mi}}{t_i} + \frac{\beta - \gamma}{t_i}.-1)]$$

After substituting m* into (*) we get

$$t_i (\max_n)(\{n \frac{t_j}{t_i}\} + [(\frac{t_{mi}}{t_i} + \frac{\beta - \gamma}{t_i} - 1)]):$$

$$: 0 \leq \{n.\frac{t_j}{t_i}\} + [(\frac{t_{mi}}{t_i} + \frac{\beta - \gamma}{t_i} - 1)] < \frac{t_{mi}}{t_i} + \frac{\beta - \gamma}{t_i})) \qquad (***)$$

Let us substitute $\{ n.\frac{t_j}{t_i} \}$ by its upper bound $\frac{t_j - 1}{t_i}$, then

$$\varphi_n^* \leq t_i (\frac{t_j - 1}{t_i} + [(\frac{t_{mi}}{t_i} - \frac{\beta - \gamma}{t_i} - 1)])$$

and since $$t_i[(\frac{t_{mi}}{t_i} - \frac{\beta - \gamma}{t_i} - 1)] \leq t_{mi} + \beta - \gamma - t_i$$

we finally have

$$\varphi_n^* \leq t_{mi} + \beta - \gamma - 1.$$

Proposition 7:

The existence of a synchronous loop in a system (P, Σ) is a sufficient condition for an information deadlock.

Proof:

To prove the proposition, we use the deadlock definition given in [Coffman and Denning (1973)]. They state there that processes p_i, $i \in D$ are in deadlock if, for each $i \in D$, the following inequality holds

$$Q_i(t) > v(t) + \sum_{j \notin D} R_j(t) \qquad (*)$$

where $Q_i(t)$ is a vector consisting of the resources required by a process p_i at the time instant t; v(t) is a vector consisting of the available resources in the system; and, $\sum_{j \notin D} R_j(t)$ is a vector of the resources which can, in principle, be redistributed (in other words, resources which have been used by processes not involved in the deadlock).

In summary, a deadlock occurs if the number of required resources is larger than the sum of available and redistributable resources. In the Q-model the only type of resources are messages. Let us consider each process as a sequence of two tasks:- the first inputs all the required messages, whilst the second outputs all the specified messages, which are the new values of the process state variables.

Vector v(t) can be computed by components

$$v_j(t) = w_j - \sum_{k=1}^{n} R_{kj}(t).$$

where w_j is the total quantity of the j-th resource and $R_{kj}(t)$ is the number of the j-th resource occupied by process p_k.

In the case of a synchronous loop, no resources exist before its activation. This implies that w = 0. Thus each of the processes in the loop has occupied at least one resource, therefore

$$\sum_{k=1}^{n} R_{kj}(t) > 0$$

and consequently v(t) < 0.

Information resources (in this case, messages) cannot be redistributed in the Q-model. Therefore we have

$$\sum_{j \notin D} R_j(t) = 0$$

Consequently, the inequality (*) holds and the synchronous loop causes a deadlock.

Proposition 8:

Let the assumptions of propositions 1 and 2 be satisfied. Let the assumptions of proposition 3 or 4 be satisfied, and $v_j > 0$, $k \leq j \leq r$.

Then, the upper and lower bounds of the time required to pass through the synchronous leg of a path are determined by the following equations:

a) the upper bound of the passing time

$$D_{sync}(\pi(p_k,p_r)) = t_a(p) \sum_{j=k+1}^{r} (v_j - 1) + (r-k)t_{max}(p) + \beta\,(p_r).$$

b) the lower bound of passing time

$$d_{sync}(\pi(p_k,p_r)) = t_a(p) \sum_{j=k+1}^{r} (v_j - 1) + (r-k)t_{min}(p) + \alpha(p_r).$$

Proof:

Suppose that a message is accepted by process p_k during the execution cycle which was activated at $t_m \in T(p_k)$. The reaction of process p_k to this message will reach process $p_{(k+1)}$ during the execution cycle activated at $t_{(m + v\,(k+1))} \in T(p_k)$.

Considering the timeset properties, we will have

$$t_a(p)\,(v_{\,(k+1)} - 1) + t_{min}(p) \leq (t_{(m + v(k+1))} - t_m\,) \leq$$
$$\leq t_a(p)\,(v_{\,(k+1)} - 1) + t_{max}(p).$$

Using the same argument for all the processes of the synchronous leg, and considering that on the output of the last process of the leg, (i.e. p_r), the reaction to the original message reaches $\zeta(p_r,t)$ time units later, we get a collection of inequalities. These inequalities characterise the time for passing through particular processes of the leg. Summing the lower and upper bounds of the individual times, we obtain the stated equations.

Proposition 9:

Let the assumptions of propositions 1 and 2 be satisfied.

Let $v_j > 0$ for $k \le j \le r$, and

$$t_{min}(p_k) \ge \max\left(\tau_{e(pk)}, \tau_{e(p(k+1))}, \ldots, \tau_{e(pr)}\right).$$

Then, the upper and lower bounds of the times required to pass through a semisynchronous leg of a path are determined by the following equations.

(i) the upper bound of passing time

$$D_{semisync}(\pi(p_k,p_r)) = t_a(p_k) \sum_{j=k+1}^{r} (v_j - 1) + (r-k)t_{max}(p_k) + \sum_{j=k}^{r} \beta(p_j)$$

(ii) the lower bound of passing time

$$d_{semisync}(\pi(p_k,p_r)) = t_a(p_k) \sum_{j=k+1}^{r} (v_j - 1) + (r-k)t_{min}(p_k) + \sum_{j=k}^{r} \alpha(p_j).$$

Proof:

By the same argument as used in Proposition 8, we compute the time for a reaction to pass between neighbouring processes.

Suppose that a message reaches the input of the first process, p_k, during an execution cycle activated at $t_m \in T(p_k)$. The reaction of process p_k will reach process $p_{(k+1)}$ during the execution cycle activated at $t_{(m + v(k+1))} + \zeta(p_k, t_{(m + v(k+1))})$, where $t_{(m + v(k+1))} \in T(pk)$.

All the processes of a semisynchronous leg are executed at the same frequency, and the transport delay of semisynchronous channels is implicitly included in the delay which occurs between the process activation and the consumption of data from the associated channel.

The time required to pass the reaction from process p_k to the next process of the path, can be estimated as

$$t_a(p_k)(\nu_{(k+1)} - 1) + t_{min}(p_k) + \alpha(p_k) \leq$$

$$\leq t_{(m + \nu (k+1))} + \zeta(p_k, t_{(m + \nu (k+1))}) - t_m \leq$$

$$\leq t_a(p_k)(\nu_{(k+1)} - 1) + t_{max}(p_k) + \beta(p_k).$$

After the summation of all the corresponding estimates, and considering that, at the output of the last process of the leg (i.e. p_r), the reaction appears $\zeta(p_r,t)$ time units later than at its input, we will get the equations of proposition 9.

Proposition 10:

Let the assumptions of propositions 1 and 2 be satisfied, let $\nu_j > 0$ for $k \leq j \leq r$, and assume that we model time by non-negative integers. Then, the upper and lower bounds of the time required to pass through an asynchronous leg of a path are determined by the following equations:

(i) the upper bound of the passing time

$$D_{async}(\pi(p_k,p_r)) = \sum_{j=k}^{r-1} \varphi_{n*}(p_j,p_{(j+1)}) + \sum_{j=k}^{r-1} (t_{max}(p_j) + t_a(p_j)(\nu_{(j+1)} - 1)) + \beta(p_r).$$

(ii) the lower bound of the passing time

$$d_{async}(\pi(p_k,p_r)) = \sum_{j=k}^{r} (t_{min}(p_j) + t_a(p_j)(\nu_{(j+1)} - 1)) + \alpha(p_r).$$

Proof:

The proof is based on the same ideas as that of propositions 8 and 9.

Suppose that the original message reaches process p_k during an execution cycle activated at $t_m \in T(p_k)$. The reaction of process p_k is ready to reach process $p_{(k+1)}$ after $\nu_{(k+1)}$ execution cycles, i.e. at the end of the execution cycle activated at $t_{(m + n (k+1))} \in T(p_k)$.

The time that passed from the acceptance of the message to the instant $t_{(m+\nu(k+1))}$, can be estimated as:

$$t_a(p_k)(\nu_{(k+1)} - 1) + t_{min}(p_k) \leq t_{(m + \nu (k+1))} - t_m \leq$$
$$\leq t_a(p_k)(\nu_{(k+1)} - 1) + t_{max}(p_k).$$

Since the processes p_k and $p_{(k+1)}$ are executed in a truly asynchronous mode, the state value which results from the execution cycle activated at $t_{(m + \nu (k+1))} \in T(p_k)$ can be accepted by process $p_{(k+1)}$ only after a non-transport delay, i.e. during the execution cycle activated at $t_m' \in T(p_{(k+1)})$.

It is known that

$$0 \leq t'_m - t_{(m + \nu (k+1))} \leq \varphi_n^*(p_k, p_{(k+1)}).$$

Thus, the reaction from process p_k reaches process $p_{(k+1)}$ at a time estimated as

$$t_a(p_k)(\nu_{(k+1)} - 1) + t_{min}(p_k) \leq t'_m - t_m \leq$$
$$\leq \varphi_n^*(p_k, p_{(k+1)}) + t_a(p_k)(\nu_{(k+1)} - 1) + t_{max}(p_k).$$

Repeating the procedure for each process in the asynchronous leg, and considering that the state of the last process of the leg changes $\zeta(p_r,t)$ time units after the message was accepted by the process, we get the stated relationship.

APPENDIX C

The Q-Model and a First-Order Predicate Calculus

A variety of different methods have been proposed for describing, studying and analysing different aspects of software. Users can face serious problems if their particular interests are not fully covered by the chosen method and will, of necessity, have to use more than one technique. In order to be able to study a problem using different methods, and hence compare the results obtained, we must also be able to compare the methods themselves. It therefore becomes important to be able to assess various methodologies and understand their fundamental natures.

For practical use we need to know which of the existing methods are equivalent, and which are generalisations or special cases of others. A serious problem, however, is that at this early stage in the development of the technology, the different specification and design methods (and where applicable, their formalisms) have seldom been properly compared to each other. This is mainly because an objective comparison is theoretically difficult and often not very rewarding. Also, restrictions imposed by proprietary rights and commercial interests make it difficult to get to the heart of many techniques.

In this appendix we will generalise the Q-model formalism into a first order predicate calculus. We would, naturally, add that this provides the possibility of comparing the method with other axiomatic approaches. However, there is an even more urgent reason to undertake this generalisation. It will have been evident so far in this book that the approach adopted has been based on empirical knowledge, which, as always, has been pragmatically filtered! The resulting formalism undoubtedly provides, as we have shown, a functional tool. However, doubts about its inner consistency and its truly formal basis, must remain. The successful generalisation of the technique into a mathematically-formal approach, such as predicate calculus, could serve to increase confidence in the approach.

At the same time the development of a first-order calculus, capable of supporting hard real-time applications, will be an independent goal. The invasion of mathematical-logic-based methods into programming has become popular recently, and Chapter 3 gave a brief review of this growing interest.

For real-time applications, a group of methods with the common denominator of temporal logic has been suggested. The group includes linear-time temporal logic, branching-time temporal logic, and many different versions of interval-temporal logic. All these temporal-logic-based methods belong to a class of "modal" logics. This name implies that, in addition to the usual logical operators, (in other words, conjunction, disjunction, quantifiers, etc.), we also have so-called "modal" operators, such as "always", "eventually", etc.

The approach taken in this chapter is different from that of temporal logic in that we do not use any modalities. Instead, we have introduced specific predicates which include time parameters. This idea is comparable with the notion of "action", (i.e. a predicate asserting "something" about pairs of states) used by Kurki-Suonio (1989) and Lamport (1990). The resulting predicate calculus is based on an extended axiom system, but still uses a conventional set of inference rules, which enables the formal proving of many time-bound properties.

The set of inference rules comes from the Gentzen's sequents calculus (see [Gentzen (1935)]). We have extended the axioms by adding those of order and arithmetic, and a set describing allowable process behaviour. These latter axioms which describe process behaviour may look cumbersome, but we should remember that the calculus is meant to be used by computers and not humans!

It must be emphasised that the text which follows is highly theoretical and can be omitted if the reader only wishes to understand the fundamental ideas of the Q-model approach. However, it is essential to a complete understanding of the techniques used, and provides a sound, mathematical basis for the formal methods described.

C.1. A LANGUAGE FOR SYSTEM DESCRIPTION (LSD)

A language used for system description, LSD, is obtained by translating a subset of the everyday language used by the computer control community, into expressions of mathematical logic. In some cases, we might need more exact data or more detailed information than the users usually provide to their programmers. Most of these detailed requirements will be necessary, in fact, because of our background understanding of the Q-model approach. So, before a formal definition of the LSD is presented, we shall go through a simple example which will provide a practical "feel" for the language.

Consider a system of three interacting processes. Processes p_1 and p_2 are activated simultaneously at a given time instant; they produce corresponding state values, called a_1 and a_2. At least one of these values is consumed by process p_3. The state value of p_3, a_3, is consumed by process p_1 when the latter is activated for the next successive time.

In terms of the Q-model, we would say that p_1 and p_2 communicate with p_3 via semisynchronous channels σ_{13} and σ_{23}, respectively, and p_3 sends its state value to p_1 via an asynchronous channel, σ_{31}. As in the Q-model, new state values a_1' and a_2', produced at the subsequent activation cycle, overwrite the previous state values.

It would be tedious to reproduce the whole translation from the above description into mathematical logic notions, so we shall demonstrate only how some of the key phrases are handled.

The *action of communication*, and also the *possibility of communication*, may be described by introducing the following symbols:

$U(1,3) \triangleq$ process p_1 is able to send information to process p_3,

$\neg U(1,2) \triangleq$ process p_1 is not able to send information to process p_2.

[In this notation $\triangleq$ means "is by definition" and $\neg \triangleq$ negation.]

From the given system, it may be concluded that state values a_1 and a_2 exist only during a certain time interval (i.e. before they are overwritten).

The endpoints of a time interval may be defined by the following expressions:

$l(d) \geq \mu \triangleq$ left endpoint of the interval is not smaller than μ

$r(d) \leq \mu' \triangleq$ right endpoint of the interval, is not greater than μ'

State values are just data items; therefore, in order to say that *state values* a_1 *and* a_2 *exist for process* p_3 *during interval d,* we use the following logical expression:

$$\forall w_1[E_3(a_1,w_1) \supset (l(w_1) \geq \mu \wedge r(w_1) \leq \mu')] \wedge$$

$$\wedge \forall w_2[E_3(a_2,w_2) \supset (l(w_2) \geq \mu \wedge r(w_2) \leq \mu')].$$

where $\wedge \triangleq$ conjunction, $\supset \triangleq$ implication, $\forall \triangleq$ universal quantifier, and $E_3(a,w) \triangleq$ data item a exists for process p_3 during interval w.

Cyclic execution is one of the main features of embedded software, as suggested by Motus (1985). Cyclic execution may cause extremely sophisticated communication patterns, both interprocess and intercycle, which are very hard to analyse and describe without ambiguity. To facilitate communications handling in the case of cyclic execution, we adopt the idea of timesets from the Q-model. A timeset includes all the activation instants of a process.

The phrase "μ is an activation-instant of process p_1" is thus denoted by $T_1(\mu)$, which means

$$T_1(\mu') \triangleq \exists x \exists y \exists w[\mu = l(w) \wedge P_1(x,y,w)],$$

where $\exists \triangleq$ the existential quantifier, and $P_1(x,y,w) \triangleq$ process p_1 produces from data item x, a state value y during interval w.

In conventional programming, a process is activated only when the initial, or input, data is available. In a control system we often cannot wait until this data appears since the environment functions according to its own laws and will not wait for the computer to solve its problems. Therefore, we have to produce a satisfactory state value even if no valid input data exists. The concept of timesets will allow us to handle such situations formally .

Formal definition of the language

By looking at the above example, it is natural to conclude that we need seven different types of symbols in our language. These are:

1) fixed or constant, values (for example, the time instant μ),

2) parameters or free variables (for example, data-item a_1, and time-interval d),

3) bound variables (for example, variables used with quantifiers, such as $\exists x$, $\forall w_1$),

4) relations or predicates (for example, $E_3(a_1,w_1)$, $T_1(\mu)$),

5) functions (for example, l(d), r(d)),

6) logical connectives (for example, conjunction ($\wedge$)), and

7) auxiliary symbols (for example, parentheses).

The following formal definition of the language, LSD, corresponds to the traditional approaches to defining predicate languages (see, for example, [Takeuti (1975)]).

Individual symbols. The alphabet of the language contains three basic sorts of individuals - data, time-intervals, and time-instants. For handling interprocess-communication in the case of cyclic execution of processes, we must be able to handle a finite sequences of variables. Each finite sequence can be considered as a function, with the domain in the form of 1,2,3, ... , n and where the range is contained in one of the basic sorts and denoted exactly as the corresponding basic sorts, only with a hat-symbol added. Therefore, we need an additional sort of individual - a sort of positive integer.

For the sake of clarity we suggest separate notations for: 1) constants, 2) parameters, 3) bound variables, and these are shown in Table Appendix C.1.

SORTS	CONSTANTS	NOTATIONS PARAMETERS	BOUND VARIABLES
Data	α, β, ν	a, b,c	x, y, z
Time Intervals	η, ζ	d, e	v, w
Time Instants	μ	q	t
Positive Integers	ν, π	m, n, i, j	s, u

Table Appendix **C.1**

Relation (or predicate) symbols of the LSD are as follows:

1) The relations, $\leq$ and $<$ for ordering time instants, and the equality relation $=$,2) The relation $\in$ $\triangleq$ an element of a finite sequence and its negation, $\notin$.

3) The predicate C(a,b) $\triangleq$ data item b contains data item a.

4) The predicate E(a,d) $\triangleq$ data item a exists in the interval d.

5) The predicate E_n(a,d) data $\triangleq$ item a exists in the interval d for process p_n.

6) The predicate I_n(a,d) $\triangleq$ process p_n inputs data item a, in the interval d.

7) The predicate P_n(a,b,d) $\triangleq$ process p_n produces data item b from data item a, during the interval d.

8) The predicate O_n(b,d) $\triangleq$ process p_n outputs data item b, in the time interval d.

9) The predicate U(n,m) $\triangleq$ processes p_n and p_m are coupled, and process p_n is able to send a message to process p_m, through the communication media.

10) The predicate T_n(q) $\triangleq$ time instant q is an activation instant of process p_n.

Note 1:
We have assumed that the predicates are defined for a system consisting of $\pi \geq 1$ communicating processes $p1, p2, \ldots, p_\pi$. A process is a notion that does not belong to the language, and formally-speaking, symbols p1, p2, and $p_\pi$and $\triangleq$ have not been included into LSD.

Note 2:
The predicate C(a,b) has some similarity with the set-theoretic relation "is subset of". These are, however, two different relationships since the sort "data" cannot always be interpreted as a set. The following examples demonstrate the importance of considering the semantic contents of data when decomposing it.

In a solution (NaCl + H_2O) we have two components - salt (NaCl) and water. A formal-minded observer would say that the solution consists of Na, Cl, H_2 and O_2. This is true, but the problem remains of how to obtain the formally-existing components!

As a second example, consider a sequence of ASCII coded symbols in a computer memory. If we partition the sequence symbol-wise, it might provide some useful information. If we partition the sequence bit-wise, the information is still there, although we will probably have some difficulties in reading it! The point made in both these trivial examples is that, when decomposing data, one cannot ignore its initial meaning, and, indeed, the semantic information one wishes to get from the decomposition itself.

The functional symbols of the LSD are as follows:

1) Constants denoting arithmetic operations (for example, "+", "-".)

2) $l(d) \underline{\underline{\Delta}}$ left endpoint of time interval d.

3) $r(d) \underline{\underline{\Delta}}$ right endpoint of time interval d.

4) $long(\hat{q}) = n \underline{\underline{\Delta}}$ sequence of time instants $\hat{q}$ contains n elements.

5) $proj(\hat{q}, n) = q_n \underline{\underline{\Delta}} q_n$ is the n-th element of the sequence $\hat{q}$.

Note 3:
Whereas d belongs to the sort "time-interval", l(d) and r(d) belong to the sort "time instant".

Note 4:
The symbol $long(\hat{q})$ always belongs to the sort of positive integers. The sort of symbol $proj(\hat{q}, n)$ depends on the sort of the finite sequence, $\hat{q}$.

The logical connectives are as follows:

$\neg$ $\underline{\underline{\Delta}}$ negation,
$\wedge$ $\underline{\underline{\Delta}}$ conjunction,
$\vee$ $\underline{\underline{\Delta}}$ disjunction,
$\supset$ $\underline{\underline{\Delta}}$ implication,
$\Leftrightarrow$ $\underline{\underline{\Delta}}$ equivalence,
$\forall$ $\underline{\underline{\Delta}}$ universal quantifier,
$\exists$ $\underline{\underline{\Delta}}$ existential quantifier.

A Term is either a constant, a variable, or an expression of the form $f(t_1, t_2, \ldots, t_n)$, where f is a functional symbol and $t_1, t_2, \ldots, t_n$ are terms. An example of a term is $l(d) + q$.

A Formula is an expression formed from terms, relational symbols and logical connectives. Examples of formulae are

$$l(d) + q < r(d) \text{ and}$$

$$C(a,b) \wedge E3(b,d) \supset \exists w\ E(a,w).$$

Formulae containing finite sequences need additional comments. Let $\hat{\varphi}$ be a finite sequence of language symbols, then

$$\hat{\varphi} = \langle \varphi_1, \varphi_2, \ldots, \varphi_n \rangle.$$

Suppose that $\hat{\varphi}$ is a parameter, then n, $\varphi_1, \varphi_2, \ldots, \varphi_n$ are also parameters; if $\hat{\varphi}$ is a bound variable, then s, $\varphi_1, \varphi_2, \ldots, \varphi_n$ are also bound variables. Whenever $B(\hat{\varphi})$ is a formula, we consider

$$(\exists \hat{\varphi})\ (\forall \varphi \in \hat{\varphi})B(\varphi) \text{ to be equivalent to}$$

$$\exists \hat{\varphi}\ \forall \varphi\ \ (\varphi \in \hat{\varphi} \supset B(\varphi)) \text{ and to}$$

$$\exists \varphi\ \exists \varphi_1\ \exists \varphi_2 \ldots \exists \varphi_u\ (B(\varphi_1) \wedge B(\varphi_2) \wedge \ldots \wedge B(\varphi_u)).$$

A sequent is an expression of the form $\Gamma \rightarrow \Delta$, where Γ and Δ are finite sets of formulae. According to Gentzen (1935), the following translations can be used:

$$A_1, \ldots, A_n \rightarrow B_1, \ldots, B_m \ \underline{\underline{\Delta}}\ A_1 \wedge \ldots \wedge A_n \supset B_1 \vee \ldots \vee B_m$$

$$\rightarrow B_1, \ldots, B_m \ \underline{\underline{\Delta}}\ B_1 \vee \ldots \vee B_m$$

$$A_1, \ldots, A_n \rightarrow \ \underline{\underline{\Delta}}\ \neg(A_1 \wedge \ldots \wedge A_n)$$

$$\rightarrow \ \underline{\underline{\Delta}}\ (A \vee \neg A) \supset (A \wedge \neg A),$$

where A, $A_1, \ldots, A_n$ and $B_1, \ldots B_m$ are formulae.

C. 2. A CALCULUS FOR SYSTEM DESCRIPTION (CSD)

A calculus is a set of inference rules for deducing new, valid assertions from a set of assertions that have already been established as valid. The set of valid assertions can further be divided into axioms and already-proved (using the same calculus) theorems.

In CSD, we use the Gentzen's set of inference rules which are usually grouped as structural (weakening and cut) rules and logical rules. These rules have been widely published, and we suggest that reference be made to [Gentzen (1935)], [Takeuti (1975)] or [Bowen (1982)].

The majority of these authors agree that the "cut" rule is difficult to apply automatically. It has been shown that all the deductions obtained using the cut rule can also be obtained without it - still using the same set of inference rules. However, since we, unlike computers, seem to manage the cut rule perfectly, many proofs are shorter when using it. Thus the cut rule has not been excluded from our calculus.

To complete the calculus it is necessary to fix the assertions that are postulated to be valid, in other words, to state the axioms. We group the axioms of CSD as either logical axioms which are necessary for the formal functioning of the calculus, or as proper axioms which will determine the a priori allowable behaviour of a process and of a system of interacting processes.

These two groups of axioms form a general theory which is assumed to be valid for the whole of the CSD application domain, and which does not tell us too much about the behavioural properties of a particular application. A specific theory for a particular application is obtained when we extend the set of axioms of the general theory by adding specific axioms, which are requirements which must be true in the particular application. Consequently, we will have a separate theory for each application.

Logical axioms of the CSD

In Gentzen's sequents calculus there is only one axiom, the initial sequence, which was also called the basic axiom for sequents calculus. The basic axiom has the following form:

$$A \rightarrow A,$$

where A is a formula of LSD.

In addition to this basic axiom (or rather, axiom schema), we need to introduce axioms for equality and ordering.

Equality axioms:. Suppose that t, t_1, ... t_n are terms of LSD, then the equality axioms can be presented in the following form:

- reflexivity $\forall t(t = t)$,
- symmetricity $\forall t_1 \forall t_2(t_1 = t_2 \supset t_2 = t_1)$,
- transitivity $\forall t_1 \forall t_2 \forall t_3(t_1 = t_2 \wedge t_2 = t_3 \supset t_1 = t_3)$,
- substitutability in functional constants

$$\forall s\{t_1 = t'_1 \wedge ... \wedge t_s = t'_s \supset [f(t_1,...,t_s) = f(t'_1,...,t'_s)]\}$$

and,

- substitutability in predicate constants

$$\forall s\{t_1 = t'_1 \wedge .. \wedge t_s = t'_s \supset [R(t_1,..,t_s) = R(t'_1,..t'_s)]\}$$

Although equality is an uncomfortable symbol for automatic deduction (see, for example, [Chang and Lee (1973)]), when manually proving theorems it often gives a degree of economy.

Ordering axioms. We need the ordering of individual symbols for "time instant" and "positive integer" sorts. For the relation "≤" we have two axioms:

- reflexivity $\forall t(t \leq t)$, and
- transitivity $\forall t_1 \forall t_2 \forall t_3(t_1 \leq t_2 \wedge t_2 \leq t_3 \supset t_1 \leq t_3)$.

For the relation "<" we have only the axiom of transitivity

$$\forall t_1 \forall t_2 \forall t_3(t_1 < t_2 \wedge t_2 < t_3 \supset t_1 < t_3).$$

Anti-reflexivity of the relation "<" -- (i.e. $\forall t \neg (t < t)$), is easy to prove when we consider that

$$q1 = q2 \triangleq q1 \leq q2 \wedge q2 \leq q1, \text{ and}$$

$$q1 < q2 \triangleq q1 \leq q2 \wedge \neg (q1 = q2).$$

The order of interval endpoints is given as

$$\forall w[l(w) \leq r(w)].$$

Making use now of the previously introduced axioms, we are able to prove that each interval has unique endpoints, i.e.

$$\forall w\ \exists t[l(w) = t \wedge (\forall\ t')(l(w) = t' \supset t' = t)],$$

$$\forall w\ \exists t[r(w) = t \wedge (\forall t')(r(w) = t' \supset t' = t)],$$

(It is interesting to note that for this proof we require the axioms of equality.)

The reflexivity of C(a,b) is given as

$$\forall x\ C(x,x).$$

Although the predicate C(a,b) and the set-theoretic one 'is-subset-of" are different relationships, we define the equality of data items in the same way as is defined the equality of sets, in other words,

$$a = b \triangleq C(a,b) \wedge C(b,a).$$

The existence of data components states that whenever a data item exists, its components will exist in the same interval:

$$\forall x \ \forall y \ \forall w \ [C(x,y) \wedge E(y,w) \supset E(x,w)].$$

The components of a data item play an important role since this is one of the ways of describing how a process can collect its input data from the output data of several other processes. We therefore define two operations which are possible on the components of a data item.

The union of two data items, b_1 and b_2, is denoted by $b_1 \cup b_2$, and the same operation can be repeated. Suppose we have a finite sequence, $\hat{b} = <b_1, b_2, \ldots b_n>$, so its union is understood to be

$$\cup\hat{b} = \bigcup_{i=1}^{n} b_i = (\ldots(b_1 \cup b_2) \cup \ldots \cup b_{(n-1)}) \cup b_n$$

The union of a finite sequence is thus expressed in LSD as

$a = \cup\hat{b} = [(\forall x \in \hat{b})C(x,a)] \wedge \forall y[((\forall z \in \hat{b})C(z,y) \supset C(a,y))]$ and $C(a, \cup\hat{b})$ is understood as

$$C(a,\cup\hat{b}) = \exists x'[(\forall x \in \hat{b})C(x,x') \wedge$$

$$\wedge \forall y((\forall z \in \hat{b})C(z,y) \supset C(x',y)) \wedge C(a,x')].$$

If the data can be interpreted as a set, the above definition of a union coincides with that of the set-theoretic union.

The *partition* of a data item is an inverse operation to the union of data. Given $a = \cup\hat{b}$ we can say that $\hat{b}$ defines a "partition" of a, and denote it as $D(a, \hat{b})$. In general, we do not impose any restrictions on a partition (in that the components may overlap, etc.). Quite often, however, it will be necessary to have a non-overlapping partition, which we will call a *strict partition.*

Thus, we introduce a formal definition of a strict-partition, step-by-step. For two components, b_1 and b_2, we have

$$\text{disj }(b_1,b_2) = \neg\exists x[C(x,b_1) \wedge C(x,b_2)]$$

and for the general case

$$\text{Disj }(\hat{b}) = (\forall y \in \hat{b})(\forall z \in \hat{b})[\neg(y = z) \supset \text{disj}(y,z)].$$

The strict partitioning of data (i.e. partitioning without overlapping components) is defined as

$$D_S(a, \hat{b}) = D(a, \hat{b}) \wedge Disj(\hat{b}).$$

Proper axioms of the CSD

In this section we will present axioms which are valid for all systems of interacting processes with imposed time constraints. To achieve this we must consider not only realistic properties of "normal" processes, but also "abnormal" processes, such as processes with instantaneous action. As a consequence, many of the time constraints which are included in the axioms, are loose. (In future versions of CSD, these time constraints should probably be reconsidered.) As a result, the set of axioms presented here provides a general theory for a system of interacting processes.

As mentioned earlier, a specific calculus for a particular application is obtained by adding special axioms to the general theory. In doing this, it becomes clear that many of the following axioms look awkward and over-sophisticated. This could be explained by the fact that the new CSD is a first attempt at formulating such a theory for interacting processes with imposed time constraints. The complex look of the axioms is also caused by the sophisticated, and maybe ill-understood, nature of the corresponding phenomena. It should be remembered, though, that the axioms only form a base for an automatic theorem prover (working in a dialogue mode) and are therefore effectively hidden from the user.

*Axiom **A1**:*
This axiom fixes the *relationship between activation instants and processing intervals*, and states that processing only takes place at specified intervals:

$$\forall t\ \exists x\ \exists y\ \exists w[1(w) = t \wedge P_n(x, y, w) \Leftrightarrow T_n(t)]$$

*Axiom **A2**:*
This axiom fixes the *order of input and processing*. Before we formulate this axiom, we need to recall that a process will not always use all the data it receives. For example, in a Q-model, a process will always input the whole state of its producer. Some of the state variables, however, are superfluous. It is not sensible to build special data transformers to eliminate the superfluous components of the input data.

Another example of such a situation is when some of the required input data is not available but the process, nevertheless, must be able to produce a new state value.

From these examples we can conclude that it is reasonable to highlight data which is vital to the successful execution of a process, even under exceptional conditions.

This vital, or inescapable, component of the input data for process p_n, is defined in LSD as:

$$Nec_n(a';a,b,d) \triangleq P_n(a,b,d) \wedge C(a',a) \wedge$$
$$\wedge\ \forall x[C(x,a) \wedge \neg C(a',x) \supset \neg P_n(x,b,d)].$$

The compatibility of the input and processing intervals for the general theory means that the input starts before the processing terminates:

$$\forall x\ \forall y\ \forall w\ [Nec_n(z;x,y,w) \supset$$
$$\supset \exists \hat{z}\ \exists \hat{v}\ (D(z,\hat{z}) \wedge (\forall z' \in \hat{z})(\exists v' \in \hat{v})[In(z',v') \wedge$$
$$\wedge l(v') \leq r(w)])].$$

*Axiom **A3**:*
This axiom handles the *ordering of output and processing*, and has the following form:

$$\forall y\ \forall w\ [On(y,w) \supset \exists x\ \exists y'\ \exists v\ (Pn(z,y',v) \wedge$$
$$\wedge C(y',y) \wedge l(v) \leq r(w))].$$

*Axiom **A4**:*
This axiom concerns *the relationship of data existence for a process and in a system,* and is expressed as

$$\forall x\ \forall w\ [E_n(x,w) \supset E(x,w)].$$

*Axiom **A5**:*
This axiom states *the existence of components of the input data*, and has the following form:

$$\forall x\ \forall w\ [I_n(x,w) \supset \exists\ \hat{x},\ \exists\ \hat{w}\ (D(x,\ \hat{x}) \wedge$$
$$\wedge (\forall z \in \hat{x})(\exists v \in \hat{w})[E_n(z,v) \wedge l(v) \leq r(w)])].$$

*Axiom **A6**:*
This axiom describes the *input of data by components* and requires that each component must exist within the input interval:

$$\forall x\ \forall z\ \forall w\ [I_n(x,w) \wedge C(z,x) \supset \exists v\ [I_n(z,v) \wedge$$
$$\wedge l(w) \leq l(v) \wedge r(v) \leq r(w)\ ]].$$

*Axiom **A7**:*
This axiom describes the *output of data by components* and requires that each component must exist within the output interval

$$\forall x\ \forall z\ \forall w\ [O_n(x,w) \wedge C(z,x) \supset \exists v\ [O_n(z,v) \wedge$$
$$\wedge\ l(w) \leq l(v) \wedge r(v) \leq r(w)]].$$

*Axiom **A8**:*
This is the axiom for *co-ordinating the existence of initial data and the results of processing*, and has the following form:

$$\forall x\ \forall y\ \forall v\ [P_n(x,y,v) \supset \exists\ \hat{b} \exists\ \hat{w}\ [D(x,\hat{b}) \wedge E(\hat{b},\hat{w}) \wedge$$

$$\wedge\ \forall \hat{v}\ \ \forall \hat{a}\,[E(\hat{a},\hat{v}) \wedge D(y,\hat{a}) \supset (\exists v_j \in \hat{v})\ (\forall w_k \in \hat{w})[l(v_j) > l(w_k)]]]].$$

*Axiom **A9**:*
This axiom declares *the uniqueness of processing* and guarantees that two executions of a process, activated at the same time-instant, give the same result:

$$\forall x\ \forall y\ \forall w\ \forall x'\ \ \forall y'\ \ \forall w'[P_n(x,y,w) \wedge P_n(x',y',w') \wedge$$

$$\wedge\ l(w) = l(w') \supset x = x'\ \wedge y = y'].$$

*Axiom **A10**:*
This axiom for *process possibilities* fixes requirements which enables the existence of the process state as a set of separate components, and also gives conditions which enable the input of initial data in the form of a set of separate components:

$$\forall x\ \forall y\ \forall w\ [P_n(x,y,w) \supset$$

$$\supset \exists\ \hat{y}\ \exists\ \hat{w}\ [D(y,\ \hat{y}) \wedge (\forall y' \in \hat{y})(\exists\ w' \in \hat{w})[E(y',w') \wedge$$

$$\wedge \exists\ \hat{x}\ \exists\ \hat{v}\ [D(x,\ \hat{x}) \wedge (\forall x' \in \hat{x})(\exists\ v' \in \hat{v})[I_n(x',v') \wedge$$

$$\wedge \exists\ \hat{x}'\ \exists \hat{v}\ [D(x'\ \ \hat{x}') \wedge (\forall x'' \in \hat{x}')(\exists\ v'' \in \hat{v})[E_n(x'',v'') \wedge$$

$$\wedge\, l(w) \leq r(w') \wedge$$

$$\wedge\, l(v') \leq r(w) \wedge\ l(v') \leq r(w) \wedge$$

$$\wedge\, l(v'') \leq r(w') \wedge l(v'') \leq r(w) \wedge l(v'') \leq r(v')\ ]]]]]]].$$

Axiom ***A11****:*

This axiom *co-ordinates input, processing and output.* Suppose that the process state, y, is represented at the output as a finite sequence, $\hat{y}$. The data from which the process output is formed is obtained from the processing, as a finite sequence, of $\hat{y}'$. Process p_n uses the finite sequence $\hat{x}$ as initial data, and the sequence $\hat{x}$ is formed inside the process from the input sequence of $\hat{x}'$. The existence-intervals for the input data are given for a partition $\hat{x}''$ of each component of the sequence $\hat{x}'$. The following axiom gives the loosest possible constraints which will enable the functioning of process p_n:

$$\forall y\ \forall w\ [O_n(y,w) \supset$$
$$\supset \exists\ \hat{y}\ \exists\ \hat{y}' \exists \hat{w}\ [D(y,\hat{y}) \wedge (\forall\ y' \in \hat{y})(\exists y'' \in \hat{y}')\ [\exists(w'' \in \hat{w}')$$
$$[C(y',y'') \wedge E(y'',w'') \wedge \exists \hat{x}\ \hat{v}[(\exists x' \in \hat{x})(\exists v' \in \hat{v})$$
$$[P_n(x',y',v') \wedge \exists \hat{x}' \exists \hat{v}'\ [D(x',\hat{x}') \wedge (\forall x'' \in \hat{x}')(\exists v'' \in \hat{v}')$$
$$[I_n(x'',v'') \wedge \exists \hat{x}''\ \exists \hat{v}''\ [D(x'',\hat{x}'') \wedge (\forall z \in \hat{x}'')\ (\exists v_1 \in \hat{v}'')$$
$$[E_n(z,v_1) \wedge l(w) \leq r(w'') \wedge$$
$$\wedge l(v') \leq r(w'') \wedge l(v') \leq r(w) \wedge$$
$$\wedge l(v'') \leq r(w'') \wedge l(v'') \leq r(w) \wedge l(v'') \leq r(v') \wedge$$
$$\wedge\ l(v_1) \leq\ r(w'') \wedge l(v_1) \leq r(w) \wedge l(v_1) \leq r(v') \wedge$$
$$\wedge l(v_1) \leq r(v'')]]]]]]]]].$$

This will conclude the calculus which forms a general theory for interacting processes with imposed time constraints. At the present moment we have not been concerned that the set of axioms for this calculus is minimal. According to our current approach it will suffice if the set of axioms is non-contradicting. This property has been proved by using the model-theoretic approach in [Tekko (1991)] and [Tekko & Uustalu (1990)].

C3. PROCESS COMMUNICATION IN CSD

When we describe embedded software, we usually fix the timing parameters in "absolute" time, where absolute time is measured from the instant of switching on the system. Its use makes it easy to compare activation-instants of all the processes. As we have discussed earlier in Chapter 2, the correspondence between "absolute" time and astronomical time can be relatively easily organised.

Intervals defined in such absolute time have been used by Allen (1984) and by Schwartz (1983). In our work, the intervals have all had endpoints, which are considered to be time-instants. The concept of a time instant, though, is merely a useful abstraction, and when we reach an implementation stage, these time instants are usually substituted by unit-intervals. (Note that these correspond to the event intervals of Schwartz (1983)).

Now, as soon as we concentrate our attention on process communication, the concept of absolute time loses its importance. This is because when we are describing the interaction of a process, the rest of the system can be considered relative to this particular process, and to the time-instant when the interaction takes place.

In other words, we are only interested in processes which participate in an act of communication. Producer- and the associated consumer-processes are executed in an endless cycle. The consumer will need to receive a finite number of producer states within each execution of the cycle. The required number of finite states must be selected from the existing, and, in theory, infinite number of producer-process's states. It is possible to identify the required states by determining a delay in respect of the instant of requesting the states.

This leads us back to the need to consider the handling of relative time in the concept of a channel.

Absolute and relative time

Given a system of processes $p_1, p_2, \ldots, p_\pi$, the moment of the "big bang", in other words, the origin of absolute time, may be defined in our LSD as:

$$\text{start}\ (q) \underline{\underline{\Delta}} (\exists\, v)\ (\exists\, s \leq \pi\ )\ (\exists\, x)(\exists\, y)[q = l(v) \wedge$$

$$\wedge\ [I_s(x,v) \vee P_s(x,y,v) \vee O_s(y,v)] \wedge$$

$$\wedge\ (\forall w)(\forall n \leq \pi)(\forall\, x')(\forall\, y')([I_n(x',w) \vee P_n(x',y',w) \vee$$

$$\vee\ O_n(y',w)] \supset q \leq l(w))].$$

When creating and analysing a system, we are usually interested only in a single origin of absolute time. Thus, the origin of absolute time can be considered to be a common, minimal element in the processes timesets, and can be denoted by μ start = q. On a time line, this absolute **time** increases from left to right.

However, relative time in CSD, just as we saw in the Q-model, takes the opposite direction. This can be justified by noting that in the real world we can communicate with the past and not with the future! Whereas absolute time can be in any metric, in relative time we can only count process activation-instants, which are usually the elements of the producer-process's timeset. Thus, relative time is by nature a logical time. It would certainly be of value if we could measure the distance between elements in a timeset; in other words, the intervals between the ticks of our logical clock.

Suppose we have a producer process, p_i, and a consumer process, p_j. The origin of relative time (q_i), assuming that the consumer process was activated at q_j, is defined in LSD as:

$$M_{ij}(0,q_i,q_j) \triangleq T_i(q_i) \wedge T_j(q_j) \wedge (\forall t(T_i(t) \Leftrightarrow T_j(t)) \supset q_i = q_j) \wedge$$

$$\wedge(\neg \forall t(T_i(t) \Leftrightarrow T_j(t)) \supset \exists x_i \; \exists y_i \; \exists v_i \; \exists z \; \exists w$$

$$[P_i(x_i,y_i,v_i) \wedge C(z,y_i) \wedge E_j(z,w) \wedge l(w) \leq q_j \wedge l(v_i) = q_i \wedge$$

$$\wedge \forall t \, \forall x'_i \; \forall y'_i \; \forall v'_i \; \forall z' \; \forall w' \; [\, l(v'_i) = t \wedge P_i(x'_i, y'_i, v'_i) \wedge$$

$$\wedge C(z', y'_i) \wedge E_j(z', w') \wedge l(w') \leq q_j \supset t \leq q_i]]).$$

The formula, $M_{ij}(0,q_i,q_j)$, determines the latest activation-instant, q_i, of the producer-process p_i, resulting in a state value which can be used by the consumer, p_j, if it was activated at q_j.

Now, suppose that the consumer-process requires, at each activation-time, (n+2) states from the producer process. A formula which points to the (n+2)-th element in the producer-process timeset (counted back from the origin of relative time) is described by the following induction schema:

$$M_{ij}(n+1,q_i,q_j) \triangleq T_i(q_i) \wedge T_j(q_j) \wedge$$

$$\wedge \; (\forall t(T_i(t) \Leftrightarrow T_j(t)) \supset \exists \; \tau \; [M_{ij}(n, \; \tau \; ,q_j) \wedge$$

$$\wedge \; q_i < \tau \wedge \forall \; \tau \; [T_i(\tau') \supset (\forall \tau' \geq \tau)(\tau' \leq q_i)]]) \wedge$$

$$\wedge \; (\neg \forall t \; (T_i(t) \Leftrightarrow T_j(t)) \supset \exists \; t' \, [M_{ij}(n, \; t' q_j) \wedge$$

$$\wedge \; q_i < t' \; \wedge \forall t \;\; \forall x_i \;\; \forall y_i \;\; \forall v_i \;\; \forall w' \;\; \forall z[\, l(v_i) = t \wedge$$

$$\wedge \; t < t' \; \wedge P_i(x_i,y_i,v_i) \wedge C(z,y_i) \wedge E_j(z, \; w') \wedge$$

$$\wedge \; (w') \leq q_j \supset t \leq q_i]]).$$

The two formulae, ($M_{ij}(0,q_i,q_j)$ and $M_{ij}(n+1,q_i,q_j)$), solve the problem of defining the origin of relative time which was described in Section 5.2, in the Q-model context.

Channels in LSD

The concept of channels has often been used in the programming context for describing message exchange between communicating processes (see, for example, [Hoare (1981)] and [Andrews (1983)]). Channels in LSD, however, will have specific features as compared, say, to those of Hoare. For example, in LSD,

- a channel will provide only a one-to-one connection,
- the buffer length in a channel is determined by the channel function, and the buffer always operates in a circular fashion in respect of writing, and

- a message destined for a consumer-process is formed in the channel, and does not necessarily coincide with the message sent to the channel by the producer-process.

Of course, the channel concept in LSD is similar to that used in the Q-model.

Most interactions between processes can be reduced to an exchange of data. We can thus say that processes p_i and p_j interact by exchanging data if

$$\exists x_i\ \exists y_i\ \exists w_i\ \exists z\ \exists x_j\ \exists y_j\ \exists w_j\ [P_i(x_i,y_i,w_i) \wedge$$
$$\wedge\ C(z,y_i) \wedge C(z,x_j) \wedge P_j(x_j,y_j,w_j)]$$

We say that processes p_i and p_j interact essentially if

$$\exists x_i\ \exists y_i\ \exists w_i\ \exists z\ \exists x_j\ \exists y_j\ \exists w_j\ [P_i(x_i,y_i,w_i) \wedge$$
$$\wedge\ C(z,y_i) \wedge Nec_j(z;\ x_j,y_j,w_j)].$$

In reality, the two processes can interact only if they have a common communication medium, and then we say that such processes are *coupled.* Although it is not sensible to connect processes by a communication medium if they are not to interact, interaction and coupling are really two different things.

The coupling of two processes implies interaction:

$$U(n,m) \supset \exists x\ \exists y\ \exists w\ \exists z\ \exists x'\ \exists y'\ \exists w'$$
$$[P_n(x,y,w) \wedge C(z,y) \wedge C(z,\ x') \wedge P_m(x',y',w')].$$

However, interaction between processes will not imply direct coupling of the processes involved

$$\exists x\ \exists y\ \exists v\ \exists z\ \exists x'\ \exists y'\ \exists v'\ [P_n(x,y,v) \wedge$$
$$\wedge\ C(z,y) \wedge C(z,\ x') \wedge P_m(x',y',v')] \supset$$
$$\supset\ (U(n.m)\ \vee\ (\exists\ s \geq 1)(\exists\ n_l)\ \ldots\ (\exists\ n_s)[\ U(n,n_l) \wedge$$
$$\wedge\ U(n_1,n_2)\ \ \ldots\ \ U(n_s,m)]).$$

The channel function will determine a finite sequence of states of the producer process p_i which are accessible via the channel to the consumer process p_j. This sequence is defined as:

$$F_{ij}(q_j,n,m,\hat{q}) \triangleq M_{ij}(n,q_1,q_j) \wedge M_{ij}(n+1,q_2,q_j) \wedge$$

$$\wedge \dots \wedge M_{ij}(n+m-1,q_m,q_j) \wedge$$

$$\wedge [q_1 \in \hat{q} \wedge \dots \wedge q_m \in \hat{q} \wedge \forall t(t \in \hat{q} \supset t = q_1 \vee \dots \vee t = q_m)].$$

Here, n determines the delay with respect to the origin of relative time of the first accessible state of the producer process, and m is the number of elements in the sequence of producer process states which form the messages for the consumer.

A channel connects a producer-process p_i and a consumer process p_j and is defined as:

$$K_{ij}(n,m) \triangleq U(i,j) \wedge \forall x \, \forall y \, \forall w[P_j(x,y,w) \wedge T_j(l(w)) \supset$$

$$\supset \exists \hat{z} \; \exists \hat{x} \; \exists \hat{v} \; (\forall z' \in \hat{z})(\exists x' \in \hat{x})(\exists v' \in \hat{v})[C(z',x) \wedge$$

$$\wedge P_i(x',z',v') \wedge F_{ij}(l(w),n,m,\hat{l}(v)) \wedge$$

$$\wedge (\forall z'' \; \forall x'' \; \forall v'' \; (C(z'' x) \wedge P_i(x'',z'',v'')) \supset v'' \in \hat{v})]],$$

where $\hat{l}(v)$ is a sequence of activation instants of time intervals from $\hat{v}$, i.e.

$$\hat{l}(v) = < l(v_1), l(v_2), \dots , \hat{l}(v_m) >.$$

As in the Q-model, we can define at least four useful types of channels.

A synchronous channel connects two processes which are activated at the same time instants:

$$SK_{ij}(n,m) \triangleq K_{ij}(n,m) \wedge \forall \, t(T_i(t) \Leftrightarrow T_j(t)].$$

A semisynchronous channel describes the case where the consumer-process is activated as soon as the producer-process completes its execution. At the same time, a message is transferred from the producer to the consumer:

$$PK_{ij}(n,m) \triangleq K_{ij}(n,m) \wedge \forall \, v \, \exists w[r(v) \leq l(w) \wedge$$

$$\wedge T_i(l(v)) \supset T_j(l(w))].$$

An asynchronous channel connects two, independently-activated, communicating processes (i.e. truly asynchronous processes). The communicating processes exchange data but do not synchronise their activities:

$$AK_{ij}(n,m) \triangleq K_{ij}(n,m) \wedge \neg SK_{ij}(n,m) \wedge \neg PK_{ij}(n,m).$$

(This is the simplest possible definition of the asynchronous channel, which might need to be changed if we add new channel types.)

A null channel is used for forcing two processes to be activated simultaneously after a triggering event from process p_k:

$$NK_{ij} \triangleq U(k,i) \wedge U(k,j) \wedge \exists z\ \exists v\ [O_k(z,v) \supset$$

$$\supset \exists x\ \exists y\ \exists w\ \exists x'\ \exists y'\ \exists w' [P_i(x,y,w) \wedge P_j(x',y',w') \wedge$$

$$\wedge\ r(v) \leq l(w) \wedge l(w) = l(w')]].$$

C.4 AN EXAMPLE OF THE USE OF LSD AND CSD

Let us return to the example of software for a direct digital controller, which was described in Section 6.1. The software structure, in terms of the Q-model, was given in Figure 6.1. The same structure can be represented in LSD as:

$$CS \triangleq U(1,2) \wedge U(2,3) \wedge U(3,4) \wedge U(4,2) \wedge U(ENV,1),$$

where ENV denotes the controller's environment which provides measurements.

In the following we will introduce the initial requirements for the controller, and also additional axioms to the CSD which are needed for handling this particular application. The following notations are used:

a_1 $\triangleq$ measurements, which serve as the initial data for the control algorithm, and are provided by the environment,

b_1 $\triangleq$ output of the control algorithm, in other words, new values for the control variable,

b_2 $\triangleq$ required change in the actuator's output value,

b_3 $\triangleq$ actual existing value of the controlled variable,

b_4 $\triangleq$ feedback signal characterising the actuator's output, and

a_2 $\triangleq$ $< b_1, b_4 >$.

Whenever we use the above notations under quantifiers, the following correspondence is maintained:

$$a_i \div x_i,\ b_i \div y_i,\ e_i \div w_i,\ d_i \div v_i.$$

The required movements of information in the controller are given as follows:

1. *Processing*:

$$PS \triangleq P_1(a_1,b_1,e_1) \wedge P_2(a_2,b_2,e_2) \wedge P_3(b_2,b_3,e_3) \wedge P_4(b_3,b_4,e_4)$$

2, *Input*:

$$IS \triangleq I_1(a_1,d_1) \wedge I_2(b_1,d_2) \wedge I_2(b_4,d''_2) \wedge I_3(b_2,d_3) \wedge I_4(b_3,d_4)$$

3. *Output:*

$$OS \triangleq O_1(b_1,d'_1) \wedge O_2(b_2,d'_2) \wedge O_3(b_3,d'_3) \wedge O_4(b_4,d'_4).$$

The relationships which must exist between time-intervals for the input, processing and output, inside a single execution cycle of the controller are fixed as follows:

$$TP1 \triangleq l(e_1) \leq l(d_1) \wedge l(d_1) \leq l(d'_1) \wedge r(d'_1) \leq r(e_1),$$

$$TP2 \triangleq l(e_2) \leq l(d_2) \wedge r(d_2) \leq l(d''_2) \wedge r(d''_2) \leq l(d'_2) \wedge r(d'_2) \leq r(e_2)$$

$$TP3 \triangleq l(e_3) \leq l(d_3) \wedge r(d_3) \leq l(d'_3) \wedge r(d'_3) \leq r(e_3)$$

$$TP4 \triangleq l(e_4) \leq l(d_4) \wedge r(d_4) \leq l(d'_4) \wedge r(d'_4) \leq r(e_4)$$

The following axioms are added to the existing set of axioms of the CSD.

Activation of the controller:
The controller is activated whenever a new measured value is received from the environment. Assuming that the timeset of the environment is known (i.e. that the domain of truth values of the predicate $T_0(q)$ is available), then

$$\forall x_1\ \forall t_0\ \exists t\ \exists w_1\ \exists y_1[T_0(t_0) \wedge T_1(t) \wedge l(w_1) = t \wedge P_1(x_1,y_1,w_1)].$$

Maintenance requirements:
The actuator might have to be replaced and, strictly speaking, is not part of the controller. It is therefore essential that the controller is able to function when the time characteristics of the actuator change, albeit within a certain interval, [u,s]. This results in:

$$\forall x_1\ \forall w_1\ \forall u\ \exists s\ \exists w_2\ \exists w_3\ \exists w_4\ \exists y_1\ \exists y_2\ \exists y_3\ \exists y_4\ [\ u <$$
$$< (r(w_3) - 1(w_3)) \leq s \wedge P_1(x_1,y_1,w_1) \wedge P_2(x_2,y_2,w_2) \wedge$$
$$\wedge P_3(y_2,y_3,w_3) \wedge P_4(y_3,y_4,w_4)].$$

The consistency of the initial requirements:
These must be guaranteed within each execution cycle of the controller:

$$\forall x_1\ \forall t_0\ \exists w_1\ \exists t_1\ \exists y_1\ \exists y_2\ \exists y_3\ \exists y_4\ \exists w_2\ \exists w_3\ \exists w_4\ [T_0(t_0) \wedge$$
$$\wedge T_1(t_1) \wedge PS \wedge IS \wedge OS \wedge TP_1 \wedge TP_2 \wedge TP_3 \wedge TP_4].$$

The designer of the controller must guarantee that it satisfies all the axioms of CSD, as well as the three new axioms. This extended set of axioms forms the special theory for the specification of this particular controller.

In the design of a controller, the designer thus has to fix the specific methods of synchronising the activation of processes in the controller, and also the timing requirements for exchanged data. Let us, again, return to the controller example given in Section 6.1. Version 1, there, which behaved similarly to the corresponding Petri-net, can be described in LSD as

$$\forall x_1\ \forall t_0\ \exists t_1\ \exists w_1\ [T_0(t_0) \wedge T_1(t_1) \wedge P_1(x_1,y_1,w_1) \wedge$$
$$\wedge D_S(x_2, \hat{y}) \wedge PK_{12}(0,0) \wedge AK_{42}(0,0) \wedge PK_{23}(0,0) \wedge PK_{34}(0,0],$$

where $\hat{y} \triangleq <y_1,y_4>$.

Version 2, which used synchronous channels with channel functions [1,1], is described here as

$$\forall x_1\ \forall t_0\ \exists t_1\ \exists w_1\ (T_0(t_0) \wedge T_1(t_1) \wedge P_1(x_1,y_1,w_1) \wedge$$
$$\wedge D_S(x_2,\ \hat{y}) \wedge SK_{12}(1,1) \wedge SK_{42}(1,1) \wedge SK_{23}(1,1) \wedge SK_{34}(1,1)]. \qquad (*)$$

Based on this description of the controller, it is possible to state and solve the tasks necessary for analysing the properties of the proposed design. The following discussion illustrates deadlock detection in a system described in terms of LSD.

Suppose we replace the channel functions of the synchronous channels. In other words, instead of

$$SK_{12}(1,1) \wedge SK_{42}(1,1) \wedge SK_{23}(1,1) \wedge SK_{34}(1,1)$$

(in expression (*)), we write

$$SK_{12}(0,1) \wedge SK_{42}(0,1) \wedge SK_{23}(0,1) \wedge SK_{34}(0,1).$$

Now, in the Q-model formalism, this substitution will introduce a synchronous loop, p_2,p_3,p_4,p_2, which, according to Proposition 7, causes a deadlock in the system.

Lorents (1986) gives two theorems which state that a deadlock in the Q-model is equivalent to the deadlock in CSD.

Theorem 8.1:
If a synchronous loop, consisting of m processes,

$$\forall j(j \leq m \supset \exists\, i[i \leq m \wedge \exists r\ \ SK_{ij}(0,r)]).$$

is built into a system of n≥m interacting processes, the system has the following property

$$\forall x\ \ \forall y\ \ \forall w\ \ (P_j(x,y,w) \supset \bigvee_{i=1}^{m} \exists x'\ \ \exists y'\ \ \exists w'\ \ [l(w) =$$

$$= l(w') \wedge P_i(x', y', w') \wedge C(y',x)]). \qquad (**)$$

Theorem 8.2:
If a system of n≥m interacting processes has the property stated in expression (**) above, then this system has a deadlock, i.e.

$$\forall w(r(w) > q_0 \supset \bigwedge_{i=1}^{m} \neg \exists x\ \ \exists y P_i(x,y,w)),$$

where q_0 is the origin of absolute time in the system.

C.5 CONCLUSIONS

This appendix has set out to illustrate how the Q-model formalism can be translated into a first-order Predicate Calculus. The objective has been two-fold; to establish a sound theoretical basis for the methodology and to provide a meaningful starting point for comparison with other proposed techniques.

REFERENCES

Abbot, R.J. and Moorhead, D.K. (1981). Software requirements and specifications: a survey of needs and languages. *J. Systems and Software*, Vol.2, No.4, 297-316.

Advances in Petri Nets (1984, 1985, 1986, 1987). Lecture Notes in Computer Science, Springer Verlag, Berlin.

Alford, M.W. (1977). A requirements engineering methodology for real-time processing requirements. *IEEE Trans. Software Engineering*, Vol.3, No.1, 60-69.

Alford, M.W. (1985). SREM at the age of eight: the distributed computing design system. *Computer*, Vol.18, No.4, 36-46.

Allen, J. F. (1984). Towards a general theory of action and time. *Artificial Intelligence*, Vol.23, No.2, 123-154.

Andrews, G. R. and Schneider, F. B. (1983). Concepts and notations for concurrent programming. *Computing Surveys*, Vol.15, No.1, 13-43.

Apt, K.R. (1984). Ten years of Hoare's logic: a survey. Part II. *Theoretical Computer Science*, Vol.28, Nos 1-2, 83-109.

Awerbuch, B. (1985). Complexity of network synchronization. *J. ACM*, Vol.32, No.4, 804 - 823.

Balzer, R. and Goldman, N. (1979). Principles of good software specification and their implications for specification languages. *Proc. IEEE Conf. on Specification of Reliable Software*, 58-67.

Belady, L. A. (1982). *Modifiability of large software systems.* Lecture Notes in Computer Science, No. 143, Springer Verlag, Berlin, 160 -174.

Bennet, S. (1988). *Real-time Computer Control.* Prentice Hall, UK.

Berzins, V. (1988). Object-oriented Techniques based on Specifications. *Proc. COMPSAC '88, 12th Int. Computer Software and Applications Conf.*, 437-438.

Biewald, J., Joho, E., Jovalekic, S. and Shelling, H. (1980). Application of the specification and design technique EPOS to process control problem. *Proc. 6th IFAC/IFIP Conf. on Digital Computer Applications to Process Control*, 517-522.

Blackledge, P. (1983). Specification languages. *IEE Proc.*, Part A, Vol.130, No.4, 185-189.

Boebert, W.E. (1980). Formal verification of embedded systems. *Software Engineering Notes*, Vol.5, No.3, 41-43.

Boehm, B.W. (1986). A spiral model of software development and enhancement. *Software Engineering Notes*, Vol.11, No.4, 14-24.

Boehm-Davis, D.A. and Ross, L.S. (1985). Program design methodologies: structuring the software development process. *Proc. IEEE Int. Conf. on Cybernetics and Society*, 371-374.

Booch, G. (1986). Object oriented development. *IEEE Trans. on Software Engineering*, Vol.12, No.2, 211-221.

Bowen, K.A. (1982). Programming with full first order logic. *Machine Intelligence,* No.10, J. Wiley and Sons, UK, 421-440.

Bull, G.M., Loomer, M.J. and Mitchell, R.J. (1986). *The design of PEACOCK paradigm of software development and associated family of languages*. School of Information Sciences, Hatfield Polytechnic, Computer Science Technical Note TN-86.

Calvez, J.P. (1990). *Embedded real-time systems: a specification and design methodology.* IRESTE La Chantrerie, CP3003 44087, Nantes, Cedex 03.

Cameron, J.R. (1986). An overview of JSD. *IEEE Trans. on Software Engineering*, Vol.12, No.2, 222-240.

Caspi, P. and Halbwachs, N. (1982). Algebra of events: a model for parallel and real-time systems. *Proc. Int. Conf. on Parallel Processing*, 150-159.

Caspi, P. and Halbwachs, N. (1986). A functional model for describing and reasoning about time behaviour of computing systems. *Acta Informatica*, Vol.22, 595-627.

Chachra, V., Ghare, P.M. and Moore, J.M. (1979). *Application of Graph Theory Algorithms.* Elsevier, North Holland, Amsterdam.

Chandy, K.M. and Misra, J. (1988). *Parallel Program Design. A Foundation*. Addison-Wesley Publishing Co., Reading, MA.

Chang, C.L. and Lee, R.C.-T. (1973). *Symbolic Logic and Mechanical Theorem Proving.* Academic Press, NewYork.

Coffman, E.G. and Denning, P.J. (1973). *Operating Systems Theory*. Prentice-Hall, New Jersey.

Corsetti, E., Crivelli, E., Mandrioli, D., Montanari, A., Morsenti, A.C., San Pietro, P. and Ratto, E. (1991). Dealing with different time scales in formal specifications. *Proc. 6th IEEE. Int. Workshop on Software Specification and Design, Como, Italy*, 92-101.

Davies, A.M. and Rauscher, T.G. (1979). Formal techniques and automatic processing to ensure correctness in requirements specification. *Proc. IEEE Conf. on Specification of Reliable Software*, 15-36.

Denbigh, K.G. (1981). *Three Concepts of Time*. Springer Verlag, Berlin.

DeNicola, R., Martelli, A. and Montanari, U. (1981). Communication through message passing or shared memory. A formal comparison. *Proc. 2nd Int. Conf. on Distributed Computing Systems*, 513-522.

DeRemer, F.L., Kron, H.H. (1976). Programming-in-the-large versus Programming-in-the-small. *IEEE Trans. on Software Engineering*, Vol.2, No.2, 80-89.

DIN 4430: Information Processing, October 1985.

Dowling, E.J. (1983). Some methods and tools for real-time software validation. *Proc. IFAC/IFIP Real Time Programming Workshop, Hatfield, U.K.*, 81-86.

Duffie, N.A. (1982). An approach to the design of distributed machinery control system. *IEEE Trans. on Industrial Control*, Vol.18, No.4, 435-442.

Emerson, E.A. and Halpern, J.Y. (1986). "Sometimes" and "Not never" revisited: On branching versus linear time temporal logic. *J.of the ACM*, Vol. 33, No.1, 151-178.

Furia, N.J. (1979). A comparative evaluation of RSL/REVS and PSL/PSA applied to digital flight control systems. *Proc. AIAA 2nd Computers in Aerospace Conference*, 330-337.

Gentzen, G. (1976). Investigations into logical deduction. *Mathematical Theory of Logical Deduction,* Nauka Publ., 9-76 (in Russian).

Giddings, R V. (1984). Accommodating uncertainty in software design. *Comm. ACM*, Vol.27, No.5, 428 -434.

Goldberg, A. and Robson, D. (1983). *Smalltalk 80: The Language and its Implementation.* Addison-Wesley, NJ.

Goldberg, R. P. (1974). Survey of virtual machine research, *IEEE Trans on Computers*, No.6, 34 - 45.

Gomaa, H. (1984). A software design method for real time systems. *Comm. ACM,* Vol.17, No.9.

Gomaa, H. (1989) A software design method for distributed real time applications. *J. of Systems and Software*, No.9, 81-94.

Greenspan, S.J. (1986). On the role of domain knowledge in knowledge-based approach to software development. *Software Engineering Notes*, Vol.11, No.4, 34-38.

Haavel, R., Motus, L. and Vain, J. (1987). Estimating the feasibility of communication network in a distributed computer control system. *Proc. 10th IFAC World Congress*, Pergamon Press, Oxford, UK, Vol. 4, 76-80.

Halang W.A. (1983). On real-time features in high-level languages and yet to be implemented. *The Euromicro J.*, Vol.12, No.2, 79-87.

Halbwachs, N. (1992). *Synchronous programming of real-time systems. The language LUSTRE*, School on Formal Techniques in Real-time and Fault-tolerant Systems, Univ. of Nijmegen, The Netherlands.

Harel, D., Lachover, H., Naamad, A., Pnueli, A., Politi, M., Sherman, R., Shtull-Trauring, A. and Trakhtenbrot, M. (1990). STATEMATE: A working environment for the development of complex reactive systems. *IEEE Trans. on Software Engineering*, Vol. 16, No.4, 403- 413.

Hausen, H.L. and Mullerburg, M. (1982). Software engineering environments: state of the art, problems and perspectives. *Proc. IEEE 6th Int. COMPSAC'82 Conference*, 297-316.

Henzinger, T.A., Manna, Z. and Pnueli, A. (1992). *Temporal Proof Methodologies for Real-time Systems*, School on Formal Techniques in Real-time and Fault-tolerant Systems, Univ.of Nijmegen, The Netherlands.

Hesse, W. (1984). A *systematics of software engineering: Structure, terminology, and classification technique.* NATO ASI Series, P. Pepper (Ed.), Vol. F8, Program Transformation and Programming Environments, 97-115.

Hoare, C.A.R. (1978). Communicating sequential processes. *Comm. ACM*, Vol.21, No.8, 666-677.

Hoare, C.A.R. (1978). Monitors: an operating system structuring concept. In *Programming Methodology,* D. Gries (Ed.), Springer Verlag, Berlin, 224-243.

Hoare, C.A.R. (1981). A calculus of total correctness for communicating processes. *Science of Computer Programming*, Vol.1, Nos 1-2, 49-72.

Hoogeboom, B. and Halang, W.A. (1991). The concept of time in software engineering for real-time systems. *Proc. 3rd International Conference on Software Engineering for Real-Time Systems*, IEE Conference Publication No. 344, 156 -163.

Hooman, J. (1992). *Compositional Verification of Distributed Real-time Systems*. School on Formal Techniques in Real-time and Fault-tolerant Systems, Univ. of Nijmegen, The Netherlands.

ISO 8802/1-5 (1987). *LAN Standards for the Data Link Layers*, IEEE/ISO.

ISO/TC97/SC6/WG1 (1986). *Draft Proposed Addendum to the ISO DIS 8802/2 Logical Link Control - Acknowledged Connectionless Service*, 14th Draft.

Izikowitz, I., Rodd, M.G. and Zhao, G. (1989). A real-time OSI based network: is it possible? *Proc. 9th IFAC Workshop on Distributed Computer Control Systems, Tokyo*, Pergamon Press, Oxford, UK.

Jefferson, D. (1983). Virtual time. *Proc. International Conference on Parallel Processing, Silver Spring, Md*, 384-394.

Jensen, K. (1981). Coloured Petri nets and the invariant method. *Theoretical Computer Science*, Vol. 14, No. 3, 317-336.

Jensen, K. (1990). *Coloured Petri Nets: A High Level Language for System Design and Analysis.* DAIMI PB-338, Computer Science Department, Aarhus University. Also published in *Advances in Petri nets* (1990), G. Rozenberg (Ed.), Lect. Notes in Comp. Science, Springer Verlag, Berlin.

Jensen, K. and Rozenberg, G. (Eds). (1991). *High-level Petri nets*. Springer Verlag, Berlin.

Joho, E. (1982). An interactive simulation system – a new component of the development support system EPOS. *Proc. 3rd IFAC/IFIP Symposium on Software for Computer Control, Madrid*, Pergamon Press, Oxford, UK, 163-168.

Kaganov, F.A. *et al.* (1984). Applying CASE system RUSA for software development. *Automation and Remote Control*, No.7, 159-168 (in Russian).

Kaplan, S.M., Campbell, R.H., Haraudi, M.T., Johnson, R.E., Kamin, S.N., Liu, J.W.S. and Purtilo, J.M. (1986). *An architecture for Tool Integration.* Lect. Notes in Computer Science, No.244, Springer Verlag, Berlin, 112-125.

Karp, R. and Miller, R. (1968). *Parallel Program Schemata.* RC-2053, IBM T.J. Watson Research Center, Yorktown Heights.

Kazmin, A.I., *et al.* (1984). *Distributed computer system for process control.* Institute of Control Problems, Moscow (in Russian).

Kelly, J.C. (1987). A comparison of four design methods for real-time systems. *Proc. 9th Int. Conf. on Software Engineering*, 238-256.

Kerridge, J. and Simpson, D. (1986). Communicating parallel processes. *Software: Practice & Experience*, Vol.16, No.1, 63-96.

Kohler W.H. (1981). A survey of techniques for synchronization and recovery in decentralized computer systems. *Computing Survey*, Vol.13, No.2, 149-183.

Kopetz, H. (1984). Real-time in distributed real-time systems, *Proc. 5th IFAC Workshop on Distributed Computer Control Systems*, Pergamon Press, Oxford, UK, 11-15.

Kopetz, H. and Kim, K.H. (1990). *Temporal Uncertainties in Interactions among Real-time Objects*. Institut für Technische Informatik, Technische Universität Wien, Austria, Research Report No. 10/90.

Kopetz, H. and Merker, W. (1985). The architecture of MARS. *Proc. 15th Int. Symp. on Fault Tolerant Computing*, 274-279.

Kramer, J., Magee, J., and Sloman, M. (1983). Dynamic system configuration for distributed real-time systems. *Proc. IFAC/IFIP Real-time Programming Workshop, Hatfield*, Pergamon Press, Oxford, UK, 81-86.

Kramer, J., Magee, J., and Sloman, M. (1984). A software architecture for distributed computer control system. *Automatica*, Vol.20, No.1, 93-102.

Kuendig, A.T. (1987). A note on the meaning of "Embedded Systems". In *Embedded Systems*, A.Kuendig, R.E.Buehner and J.Daehler (Eds). Lecture Notes in Computer Science, No.284, Springer Verlag, Berlin, 207.

Kuo, J.H.C., Leslie, K.J., Maggio, M.D., Moore, B.G. and Tu, H.-C. (1986). *Information Structuring for Software Environments*. Lecture Notes in Computer Science, No.244, Springer Verlag, Berlin, 97-111.

Kurki-Suonio, R. and Jarvinen, H.-M. (1989). Action system approach to the specification and design of distributed systems. *ACM Software Engineering Notes*, Vol.14, No.3, 34-40.

Kurki-Suonio, R. (1991). Some thoughts for the Real-time Session in the Como Workshop, *6th Int. Workshop on Software Specification and Design - private communication.*

Kurki-Suonio, R., Systa, K. and Vain, J. (1991). Real- time Specification and Modeling with Joint Actions, *Proc. 6th IEEE Int. Workshop on Software Specification and Design, Como*, 84-91.

Lamport, L. (1985). Solved problems, unsolved problems and nonproblems in concurrency. *Operating Systems Review*, Vol.19, No.4, 34-44.

Lamport, L. (1990). *A temporal logic of actions*. DEC Systems Research Centre, No.57.

Lauber, R.J. and Lempp, P.R. (1983). Integrated development and project management support systems, *IEEE Int. COMPSAC'83 Conf.*

Lawson, H. (1981). New directions for micro- and system architecture in 1980's, *AFIPS National Computer Conf.*, AFIPS Press, Vol.50, 57 -62

Lehman, M.M. (1980). Programs, life cycles, and laws of software evolution. *Proc. IEEE*, Vol.68, No.9, 1060-1076.

LeLann, G. (1983). On real-time distributed computing. *Information Processing '83*, R.E.A. Mason (Ed.), Elsevier Science Publishers, Amsterdam, 741-753.

Linger, R.C. and Mills, HD. (1977). On the development of large reliable programs. In *Current trends in Programming Methodology*. R.T.Yeh (Ed.), Vol.1, Prentice-Hall, New Jersey, 120-139.

Lorents, P., Motus, L. and Tekko, J. (1986). A language and a calculus for distributed computer control systems description and analysis. *Proc. 4th IFAC/IFIP Symposium on Software for Computer Control*, Pergamon Press, Oxford, UK, 139-146.

Ludewig, J. and Streng, W. (1978). *Methods and Tools for Software Specification and Design – a Survey*. EWICS TC on Safety and Security, No.149.

Ludewig, J. (1980). *PCSL - a Process Control Software Specification Language*. Kernforschungszentrum Karlsruhe, Institut für Datenverarbeitung in der Technik, KfK 2874.

Ludewig, J. (1981). *Zur Erstellung der Spezifikation von Prozessrechner Software.* Diss. Dokt. (Fakultät für Mathematik und Informatik der Technischen Universität), Munich.

Ludewig, J. (1983). ESPRESO - A system for process control software specification. *IEEE Trans. Software Engineering*, Vol.9, No.4, 427-436.

Lynch, N.A. and Fischer, M.J. (1981). On describing the behaviour and implementation of distributed systems. *Theor. Computer Sci.*, Vol.13, No.1,17-43.

Ma, R.P. (1984). A model to solve timing-critical application problems in distributed computer systems. *Computer*, Vol.17., No.1, 62-65, 67-68

MacLeod, I.M. (1983). *A Study of Issues Relating to Real-time in Distributed Computer Control Systems.* PhD Thesis, University of the Witwatersrand, Johannesburg.

MacLeod, I.M and Rodd, M.G. (1982). Interprocess communication primitives for distributed process control. *Proc. 3rd IFAC/IFIP Symp. on Software for Computer Control, Madrid,* Pergamon Press, Oxford, UK.

Magel, K. (1984). Principles for software environments. *ACM Sigsoft, Software Engineering Notes*, Vol.9, No.1, 32-35.

Maiden, N. (1991). Analogy as a paradigm for specification reuse. *Software Engineering Journal*, Vol.6, No.1, 3-15.

Mellor, S.J. and Ward, P.T. (1986). *Structural development for real-time systems*, Vols 1-3. Prentice-Hall, New Jersey.

Mesarovic, M.D., Macko, D. and Takahara, Y. (1970). *Theory of Hierarchical, Multilevel systems.* Academic Press, New York.

Miller, G.A. (1955). The magical number of seven, plus or minus two. Some limits on our capacity for processing information. *The Psychological Review*, Vol.63, No.2, 81-97.

Milner, R. (1980). *A calculus of communicating systems*. Lecture Notes in Computer Science, No.92, Springer Verlag, Berlin, 80-110.

Milner, R. (1983). Calculi for synchrony and asynchrony. *Theor. Computer Sci.*, Vol.25, No.3, 267-310.

Motus, L. and Vain, J. (1982). A set of tools for designing and evaluating communication protocols in industrial computer networks. *Proc. 3rd IFAC/IFIP Symposium on Software for Computer Control*, Pergamon Press, Oxford, UK, 101-109.

Motus, L. and Kaaramees, K. (1983). A model based design of distributed computer control system software. *Proc. 4th IFAC Workshop on Distributed Computer Control Systems*, Pergamon Press, Oxford, UK, 93-101.

Motus, L. and Lomp, A. (1984). Distributed computer control system's software dynamics specification. *Proc. IFAC 9th World Congress*, Pergamon Press, Oxford, UK, Vol.2, 144-148.

Motus, L., Tchugunov, V. and Artemyeva, N. (1984). Selection of the formal model for a batch chemical process control system software specification. *Preprints 9th IFAC World Congress, Budapest*, Vol.3, 196-201.

Motus, L. (1985). Specific problems of software modelling in embedded multiprocessor systems. *Proc. USSR Academy of Sciences, Technical Cybernetics*, No.4, 149-155 (in Russian).

Motus, L. (1986). Semantics and implementation problems of interprocess communication in a DCCS specification. *Proc. IFAC Workshop on Distributed Computer Control Systems*, Pergamon Press, Oxford, UK, 31-38.

Motus, L. (1990). *Dynamics of Software for Embedded Systems.* Valgus Publ., Tallinn (in Russian).

Ohno, Y. and Agura, K. (1982). A survey of software engineering in Japan. *Japan Ann. Rev. in Electronics, Computers and Telecommunication: Computer Science and Technology*, 102-109.

Ostroff, J. (1989). *Temporal Logic for Real-time Systems*. Research Studies Press/ John Wiley and Sons Inc., New York.

Pattison, H.E., Corkill, D.D. and Lesser, V.R. (1987). Instantiating descriptions of organisational structures. In *Distributed Artificial Intelligence*, M.N. Huhns (Ed), Pitman, UK, 59-96.

Peterson, J.L. (1981). *Petri-net Theory and the Modeling of Systems*. Prentice Hall Inc., New Jersey.

Petrov, B.N. and Krutko, P.D. (1980). Inverse dynamic problems of controllable systems. Linear models. *Proc. of Academy of Sciences of the Soviet Union, Technical Cybernetics*, No.4, 147-156 (in Russian).

Pizzarello, A. (1982). Liveness properties in distributed systems. *Proc. IEEE Int. Conf. on Computers and Communications*, 267-270.

Pogrebnyi, V.K. and Komagorov, V.P. (1981). *Modular Design Technology of Complex Programs, Software for CAD.* Gorki State University, 156-164, (in Russian).

Prieditis, A. (Ed.) (1988). *Analogica.* Pitman, UK.

Prieto-Diaz, R. and Neighbors, J.M. (1986). Module Interconnection Languages. *J. Systems and Software*, Vol.6, 307-334.

Quielle, J.P. and Sifakis, J. (1982) *Specification and verification of concurrent systems in CESAR*. Lecture Notes in Computer Science, Vol.137, Springer Verlag, Berlin, 337-351.

Quirk, W.J. and Gilbert, R. (1977). *The Formal Specification of the Requirements of Complete Real-time Systems.* AERE, Harwell, No.8602.

Quirk, W.J. (1978). *The Automatic Analysis of Formal Real-time System Specification.* AERE, Harwell, No.9046.

Rationale (1979). Rationale for the design of the ADA programming language, *SIGPLAN Notices*, Vol.14, No.6., Part B, 11.1-11.54.

Reghbati, H.K. and Hamacher, V.C. (1980). A constructive solution to the extensibility problem in real-time computer systems. *Auerbach Annual Best Computer Papers*, Auerbach, USA, 35-56.

Reingold, M., Nievergelt, J. and Deo, N. (1977). *Combinatorial Algorithms: Theory and Practice*. Prentice-Hall Inc., New Jersey.

Riddle, W.E. and Williams, L.G. (1986). Software Environments Workshop Report. *ACM Sigsoft, Software Engineering Notes*, Vol.11, No.1, 73-102.

Rodd, M.G. and Deravi, F. (1989). *Communication Systems for Industrial Automation.* Prentice-Hall, UK.

Roman, G.C. and Israel, R.K. (1983). Functional specification of distributed systems, *Proc. Int Conf. on Parallel Processing*, 503-505.

Roman, G.C. (1985). A taxonomy of current issues in requirement engineering. *Computer*, Vol. 18, No.4, 14-24.

Ross, D.T. (1985). Applications and extensions of SADT. *Computer*, Vol.18, No.4, 25-35.

Scheffe, P.A., Stone, A.M. (III), and Rzepka, W.F. (1985). A case study of SREM. *Computer*, Vol.18, No.4, 36-46.

Schiel, U. (1985). The time dimension in information systems. In *Information Systems: Theoretical and formal Aspects*, A. Sernades, J. Bubenko (Jr) and A. Olivet (Eds.), Elsevier Publ., Amsterdam, 67-76.

Schtrik, A.A. (1984). RUSA – control software design system. *Microprocessor Devices and Systems*, No.2, 46-49 (in Russian).

Schwan, K., Bihari, T., Weide, B.W. and Taulbee, G. (1985). GEM: Operating system primitives for robots and real-time control systems. *Proc. IEEE Int. Conf. on Robotics and Automation*, 807 -813.

Schwartz, T.L., Melliar-Smith, P.M. and Vogt, F.H. (1983). Interval logic: A higher level temporal logic for protocol specification. In *Protocol Specification, Testing, and Verification III*. H. Rubin, C.H..West (Eds), Elsevier Science Publ., Amsterdam, 3-18.

Shoham, Y. (1988). *Reasoning about Change. Time and Causation from the Standpoint of Artificial Intelligence.* MIT Press, Cambridge, MA.

Sifakis, J. (1979). Use of Petri nets for performance evaluation. *Acta Cybernetica*, Vol. 4, No.2, 185-202.

Stankovic, J.A., Ramamritham, K. and Cheng, S. (1985). Evaluation of a flexible task scheduling algorithm for distributed hard real-time systems. *IEEE Trans. on Computers*, Vol. C-31, No.12, 1130-1143.

Stankovic, J.A. (1988). Misconceptions about real-time computing. A serious problem for next-generation systems. *IEEE Computer*, Vol.21, No.10, 10-19.

STARS (1983). Software technology for adaptable, reliable systems (STARS), Program Strategy. *Software Engineering Notes*, Vol.8, No.2, 56-108.

Takeuti, G. (1975). *Proof Theory*. North Holland, Amsterdam.

Teichroew, D. and Hershey, E.A. (1977). PSL/PSA: A computer aided technique for structural documentation and analysis of information processing systems. *IEEE Trans. on Software Engineering*, Vol.3, No.1, 41-48.

Tekko, J. (1988). The Q-model language for comparing the Q-model and Petri nets. *Proc. Estonian Academy of Sciences, Series of Math., Phys. and Techn.*, Vol. 37, No.1, 18-25 (in Russian).

Tekko, J., Uustalu, T. and Lorents P. (1990). *A Model Theoretic Study of the Calculus for System Description*. Estonian Academy of Sciences, Institute of Cybernetics, Research Report Math. 24/90.

Tekko, J. (1991). A model for interpreting the language LSD and calculus CSD. *Proc. Estonian Academy of Sciences, series Math., Phys.* Vol.40, No.4, 266-278 (in Russian).

Thorelli, L.E. (1983). A linker allowing hierarchic composition of programs. In *Information Processing '83*, R.E.A.Mason (Ed.). Elsevier Science Publ., North-Holland, Amsterdam, 101-106.

Tyugu, E.H. (1970) Problem solving on computational models. *J.of Computing Mathematics and Mathematical Physics*, Vol.10, No.3, 716-733 (in Russian).

Vain, J. (1987). Comparison of the Q-model and Petri nets using modelling power. *Proc. Estonian Academy of Sciences, series of Math., Phys., and Techn.*, Vol.36, No.3, 324-333 (in Russian).

van Benthem, J. (1991). *The Logic of Time. A Model-theoretic Investigation into the Varieties of Temporal Ontology and Temporal Discourse.* Kluwer Academic Publishers, Boston, MA.

Varshavskii, V.I. (Ed.) (1986). *Control automata for asynchronous processes in computers and discrete systems*, Nauka Publ., Moscow (in Russian).

Welsh, J. and Lister, A. (1981). A comparative study of task communication in ADA. *Software:Practice and Experience*, Vol.11, No.3., 257-290.

Winograd, T. (1979). Beyond programming languages. *Comm. ACM.*, Vol.22, No.7, 391-401.

Wirth, N. (1977). Towards a discipline of real-time programming. *Comm. ACM*, Vol.20, No.8, 577-583.

Zave, P. (1976). On the formal definition of processes. *Proc. Int. Conf on Parallel Processing*, 35-42.

Zave, P., (1982). An operational approach to requirements specification for embedded systems. *IEEE Trans. on Software Engineering*, Vol.8, No.3, 250-269.

Zave, P., (1984a). The operational versus the conventional approach to software development. *Comm. ACM*, Vol.27, No.2, 104-118.

Zave, P. (1984b). An overview of the PAISLey Project - 1984. *Software Engineering Notes*, Vol.9, No.4, 12-19.

INDEX